MA

The pretty, ~~v~~ ... ~~was walk~~ing alone to a convenience store when the handsome, long-haired, bearded stranger forced her into the sleeping compartment in the back of his semi-truck. There he violated her again and again and again, in ever more ingeniously perverted ways to recharge his sexual batteries, in a horrifying ordeal she thought would never end.

Still, she was lucky. The man let her live.

That was more than the savage Darren Dee O'Neall did for beautiful young Robin Smith, whom he first deftly separated from her fiancé, then bestially abused and killed.

Why did he do it? How did he do it? Here is the riveting true-crime story that takes you into the mind of an evil murderer, into the agony of his victims, and into the core of the massive manhunt that pulled out all stops to track down a vicious sex slayer.

BLIND RAGE

"A solid, absorbing true-crime book that depicts the depths of a remorseless mind."
—Clark Howard, author of *City Blood*

BLIND RAGE

GARY C. KING

AN ONYX BOOK

ONYX
Published by the Penguin Group
Penguin Books USA Inc., 375 Hudson Street,
New York, New York 10014, U.S.A.
Penguin Books Ltd, 27 Wrights Lane,
London W8 5TZ, England
Penguin Books Australia Ltd, Ringwood,
Victoria, Australia
Penguin Books Canada Ltd, 10 Alcorn Avenue,
Toronto, Ontario, Canada M4V 3B2
Penguin Books (N.Z.) Ltd., 182–190 Wairau Road,
Auckland 10, New Zealand

Penguin Books Ltd, Registered Offices:
Harmondsworth, Middlesex, England

First published by Onyx, an imprint of Dutton Signet,
a division of Penguin Books USA Inc.

First Printing, August, 1995
10 9 8 7 6 5 4 3 2 1

For the memory of Robin Smith,
Larron Crowston, Wendy Aughe,
and Lia Szubert.

Acknowledgments

Much of the information contained in this book was obtained by numerous interviews of the principals of the case and by countless hours of study of the police files and public information surrounding the disappearances and subsequent homicides of Robin Pamela Smith, Wendy Aughe, and Lia Elizabeth Szubert. Some of the biographical background information on suspected serial killer Darren Dee O'Neall, a convicted rapist and the confessed killer of Robin Smith, was obtained as a result of the author's correspondence with O'Neall himself.

The author is especially grateful to the following people for their assistance, cooperation, and candor during the research and writing of this book:

Edna Smith, for graciously inviting me into her home to share with me her fondest memories of her daughter, Robin, and for also sharing with me the terrible repercussions of Robin's untimely and senseless death and the nearly insurmountable toll that it has taken on Edna and her family. Although the meetings and follow-up telephone conversations were often unsettling experiences for me, just as I am certain that they were even more so for her, I am deeply grateful to Edna for enabling me to not only see but *feel* her pain and anguish and for allowing me to relate in the pages of this book just what she went through in the search for and the eventual discovery of what happened to her daughter. I am also thankful to Edna for introducing me to members of her family, each of whom, like Edna, shared with me their innermost memories and feelings: Laurie Garl, Robert J. Sharp, Albert B. Smith, II, Deana Smith, Brenda Baker, and Mike Baker. Never have I encountered such a fine, compassionate, and emotionally strong group of people. I am also deeply indebted to James M. Chaney, Jr., a Smith family friend, for providing his valuable insight into the case and for pointing out and directing me to the numerous locations and points of interest associated with this unusual case. Much gratitude also to Judy Crowston for allowing me to write about the tragedies that have also adversely affected her life and that of her family.

I am also sincerely grateful to Sheriff John H. Shields, Detective Terry Wilson, and Public Information Officer Curt Benson, Pierce County Sheriff's Department, all of whom pledged their support, assistance, and valuable time during the research and writing of this book. They came through beneficently for me on all counts. Also deserving of special acknowledgment for their work and diligence on this difficult case are: Detective Walt Stout, retired, Pierce County Sheriff's Department; Emmanuel Lacsina, M.D., M.E., Pierce County Medical Examiner's Office; William D. Haglund, Chief Medical Investigator, King County Medical Examiner's Office; Pierce County Superior Court Judge Tom Felnagle, who was at the time of this case's investigation and adjudication Pierce County's chief criminal deputy prosecutor; detectives Carlotta Jarratt and Fred Nolte, Bellingham, Washington, Police Department; Detective Bill Carter, Sex Crimes Unit, Portland, Oregon, Police Bureau; Deputy District Attorney Charles Sparks, Multnomah County, Oregon, District Attorney's Office; Dave Trimble and Steve Nelson, then both serving as lead investigators in the still unsolved disappearance of 18-year-old high school girl Kimberley Kersey, for the Clark County, Washington, Sheriff's Department; the Nampa, Idaho, Police Department; the Oregon State Police; Federal Bureau of Investigation; the Lakeland, Florida, Police Department; the Jefferson Parish, Louisiana, Sheriff's Office; and the many other fine law officers, investigators, explorer scouts, family members and friends of the Smith family, and others, many of whom were complete strangers to the Smiths and who through their compassion and sensitivity gave unselfishly of themselves to try to help the Smiths bring this case to a close.

Deserving of a very special acknowledgment is Kathleen Dremillion, who was a junior technician or "rookie" with the Louisiana State Police Bureau of Criminal Identification when the case finally broke. Just as Darren O'Neall was about to attend a bail hearing and possibly be released from police custody,

Ms. Dremillion, armed with a computerized fingerprint-identification system, discovered that O'Neall, who was incarcerated for car theft under one of his many aliases, was on the FBI's Ten Most Wanted list. If not for Dremillion's keen eye and masterful fingerprint-identification abilities, Darren O'Neall might still be at large, leaving a trail of missing persons and unidentified bodies in his wake.

Thanks also to Jim Bosley, Mary Starrett, Nancy Bolton, Janice Bangs, Peter Clem, and everyone else at Portland's KATU-TV and *A.M. Northwest* for their support; to Fiona Martin of *The Oregonian;* Elisa Jaffe and Dick Foley of *Northwest Afternoon,* KOMO-TV, Seattle; and Gary Christenson for *The Jim French Show,* KIRO-Radio, Seattle.

I am also deeply indebted to my editor, Michaela Hamilton, for her patience, but most of all for believing in this project from its outset and for skillfully guiding me through it to its completion, to her assistant, Jory Des Jardins, and to everyone else at Dutton Signet who played a part, whether major or minor, in this collaboration; to Susan Crawford, my literary agent; to Ivola "Vodee" Selis, a dear friend and a real sweetheart of a person; to Laurie McQuary, who gave generously and freely of her time and her much substantiated psychic abilities; to my endearing, not to mention enduring, wife, Teresita, who assisted me with the legwork and accompanied me every step of the way; and finally, to the primary sources of my inspiration, Kirsten and Sarah.

Author's Note

True-crime books such as this one are, of course, works of nonfiction and as such are in many ways historical in nature. Although tragic, they become a permanent record of the events of a given case. Even though historical events are subject to some interpretation, I have not made things up nor have I deliberately omitted significant details, as so often happens with the work of a few writers in this exacting genre who dilute its properties in a misguided attempt to reach a wider, mainstream audience. I have made every effort to remain true to the readers of this genre and have not altered the facts under the guise of sparing the survivors' feelings. Anyone who has read my work before knows that I always include the unpleasant details of the cases that I write about; I have not "looked the other way" here.

These unpleasant details must be included to show the reader how the crimes occurred, to describe the perpetrator accurately, and to show the killer through his despicable actions as the cowardly monster that he really is. Sociopathic killers should never be glorified, even minimally, by leaving out details of their crimes or by sugarcoating their actions. Such an approach to telling a true-crime story only lessens the severity of what the killer has done and can inadvertently glamorize him and make him seem "not that bad of a guy" to the reader, which is something that I do not want to do in any of my books. True-crime readers need to see the killer in an accurate light, and the families of crime victims, in this case and in others that I have written about, have indicated to me that before they will agree to cooperate with me they need to be assured that the story of what happened to their loved ones will be told in a truthful and forthright manner. Families of crime victims already know the gruesome details of their cases and have relived them time and again, both inside and outside the courtroom, and will carry the vivid details of what happened to their loved ones to their graves. To omit the unpleasant details would only serve to do them yet another injury.

I have tried throughout this book to include the *what happened* or the *how* of the crimes because that is what almost always sheds the most light on and often leads investigators directly to the criminal. It also helps them answer the question of *why* the crimes happened in the first place. The *how* and the *why* clearly go hand in hand, and I have made every effort to consider each of equal importance, just as they are considered by the investigators who solve such cases. It is difficult, if not impossible, to address the *why* behind a case without dealing with the *how* and still maintain a high level of credibility and integrity.

I can only hope that I have achieved those levels here.

I would also like to point out that there is a significant amount of spiritual and psychic phenomena that seems to be associated with this case, which I neither entirely support or necessarily disbelieve. I have merely incorporated into the story such details as they were related to me by people who, I am convinced, very much believe what they have told me. I have taken the position that it should be left up to the individual reader to decide whether to believe these unusual incidents occurred or not. That is why I have included them herein.

For murder, though it have
no tongue, will speak
With most miraculous organ.

—William Shakespeare
Hamlet, Act II, Scene 2

A man that doeth violence to
the blood of any person shall flee to
the pit; let no man stay him.

—Proverbs 28:17

Prologue

Saturday, January 17, 1987

Fawn Creswell,* 14, shivered from the January chill the moment she stepped out the front door of her home on Portland's southeast side. Although there was no ice or snow on the ground, the Arctic air from Alaska had pushed the temperature into the low thirties, as it frequently does at that time of the year, and the raindrops that pelted her face early that evening felt more like ice pellets than rain. She could see her breath as she pulled her insulated multicolored nylon jacket, the kind that teenage girls everywhere seem to like to wear, up tightly around her neck for the short walk to the convenience store a few blocks away. Although it had been nearly a month since the winter solstice occurred and each

---

The names of some individuals in this book have been changed, though such changes have been kept to a minimum. An asterisk (*) appears after a fictitious name at the time of its first occurrence.

successive day had slowly given way to small incre-
ments of more and more daylight, it was still dark at
six o'clock throughout the Pacific Northwest on that
January evening. But Fawn paid the darkness no
mind. It was Saturday night and, like most teenagers,
she was bored. There was nothing that she wanted to
watch on television, and despite the inclement
weather she had decided that she just had to get out
of the house for a while. She reasoned that a walk to
the store would at least give her something to do. It
would kill some time, relieve her boredom even if
only for a short while, and there was always the
chance that she might run into a friend along the
way.

An attractive girl with a well-endowed body for her
age, Fawn minded her own business and sang to herself as she walked along the dark, not-so-busy avenue. Having never been a victim of violent crime
before, Fawn, like most other people, had no reason
to fear for her safety that evening. Bad things, she
had always believed, happened to other people, but
not to her. As a result of her innocent, still childlike
way of thinking, appropriate for her age by most people's standards, she never even noticed the large
semi-trailer with an attached sleeping compartment
when it passed slowly by her as she walked along the
freeway overpass. Similarly, she never noticed the
truck's long-haired, bearded driver leering at her on
that first pass along the block. But she would notice
him soon enough. He was just in time on his second
pass, after circling the block, to see Fawn as she

walked into the convenience store, located just beyond the overpass.

This was too good to be true, or so the driver reflected. After all, he had just driven south for 135 miles on Interstate 5, from Tacoma, Washington, to Portland, Oregon, the City of Roses, and he had already found a perfect victim. While it was certainly bad luck for the girl, a concept that he would never have even considered due to his inherent and severe inability to feel compassion for others, it was indeed good luck for him. Rarely was finding a victim so easy. Fate was clearly on his side once again. With his libido now dictating his actions, he turned his truck around and parked at a location where he knew she would soon have to pass. Once he had her under his control, he decided, it would all be worth the trip. He lit up a Camel filter, his favorite brand of cigarette, and drew the harsh smoke deep into his lungs as he waited for the girl to come out of the store.

Five minutes passed. As he waited for her to return, he became more anxious, excited, and his breathing grew heavier, more intense with each second that ticked by. Three minutes later he lit another Camel from the one he was smoking, and flicked the finished one out into the street. He continued to wait, and he took out one of the long-bladed hunting knives that he always carried with him as he began to fantasize about what he would soon be able to do with the girl. He turned the knife over and over in his hands, feeling the sharp, turned-up tip as he gazed with a far-off look in his eyes at the reflection of a streetlight in the knife's polished, glinty steel. The things he planned to do to the girl were terrible, unthinkable by most people's values, but not to his. People, to him, were objects to be used for his pleasure alone, to be discarded like refuse when he was finished with them. He didn't care whether she had a family or what kinds of repercussions his actions would have on them or the girl. Thoughts of decency were foreign to him. All he cared about was himself, what he needed, what he wanted. Even more frightening, there was a part of him that understood all of this.

Although he was not yet versed in the legality of what he was about to do, by definition he was going to interfere with a person's personal liberty and commit the crime of kidnapping in the first degree with the sole purpose of causing physical and psychological injury to his chosen victim. He was going to confine her secretly so that he could terrorize her without being disturbed, ultimately for his sexual pleasure and the delight he would enjoy of having her under his power, under his total control. He knew what he was doing, and he knew right from wrong. But he didn't care. He was evil.

Finally, there she was, coming out of the store. She was carrying an open bottle of soda pop in one hand and a small sack of candy and other treats in the other. There was no time to lose. The man moved quickly into action. He climbed out of the cab of his big rig, the half-burned Camel hanging from his lips, and moved toward the truck's sleeping compartment door, pretending that he was attending to some kind of a problem with his rig. Such tactics had worked for him before. There was no reason for him to believe they wouldn't work this time.

When Fawn was alongside the truck, the hairy man, without any warning, pulled on the outside handle of the sleeping compartment door and swung it open, then stepped onto the sidewalk in front of her and effectively blocked her path, all in one swift action. It was imperative that he move quickly. He couldn't risk anyone seeing him kidnap the girl.

Puzzled and somewhat startled at first, Fawn stopped in her tracks and looked up quizzically at the man. Not wanting the girl to scream and cause a scene before he could get her under his control, the man attempted a halfhearted smile as he leered at her with Charlie Manson eyes. Quick as a snake he reached out and grabbed her by the front of her nylon jacket. Terrified, Fawn stiffened and froze, unable to scream or fight back. The man lifted her off the sidewalk and pushed her forcefully into the truck's sleeping compartment. He leaped inside after her and pulled the door shut behind him, brandishing the hunting knife for the girl to see. He also told her that he had a gun, but Fawn didn't actually see the .357 Ruger he was carrying.

"If you scream or try to get away, I'll kill you," said the man, brimming with a matter-of-fact, arrogant confidence. Fawn, wild-eyed with fear, couldn't take her eyes off the knife. The knife was having the effect that he wanted it to have, and he seemed aroused by her wild display of fear. Although terrified, she kept quiet and involuntarily allowed the man to stuff a gag inside her mouth and to bind her hands and feet. Squirming from discomfort and crying uncontrollably, Fawn's young mind instinctively told her that it would be futile, and possibly very dangerous, to resist. When he was certain that the bindings were tautly in place and was confident that she couldn't get away or cause him any trouble, the man exited the sleeping compartment and climbed back into the driver's seat. Certain that he had drawn no attention from passersby, he calmly started the engine and pulled unobtrusively away from the curb. He crossed the overpass, then took the freeway on-ramp that headed him south into rural Clackamas County, his predetermined destination. He wanted his privacy, and he knew that he would get it there.

Fifteen minutes later, he pulled off onto a dark, tree-shrouded unpaved road and parked. No one would bother him there, of that he was certain. With steady hands he reached into a sack on the floorboard and pulled out a lukewarm can of Black Label beer, next to the last can of a six-pack that he had purchased just before leaving Washington state. He lit another Camel, climbed out of the truck, and listened intently. All he could hear was the wind-driven rain pelting the metal of the cab's roof. He was alone with the girl in a silent forest, and though her tears flowed like the rain coming down outside and he could hear her whimpering in the compartment behind him, he made not a sound. He was feeling good, strong, and in control. After several minutes of savoring the moment, he climbed inside the sleeping compartment and sat down next to the frightened, whimpering girl, a mere child who was only now beginning to learn about life's darkest side.

Keeping the knife where she could see it, he carefully removed her restraints. He drew back his hand at one point, as if he was going to slap her hard across the face with the palm of his hand. The display was to show her that he meant business, and that he would have his way with her. But for some reason he didn't strike the girl. Perhaps it was the way she had flinched sharply in anticipation of the pain that the slap would have caused, or perhaps it was because she had promptly nodded in affirmation that she would do just as she was told, everything that he instructed her to do as long as he promised not to kill her. But the only promise he made to her was that if she didn't obey, she would suffer dearly for it. She believed him, and slowly followed his instructions by removing all of her clothing.

Fawn slowly unbuttoned her blouse and slipped it off, revealing the swell of her breasts that were pushed up firmly by the brassiere she was wearing. She next unfastened her jeans and, from a sitting position, slipped them down. She paused long enough to remove her shoes, then removed her legs one at a time from her pants. She looked at him for a moment, as if waiting or hoping that he would change his mind.

"Go on, get the rest of those off," he commanded as he showed her the knife again. "What the fuck are you waitin' for?"

Fawn unfastened her bra in the back, and let the straps fall from each shoulder. Attempting to cover her breasts with one arm, she removed the bra the rest of the way with the other. She then slipped her panties off and kneeled on the floor, her thighs held tightly together in an attempt to hide her private parts from the man. He pushed her onto her back, but she remained rigid.

He ran his large, rough hands across her young, tender breasts, and took the hunting knife and ran its tip slowly and ever so lightly across her stomach. With careful, deliberate movements he continued dragging the knife in a downward motion, across her abdomen and pelvic area to, finally, between her thighs. Fawn shivered involuntarily and cried as he parted her legs and placed one of his hands on her soft, sparse patch of pubic hair. He felt himself become hard, and it felt good, all-powerful. He wriggled out of his own pants, and Fawn was suddenly aware of his largeness. It was not that he was particularly well endowed; it was just that the sight of an erect penis to the 14-year-old girl was enough to give her the impression of largeness. He spat into the palm of his left hand, the one with the word J-U-N-E tattooed across the knuckles, and excitedly rubbed the saliva all over his penis. He forced himself on top of the helpless child and entered her forcefully, all within a matter of seconds. She grunted with pain and cried out momentarily, but otherwise tried to remain quiet. She knew better than to do anything to anger this bastard. His breath stank of beer and cigarettes, and he panted repulsively as he pushed and pulled his less than adequate organ in and out of her body. It didn't take long for him to climax, and he ejaculated inside her vagina.

"I could fuck you all night," he lied, trying to bolster his much inflated ego. His manhood was important to him, even if he really wasn't the man he wanted everyone to think that he was. He had to maintain the image. It was all an extension of his fantasy, which he believed he had to keep alive to get along in the world.

Desirous of another erection, he fondled the girl's breasts and buttocks. At one point he forced her mouth onto his organ and demanded that she fellate him.

"You're going to have to give me a blow job now, you little bitch!" He laughed disrespectfully.

When she tasted the saltiness of her own vagina, it sickened her and she gagged with revulsion, but she complied as best she could. His body smelled badly, like several days worth of old, built-up sweat, which didn't make it any easier for her to accomplish the deviant act that he was demanding. When he ejaculated and filled her mouth with his semen, she thought that she would vomit. But she didn't want to take any chances of angering him by protesting and so continued the deviant act until he backed away on his own. She didn't know what he might do with the knife.

He would enter her again and again over the next two hours, and would repeat the process of ejaculating both inside and outside her body. At one point, when it appeared that he would not be able to attain another erection, the man grabbed the now empty soda pop bottle that the girl had been carrying when he kidnapped her and placed it angrily between Fawn's legs.

"Bet you know what I'm doing to do with this, don't you?" he laughed. Fawn remained silent, and only stared at him with wild, frightened eyes.

He carefully, but forcefully, worked the bottle's neck into her vagina, the tip of which was lubricated only with the girl's bodily fluids and the man's semen that had dripped from her vagina. He pulled it out and reinserted it until he established a rhythmic motion and the process became easy for him. Though it was painful, Fawn knew that she had no choice but to let him have his way. Abusing her body with the pop bottle amused him at first, but finally became erotic to the point that he was able to get yet another erection. He pulled the bottle out and in its place inserted his penis. Grunting primitively, he raped her once again.

When the man realized that he was finished with the girl, he also knew that he had the problem of deciding what to do with her. He had kidnapped, repeatedly raped, and sexually penetrated the body of a juvenile female with a foreign object, among other crimes. If he let her go, he knew that she would likely be able to identify him at some point. He thought and talked of killing her, but she cried and pleaded with him to let her go.

"I promise I won't tell anyone what happened if you'll just let me go," she cried. "Please don't kill me!"

"I could sell you to pimps in California," he said after several minutes of silence, an evil gleam in his eyes. He seemed lost, deep in thought for several more minutes before finally breaking the quietude. After taunting her by telling her the horrible things that he could do to her, he demanded that Fawn promise, again, not to tell anyone about what had happened to her. After threatening to find her if she did, the man, miraculously, agreed to let her go. He allowed her to dress, drove her back to the city, and dropped her off at a location where she could easily find her way home.

When Fawn arrived home, she discovered that her parents were still up, frantic with worry. They had already called the police, but, they had been told, there wasn't much that they could do until more time had passed. She hadn't been missing long enough to qualify as a missing person. Trembling uncontrollably, Fawn tearfully recounted to her parents the horror she had been subjected to over the past few hours. They promptly reported the crimes that had been committed against their daughter to the Portland Police Bureau, and Fawn was taken to a local hospital for examination. A standard rape kit, which includes a comb, swabs, and evidence containers, was used to collect the evidence.

A physician swabbed Fawn's bodily orifices and tested them with acid phosphatase. The swabs turned a pinkish purple from the enzyme, a positive chemical reaction that revealed the presence of semen inside her vagina and mouth. Her underpants, which also contained semen stains, were collected, along with the swabs, as evidence. Her pubic hair was combed in search of stray or foreign hairs, and samples of her own pubic hair were collected for purposes of comparison. In addition, a pubic hair was found on her sweater during the examination.

Following the medical examination, Fawn was interviewed at length by Portland Police Bureau Detective Bill Carter. She described her attacker as a white male, approximately 25–30 years of age, nearly six feet tall, and about 160 pounds. She said that he had a thick mustache and beard, and somewhat crooked teeth. However, despite the investigation that was initiated as case number 87-12-37738 that evening, it would be nearly six months before Fawn would identify her attacker as one Darren Dee O'Neall.

In the meantime, Fawn would begin to despise and distrust nearly all men because of what happened to her on the night of January 17, 1987, and would grow up harboring such feelings despite the therapy sessions she would undergo. And, like so many others who had become victims of violent crime, she would become afraid of the dark.

Chapter 1

Darren Dee O'Neall, 27, arrived virtually unnoticed in the rugged Twin Peaks backwoods of Washington State on November 3, 1986, an unseasonably warm Monday. Known as a drifter to his family, friends, and law enforcement agencies across the country, O'Neall had traveled extensively throughout the United States. As the product of an army household, his travels had begun in his youth and continued until his father, Darrell, finally retired from the military and settled with Darren's mother, Christa, in Colorado Springs, Colorado. But for reasons, dark, macabre reasons that no one yet fully understood, Darren O'Neall continued to travel in his adult life entirely of his own doing, out of necessity in most cases in order to stay one step ahead of the law, as he was doing now. On the move almost constantly, he never remained in one location for very long. As a result, he did little bonding with others and knew few people whom he could call friends. When he chose to associate with anyone, he did so mostly with street people, "animals of the street" as O'Neall himself was known to call them. He didn't form such alliances out of a yearning for companionship but out of a need to score illicit drugs or to launch a new scam of some sort. Mostly, however, he made contacts in the streets because he blended in so smoothly with what he termed "society's rubbish," which is how he sometimes thinks of himself, and because he knew that such people would be the least likely ever to turn him in to the law. He was gutsy and daring, which should not be construed as bravery or gallantry but instead should be understood in the vein that he would do what he had to do to get what he wanted. In that sense, some would say, he had more nerve than a government mule. But he was a loner for the most part, afraid to face life responsibly and on the right side of the law, and that seemed to suit him just fine.

He had spent varying amounts of time, anywhere from six weeks to six months in each of the states of Pennsylvania, New Jersey, Delaware, Georgia, Florida, Louisiana, Tennessee, and most recently he had wandered through the Rocky Mountain states where not only his father and mother resided, but where other family members lived, too. But now O'Neall was in the Evergreen State, so named because of its vast, extensive forests, a place of natural beauty and serenity where he was not yet known in law enforcement circles. He was there not by accident but out of design. He had planned it that way, just as he planned almost everything that he did. Driving a butterscotch-colored 1972 Chrysler New Yorker with

Montana license plates, he was there to contact an old high school acquaintance, Frank Wilhelm.* O'Neall didn't want to see Wilhelm because he particularly liked him or wanted to befriend him. He was looking him up because he desperately needed a place to stay, a place where he could lie low for a while, rethink his situation, get back on his feet, all the while staying out of reach of the long arm of the law. Wilhelm, O'Neall had learned from a relative before setting out on this latest trek, had also only recently moved into the state and was running his own business. O'Neall hoped that Wilhelm would be happy to see him again, if only for a while.

O'Neall and Wilhelm had first become acquainted when they were both teenagers in the mid-1970s, and their association, for that is all that it could be called, had grown out of Wilhelm's close friendship with O'Neall's older brother, Kevin. O'Neall's father and Wilhelm's stepfather had both been in the military back then, stationed at Fort Polk, Louisiana, and they had lived across the street from each other. Even though O'Neall was a couple of grades behind Wilhelm, they nonetheless had become "buddies" of a sort.

Pretending to be insecure, unsure of himself, always wondering aloud about what he wanted to do with his life, O'Neall preyed on whatever sympathy he could muster from Wilhelm and his wife to get into their home. As a ruse, he sought solace and advice from Wilhelm upon his arrival in Washington. Not that he would take or heed any advice even if it was offered to him. He just wanted to appear as down and out as possible in Wilhelm's eyes, and to be able to use him in any way that he could before moving on. Darren O'Neall didn't know how *not* to take advantage of someone's good nature.

After renewing their friendship and getting to know each other all over again on a more or less superficial basis, superficiality being one of the major distinguishing characteristics of O'Neall's relationships with others, Wilhelm easily convinced O'Neall that life and women were indeed good in the Pacific Northwest. Since O'Neall had little money, no place to stay, and was a virtual stranger to the area, Wilhelm apparently felt sorry for him and agreed to put him up in his home for two weeks. O'Neall's cunning had worked once again, just as he had known it would when he began going over the plan in his mind prior to meeting with Wilhelm.

Within the two weeks that O'Neall stayed with Wilhelm, he discovered, after familiarizing himself with the region, that he really did like it there, especially the vast outdoors. He could implement all of his plans, carry out more of the evil carnage that he lived for, all with less chance of being caught as long as he remained careful. Once again he would soon be able to release the diabolic entity that writhed deep within the further reaches of his tortured soul, from within his very psyche, that evil from inside that ultimately dictated in its cyclic fashion just what O'Neall, and others like him, would have to do. Thinking ahead and making plans that, as yet unknown to him, would ultimately go awry and send him on the lam again, he quickly decided during those two weeks with Wilhelm that he needed an apartment of his own, a safe haven that could serve as his home base after carrying out his acts of profane handiwork, whatever they turned out to be. Like Wilhelm, he would stay in the Pacific Northwest, too, at least for a while. But he would stay for all of the wrong reasons.

With barely $200 in his wallet when he arrived, O'Neall worked at odd jobs, ran scams with street people, and occasionally robbed a three-time loser who was too drunk to know what was happening to him, all so that he could accumulate enough money to put down on a place of his own. He soon found such a place, a reasonably priced duplex apartment that he saw while studying the classified ads in the local newspaper. It was located at 10224 13th Court East in the Edgewood section of Puyallup, near Tacoma. When he drove over to see it, he would have been the first to admit that it didn't look like much. From all outward appearances, the apartments could easily have qualified as low-income Section 8 housing had the owner wanted to participate in the government program. But O'Neall didn't care. He wasn't, after all, particularly choosy about where he lived, and he had certainly lived in places far worse than this. After giving it a cursory once-over and deciding that it would adequately serve his needs, he told the manager that he would take it. He reasoned, correctly, that the manger wouldn't hassle him about references. He paid part of the deposit at that time and promised to pay the rest later, and also paid two weeks' rent for the one-bedroom unit that would become his home for the next five months. In need of a steady income, he immediately began searching for a full-time job. He realized that he needed something substantially better than what scamming people and rolling drunks could provide.

Having worked as a casual laborer, cook, bartender, dishwasher, warehouseman, salesperson, and a wood laminator, O'Neall wasn't too worried about finding a job. As soon as he left Wilhelm's home and moved into his own apartment, he knew that he would take the first firm offer that came along regardless of the pay. That first offer turned out to be a job as a laminator at Interior Form Tops, a countertop-manufacturing firm located at 1420 Meridian East, also in Puyallup and only a short drive from O'Neall's apartment. O'Neall obtained the job after Frank Wilhelm, himself a businessman in the community, put in a good word for him with the shop's owner.

Interior Form Tops was set back away from the street, just across the road from a place called Baldy's Tavern, a beer and wine haunt that sometimes featured live music. The close proximity of the tavern to O'Neall's place of employment naturally pleased him, since he liked to guzzle beer and associate with the tavern crowd. He soon found that he could take some of his lunches there, and would sometimes sneak out in the afternoon for a fast beer break whenever he knew that the boss was away. And after work Baldy's would become a favorite hangout of O'Neall's. Unfortunately, the tavern would ultimately figure significantly as the starting point in what would be remembered as one of Washington state's most intensive missing-person-turned-murder investigations.

Sylvan in its natural beauty, the state of Washington was named in honor of the nation's first president. Ideally located in the extreme northwestern corner of the continental United States, Washington is conveniently situated geographically to the Canadian province of British Columbia to the north, and the states of Idaho and Oregon form its eastern and southern borders, respectively. A large body of water known as Puget Sound lies to the west and leads directly into the Pacific Ocean via the Strait of Juan de Fuca and other scenic waterways. The Olympic Peninsula, which lies to the north near British Columbia's Vancouver Island, boasts its own national park, the interior of which is accessible only to foot traffic. Within the park's boundaries lies a dense rain forest, rimmed by the snowcapped and hauntingly beautiful Olympic Mountains. It is only a short ferry ride from the Washington peninsula to Victoria, a city popular with tourists from around the world.

East and southeast of Puget Sound lies a coastal plain, the Puget Sound lowland. Farther due east, however, the lowland soon gives way to the Cascade Range, the highest peak of which is Mount Rainier, which majestically looms over the region at 14,410 feet and can easily be seen from Seattle and Tacoma on clear days. It is an area that has been both sullied and beautifully molded by eons of movement of the prehistoric glaciers and ice sheets and which is now dominated by dormant volcanoes. There is, of course, the one non-dormant exception known as Mount St. Helens, which awakened after 123 years of sleep and erupted in 1980, causing extensive damage to the surrounding areas, mostly from volcanic ash, and left frequently recurring low-level seismic activity in its wake.

Under the influence of the prevailing westerly winds, western Washington is a moist, temperate zone that receives up to 150 inches of precipitation annually. Temperature in the Cascades and the surrounding national forests fluctuates between 45 and 50 degrees nine months out of the year. In the summer it is considerably warmer and drier, of course, than in the other seasons. It is just such extremes in the fluctuation of atmospheric conditions that provides for the rapid decomposition of human remains left in the outdoors, which is one of the reasons why, perhaps, that the Pacific Northwest has played host to a number of notorious serial killers in recent years and has provided them with such a favorable dumping ground. And now it was providing the perfect backdrop for the likes of Darren O'Neall to carry out his frenzied fits of *blind rage*.

* * *

Darren O'Neall partied heartily during the remaining days of 1986 and into early 1987, mostly at Baldy's Tavern and at after-hours parties held at the homes of acquaintances, many of whom he had met at Baldy's. He preferred to listen to modern country and western music, which Baldy's frequently featured. He stayed drunk on Black Label beer much of the time but, in addition to his heavy drinking, soon worked his way into Tacoma's drug underworld and resumed smoking marijuana and injecting cocaine and tar heroin. He had been using illicit drugs on and off since he was a teenager and, being well versed in the drug subculture that is so prevalent in our cities and urban areas, it had not taken him long to find the right connections in Pierce County, Washington.

On the few occasions when he wasn't drunk or high on drugs during this period, O'Neall spent his time reading western novels by Louis L'Amour, his favorite author, and the pulp-type western and outdoor magazines that are often found on convenience store and drugstore newsstands. He soon began posturing as an outdoorsman to those with whom he associated, as both a "mountain man" and an "urban cowboy." As it became increasingly difficult, and eventually impossible, for O'Neall to separate his fantasies of becoming an outdoor survivalist from reality, it naturally became important for him to exhibit even more of a "Marlboro Man" persona to everyone he met, all despite the fact that he had been raised in a number of cities. He made no secret of his unusual fascination with knives and hatchets, and nearly always carried one knife in a sheath on his belt and another knife concealed in one of his boots. He often carried several others in his car, and is known to have been also in possession of a .357 Ruger during this period of his life.

A fast and smooth talker, O'Neall always made quite an impression on the women he met. While frequently cleaning his fingernails with the knife he kept in his boot, he would talk nonstop about being a survivalist with past military experiences as a Ranger and Green Beret. He nearly always mentioned to the women he had just met that he was from Louisiana and was "just passing through." He was there, he said, only so that he could earn enough money to get to Alaska, where he would live out the rest of his life in the great outdoors. It was all a line of bullshit, of course, but people tended to believe him, at least until they got to know him well enough to see through some of his deceptiveness.

As part of the image that he wanted to project, O'Neall always wore cowboy boots, jeans, and a western-style shirt. He sported a small, barely detectable five-point star tattoo at the outer corner of his left eye, and the name "J-U-N-E" was tattooed across the knuckles of his left hand, one letter permanently inked on each knuckle beginning with the J on his index finger. Although the tattoos looked like hell, they were distinguishing features that people who came in contact with him would always seem to remember, which in turn would end up greatly aiding law enforcement authorities in tracking his movements. He also had a small vertical scar on his right cheek, evidence, he always bragged, of his getting into brawls. Outwardly, he was a *real man,* or so he wanted everyone to believe. He was always out to prove himself to others, to make them see his manliness, even if it meant "getting the shit" kicked out of himself after drunkenly starting a fight with someone that he knew he couldn't possibly defeat. He somehow justified it all, at least to himself, because it bolstered his manly self-image that was all-important to him. Inwardly, however, as most of his associates would eventually learn, he was a lonely, frightened, even cowardly man with an intense inferiority complex who lived mostly in a world of make-believe. He liked to pick on women, especially those he perceived as a threat to his manhood.

O'Neall frequently wore his dishwater blond hair in a perm, though at times, especially when he was on the move, he would wear it long and stringy. When the need arose he could also take on a neat and trim appearance, sometimes parting his hair either in the middle or on the left side of his head. He sometimes wore a well-trimmed beard and mustache, and sometimes only a mustache. Depending upon his mood and the effect he desired to project at any given time, O'Neall sometimes wore gold wire-rimmed glasses. At 5 feet 11 inches, 160 pounds, with clear blue eyes, women seemed to be naturally drawn in by O'Neall's rugged, masculine facade. He frequently spoke of wanting to find the perfect woman for himself, a woman he hoped he could take back into the woods and with whom he could live out the rest of his life. A master at manipulation, as most sociopaths are, it was difficult, if not impossible, for those who came in contact with Darren O'Neall to see the deceit that lurked beneath his skin until after they had been completely drawn in. And by then it was usually too late to avoid becoming one of his victims.

Although involved in a number of drunken brawls, most of which he started himself, during this same period O'Neall managed to keep away from law enforcement authorities. Even after committing the January 17, 1987, kidnapping and rape of Fawn Creswell in Portland, O'Neall was soon confident that the authorities in Tacoma and Pierce County had no interest in him. Unaware that the girl hadn't heeded his warnings about turning him in to the police, O'Neall had no way of knowing yet that Portland detective Bill Carter had called in police sketch artist Jean Boylan, one of the best sketch artists in the country, from her home in Bend, Oregon, to work up a composite drawing based on Fawn's description of her attacker. Interestingly, Carter and others would note years later, in 1993, that it was Boylan's talent and expertise that provided Petaluma, California, investigators a sketch of their suspect in the Polly Klaas abduction/murder, which resulted in an arrest in that well-known case. With Boylan's help in Fawn's case in 1987, the wheels of justice began moving, albeit slowly, against Darren O'Neall soon after she put pencil to paper. But the important thing was that the wheels were indeed turning and would eventually lead Detective Carter to focus on O'Neall in Fawn's rape. It is not known how many other rapes and/or sexual assaults that O'Neall might have been responsible for in the Pacific Northwest during this period. However, based on his past history of rape and sexual assault that would eventually be uncovered, many law officers would remain convinced that O'Neall was likely responsible for many.

Although Darren O'Neall had begun dating a number of young women after his arrival in Washington, dates that rarely amounted to anything more than one night out and with no sex involved, it wasn't until March 1987, after he became acquainted with Mary Barnes,* 27, that anything even resembling a relationship began to emerge. Mary would decide later that it was her bad luck working against her when she met O'Neall at Baldy's Tavern shortly after she began working there as a part-time bar maid.

Mary wasn't on duty, however, on the day that she met O'Neall. Mary's mother, who was battling Mary for the custody of her young daughter, purportedly over what she considered Mary's opprobrious conduct and lifestyle, had just kicked Mary out of her house. With nowhere to go and mentally depressed, Mary climbed into her old, gold Plymouth Duster and drove to Baldy's at approximately five that day in early March to drown her sorrows in a few drinks. Tall, skin-and-bones Mary was neither particularly attractive or unattractive. On a scale of one to ten she probably figured somewhere in the middle. Her long auburn hair, naturally wavy, contrasted her lily-white skin, and her high, rouge-dotted cheekbones, an aquiline nose, and white straight teeth were often more than enough to offset any of her negative features. Hoping to forget her troubles, Mary slid quietly into a bar seat next to O'Neall. Looks aside, O'Neall, with a belly full of beer, was instantly attracted to her much as a sire would be attracted to a bitch in heat. Having been a while since O'Neall had been involved sexually with a "willing" woman, he quickly struck up a conversation with Mary. He needed a female companion for show, someone who could unwittingly help him establish somewhat of an image of normalcy in the community.

Pathological liar that he was so known for, O'Neall began bragging to Mary about all the money that he supposedly had in his bank account. At one point he pulled out his checkbook and showed her some impressive figures. Later, however, in retrospect, Mary would recall how all of the numbers just seemed to have been hastily "written in," like he was "just out trying to impress someone," to win them over with money that he supposedly had in the bank. The ruse didn't always work, but his psychopathic "instinct" kept telling him that it would work in Mary's case.

Several drinks later that evening, Mary told O'Neall all about her problems and how she had no place to go. O'Neall, recognizing that he must seize the opportunity, quickly offered Mary a key to his apartment. Attracted to O'Neall's facade of manliness, she moved in that same night. Over the next three weeks she would get to know O'Neall about as well as anyone could, and would satisfy him sexually, at least at first. But by the third week in March, she became starkly aware of a definite, observable transformation occurring within the man with whom she was living. She discovered that her companion had a frightening and dangerous dark side that he tried to keep hidden beneath a thin veneer.

"He was always pacing and looking out the curtain, nervous, like he was paranoid all the time," Mary would later tell the police. "It hit him real bad when he, you know, used the needle, shot up. He kinda scared me, you know, when he shot up."

Although Mary didn't understand what was happening to her new companion, O'Neall in fact was beginning to metamorphose again, entering the first of several stages of transformation. Unconsciously, he was moving dangerously toward a new cycle or phase in his mental state. In Mary's words he began acting "weird," and he grew "meaner" with each new day.

He began to take a knife to bed with them, and kept another on the floor beneath their bed. While sitting on the living room couch, he always kept a knife hidden underneath it or lying nearby, always within easy reach. Alarmed, Mary spoke up one day about O'Neall's unusual passion for knives.

"I don't like those knives you carry all the time," she said. "Why are you so paranoid?"

"I just like to keep them for protection," he answered curtly, without elaborating.

O'Neall began spending most of his spare time re-reading his collection of Louis L'Amour novels and western magazines, and Mary observed a nearly constant faraway look in his eyes that began to frighten her. When he wasn't reading, she watched him as he mainlined cocaine and tar heroin, which he began spending all of his money, and soon most of hers, on. As his life continued its downward spiral, Mary would soon bear witness to his rage within.

"Why don't you read one of these books, Mary?" O'Neall urged his companion one day in late March as he looked up momentarily from the yellowed pages of one of L'Amour's Sackett family novels. Although he was in one of his infrequent sober states of being, he still had that strange, faraway look in his eyes that had by then begun to frighten Mary.

"No," she responded. "You know I don't read that kind of stuff. I'm just not interested in 'em."

"But don't you want to learn how I want to live, baby?" O'Neall sarcastically asked. For one brief, fleeting moment Mary thought that she had glimpsed hatred in O'Neall's eyes. Checking himself, he quickly flashed her a halfhearted grin. After a few moments of reflection, O'Neall continued: "I just want to get away. I want to go walk up into the mountains. Have you ever lived in the hills?"

"No," Mary said dryly.

"You want to come live in the hills with me?" he asked.

"No, I don't want to live out in the mountains,"

she responded in an uninterested monotone. Sensing that her answer had displeased him, Mary smiled in an attempt to placate O'Neall's ranting about living in the outdoors. She hoped that he wouldn't go on so, but he wouldn't give up.

"You won't need much," he persisted. "Just a couple of pairs of pants, some shirts, boots, a backpack. It won't take much. We could hunt our food."

"No, I can't," Mary said emphatically. "I got a daughter that I've gotta get back, and I can't go with you."

O'Neall withdrew further into himself after being rebuffed by Mary. He began to read even more, which annoyed her immensely, and he started ignoring her almost constantly. When she tried to talk to him, he acted as if she wasn't even there.

They still engaged in sex, but even that wasn't like it had been at first. O'Neall began to have difficulty attaining an erection, and when he did manage to get it up, he couldn't maintain it for very long. It seemed to Mary that he was becoming impotent. On the ever increasing occasions in which he managed to reach a climax and in which Mary didn't, O'Neall would became angry.

"How come you didn't get off?" he would ask her afterward. It seemed as if his continued premature ejaculations and failure to please Mary sexually was hurting his ego, and he began to take his resulting anger out on her by verbally abusing her. At times his anger caused her to wonder if he hated all women or just her. She tried not to think about it too much because when she did, it always brought out a definite fear of O'Neall in her, a fear that she didn't understand and that was difficult for her to cope with.

Thinking that what they needed was to try something different sexually, Mary took control during one of their episodes by mounting *him*. O'Neall, accustomed to being in control, seemed shocked at Mary's sudden aggressiveness. Instead of improving O'Neall's performance in bed, however, Mary's aggressiveness actually made matters worse. Although he had started out with a partial erection on that occasion, O'Neall's organ suddenly went completely limp when Mary climbed on top of him.

"What's the matter, baby?" she asked. "Am I not doing enough for you?" His ego hurting again, O'Neall didn't answer her. Instead, he indicated that he wanted to quit that particular attempt at sex. Mary didn't understand. She didn't know if the problem was with her, or if it was just some male problem that affected only certain men. Mary didn't realize that it was the power, of being the one in control and not necessarily the sexual acts themselves, that meant everything to O'Neall. If he couldn't be the aggressor when it came to sex, he didn't want it at all.

From that point on, their relationship continued to deteriorate. On the few occasions that they talked to each other at all, the conversation almost always turned into a heated argument. Sex became less and less frequent, mechanical and with little emotion. It finally got to the point that she had to talk him into having sex because he no longer seemed interested.

On one occasion Mary interrupted O'Neall's reading and began telling him about her background. She thought, mistakenly, that if O'Neall knew more about her and she knew more about him, their sexual relationship might improve. She had no way of knowing that getting to know her was the last thing that O'Neall wanted. To know her, that is, to know her well, would mean she would become a real person to him. She would no longer be merely an object for him to use, something that could satisfy his every whim without requiring any sense of moral decency or responsibility on his part.

She began by telling him how she had been abused and raped by her father when she was younger, and hoped that he would react sympathetically. Instead he got up, pulled out one of his knives and, without warning, threw her to the floor. Mary, shocked and frightened, didn't know what had suddenly come over him. O'Neall held her there, pinned to the floor, and remained silent for about a minute.

"Maybe I should take you down and hold you down, abuse you for maybe ten minutes a day," O'Neall said, his voice now angrier than she had ever heard it before.

"You better not," Mary responded, scared and trembling. She couldn't take her eyes off the knife. It terrified her.

O'Neall seemed to be going into a rage. He placed one hand, the one that held the knife, across Mary's neck, and twisted her head to the right with the other. She thought that he was trying to break her neck, and feared that her frail bones might snap at any moment. She also feared that he might take the knife and just slit her throat.

"You're just like the rest of them cunts," O'Neall screamed. "You're all good-for-nothing whores. You're all useless."

Mary saw an evil look in O'Neall's eyes. It scared her even more, and she suddenly realized that she had better do something, anything, to defuse the situation because she didn't know what he might do next. For the first time since she had known him, she thought that he would kill her. She began yelling back at him.

"You sonofabitch!" she screamed. "You get off me! I cook and clean for you. I'm working part-time. I'm trying. If you don't like it, I don't know what to tell you, but you best get the fuck off of me."

O'Neall seemed shocked by Mary's sudden display of aggression and control, and he sat up. He slowly moved the knife away from her throat, and simply stared at her for a few seconds with that strange, far-off look in his eyes. Finally, after what seemed like an eternity but what in actuality amounted to only a few seconds, O'Neall shook his head and then slowly moved off her. Mary had won, and he knew it. She had taken the wind out of his sail, so to speak, and in so doing she had likely saved her own life. Mary knew at that moment that it was time for her to move on, but she had nowhere to go. She realized that she couldn't risk staying with O'Neall for even a few more days. She had to begin making plans to get out. If she didn't leave him, she feared that he might kill her the next time he flew into a rage.

Chapter 2

Robin Pamela Smith was born in New Britain, Connecticut, on April 4, 1965, to Edna and Stuart Smith. A tiny baby, not much larger than a child's doll, Robin weighed a mere four pounds, four ounces. Her mother described her as a good baby, which, in any mother's language, translates into a quiet baby, and the placidity that followed her into adolescence and adulthood would be but one of several traits for which she would be remembered. Somewhat prissy as a little girl, she borrowed her sisters' clothes all the time, and these, too, were characteristics that she would carry with her into young adulthood.

Robin's mother, Edna, grew up in New Britain, having moved there when she was five, and she lived there for approximately 25 years. Later, after marrying Stuart, her second husband, and giving birth to Robin, Edna and her family moved to Meriden, Connecticut, where they lived on Crown Street for 12 years and made their living for a while by operating a restaurant and bar. Shortly after Robin's twelfth birthday, the Smiths decided to leave New England. After considerable soul searching and planning, they packed up their belongings and moved to the state of Washington, leaving behind their friends and relatives to start a new life in the Pacific Northwest.

Although Robin was considered a generally serene and private teenage girl, she did like to dance. While growing up she often was affectionately called "Rockin' Robin" by her friends, a nickname that was inspired by the old Michael Jackson song bearing that same title, because she always rocked and danced to the music on the radio. But Robin, in actuality, was no rocker at all, at least not in the true sense of the word. She liked to listen to the tunes and move to the beat, but she was not lost in the world of rock 'n' roll. She liked other music as well, as long as it pleased her ear and she could dance to it.

On the surface Robin, in her youngest years, was not always perceived as a friendly child, as often happens to people who are shy. People often mistake shyness for coldness or aloofness, when it is usually nothing of the sort. Deep down, Robin was really a very warm and loving young girl who was devoted to her family and friends. Although beheld by some in her later teenage years as a happy-go-lucky girl, those closest to Robin knew her as being quieter and more reserved than many young girls her age. The shyness, say members of her family, never really left her, and it always took some doing for anyone even to get to know her. She consistently moved slowly with new acquaintances, especially males, perhaps because of the pain that she had watched her mother go through during the trauma of divorce. It was only after Robin had become comfortable with someone that she would open up and talk to them, and even then only rarely would she reveal her innermost feelings and secrets to anyone outside her immediate family.

Like many kids, Robin grew up being afraid of the dark. At first it seemed natural enough to her parents, as if it was only a childhood phase that she was going through. But as time went on she began to dwell upon her as yet unfounded fears, and often had disturbing thoughts that something terrible was going to happen to her someday. Family members believed that might have been one of the reasons why she always kept very much to herself. That is not to say, however, that she did not have friends. She did, of course, and she loved them dearly, just as they loved her. But she was always very selective about the people with whom she chose to associate, and she always remained close to her family.

Perhaps more of a homebody type than many of her peers, Robin tried hard to be a typical teenager during her high school years. Like most teenagers, she wanted acceptance from kids her own age and sometimes bowed to pressure, such as taking up the habit of smoking cigarettes. But she never did anything to cause her parents any real problems or grief. Even though she made good grades in school, she didn't particularly like school, and as time went on it became tough for her mother to get her out of bed in the morning. But even that, aside from occasionally showing up late for school, never really became a problem for anyone. If she had a problem that she couldn't solve herself or if something bothered her, she would always go to her mother with her troubles, just as all of Edna's kids would. Of course, she had the usual fights with her three brothers and two sisters, and there was a certain amount of sibling rivalry among all of them, just as there is in any large family, but when it came down to the nitty-gritty they were always there for one another just as their mother had always taught them to be.

Despite the love and positive reinforcement that Robin received at home, she did not grow up being overly confident. She often worried about her looks and became self-conscious, which, again, was typical for a teenage girl. She was pretty, but she didn't really think of herself as being very pretty. She had had a hernia on her navel when she was a baby, not a "normal belly button," which, even though surgically repaired when she was an infant, transformed into a rather small line with an indentation as she grew up. Although it wasn't particularly noticeable and didn't mar her attractiveness, she didn't want people to see it. For reasons that no one really understood, she developed an almost unnatural fear of having her body exposed, perhaps because of her herniated navel. She even dreaded going to the doctor out of fear that she would be asked to disrobe for an examination, and would see a doctor only when it became absolutely necessary.

There was also a certain inexplicable dark or grim side to Robin that bordered on the macabre. Besides being afraid of the dark, which might have stemmed from her fondness for a country and western song, "Jeannie Is Afraid of the Dark," that she listened to constantly as a child, Robin withdrew into her own little shell when her mother divorced her second husband, Robin's father, Stuart, in 1978. As if being withdrawn wasn't a serious enough problem for her to cope with, she began having recurring nightmares of being held captive in a crowded, dark place, nightmares that her mother now believes, in retrospect, were a chilling foreshadowing of what was to come.

Within a year or so, as she began to accept her parents' divorce, Robin started coming out of the protective shell that she had constructed around herself. By then she had become close friends with two other girls, Julie and Trish, and the trio was inseparable. Together almost constantly, everybody soon began calling them the Three Musketeers.

Then, in 1982, Trish suddenly announced to Robin and Julie that she was moving to California. She was going to stay with a friend there and find a job, she told her friends. Robin, then 16, was deeply saddened to see her friend leave, but she nonetheless wished Trish luck and issued her a stern warning not to get drawn into the nether world of drugs or prostitution. Trish promised her friends that she wouldn't, and assured them that she would behave herself and that she would stay in touch. Following a tearful going-away party, Trish departed her friends' lives.

Two months later, however, Trish called Robin. Robin, of course, was ecstatic to hear from her. But there was something about the fact that Trish had called that troubled her. Robin asked her what was wrong, not really expecting Trish to tell her but nonetheless hoping that she would. Everything was fine, said Trish. She had a job, she was happy, and she said she liked living in California. But she somehow didn't sound normal to Robin, and Robin continued to sense that something was wrong.

"Are you sure that you're not on drugs or involved in prostitution?" Robin asked. "If you are, I'll kick your butt because I don't want you doing things like that. Come home if things are going wrong for you." Still Trish insisted that everything was fine.

Two days later, while watching television, Robin saw a news report about a girl who had been murdered at an apartment complex down on the Sea-Tac Strip, a busy boulevard of hotels, motels, and restaurants so named because of its close proximity to the Seattle-Tacoma International Airport. Some of the establishments were classy, but for every classy hotel or motel there were two that were seedy. Hookers, young and over-the-hill alike, commonly walked the Strip at all hours of the day and night, looking to turn a trick and make a few bucks for their next fix of heroin, speed, or whatever. Some of the girls worked independently, and others had pimps. But it didn't matter. They were always there, rain or shine, and many of them often fell victim to a sex criminal of one kind or another while plying their trade in the world's oldest profession. Most were either released or escaped with only minimal physical harm after having been forced to engage in any number of sexual fetishism, some violent. But one such sex criminal, however, showed them no mercy. He would eventually be dubbed the Green River Killer, a vicious psychopathic murderer who wanted more of the prostitutes, much more, than they were willing to sell to him. The Strip would become the focal point of the police, from where so many of that serial killer's street-walking victims were plucked off the boulevard and driven to their violent, horrible deaths.

Naturally, when the girl was found dead at the apartment complex, most people never thought much about it at the time. By then the murders attributed to the Green River Killer had become more or less commonplace, and the public at first just chalked up the murder of this latest young female as another of the elusive serial killer's victims, just another prostitute who had met an unpleasant end. But the police knew right away that the girl wasn't a Green River Killer victim. Although the girl was indeed quickly labeled a hooker by the police, her murder simply did not fit that serial killer's modus operandi, his method of operation. And when Robin saw the news reports of the murdered girl, her thoughts turned to Trish. But she soon convinced herself that the girl couldn't have been Trish. She was in California.

The police couldn't immediately identify the young girl. The news reports said that she had been raped and murdered in an upstairs apartment unit, stabbed to death, and her nude body had been tossed off one of the balconies. Soon, however, the police had a photo taken of the dead girl, just of her face, and had it published under the Crimestoppers heading in the local newspapers. One of the victim's former classmates recognized her, and positively identified her for the police. It was Trish, all right, and when Robin learned that one of her closest friends had been brutally raped and murdered, it was almost more than she could take.

Robin literally came unglued, as did her friend Julie, the sister of close family friend Jim Chaney. Despite warnings from her family and friends, Robin went down to the apartment complex where the murder occurred and started knocking on doors, asking questions of the tenants in an attempt to find out who had done such a horrible thing to her girlfriend. Fearing that Robin might roust the killer out during one of her irrational outbursts, Edna called a police friend and asked him to speak to her. Although Robin at first resisted the police officer's efforts to talk some sense into her, he eventually was able to convince her to let the police do their job. Even after the case was eventually cleared, Robin and Julie would find it difficult to return their lives to normal.

Following Trish's murder, Robin's nightmares resumed and actually intensified. No longer did she merely dream that something horrible was going to happen to her. Her dreams became more specific than that and intensified to the point where she frequently dreamed of *dying* at the hands of another, horribly, just like Trish. Although everyone tried to console her and attempted to pump positive thoughts into her mind, the nightmares only grew worse. Concerned for her safety after Trish's murder, and seeing how adversely the murder had affected her, Robin's brothers and sisters began cautioning her about the many dangers lurking on the city's streets. If anyone ever tried to rape her, they told her, just give it up if it otherwise meant losing her life. But Robin always remained steadfast.

"Never. Over my dead body. I'll fight. I'll go down with a fight," she told them. Although she never fully got over Trish's brutal and untimely death, she tried hard to get on with her life. It wasn't easy, but the fact that she and Julie were there for each other to lean on helped them both to eventually accept what had happened to Trish.

Though certainly no "party animal" like so many of the other girls her age, Robin was known to take part in a little merrymaking with her friends as she grew older, but only occasionally. She enjoyed the occasional "kegger," as all high school and college-age teenagers do, and after turning twenty-one she became fond of occasionally going out dancing. Which is precisely what she had made plans to do on Friday evening, March 27, 1987, a week shy of her twenty-second birthday.

Having recently quit her job at Heath Tecna Aerospace Company in nearby Kent, a Seattle suburb, where she had worked for a time with her mother, Robin was currently earning money by baby-sitting her young niece, her sister Laurie's daughter, five days a week. She adored children, and baby-sitting to her was more rewarding than working at a regular job. She wanted to have children of her own eventually, and she viewed baby-sitting as an experiential precursor to starting her own family someday. On that Friday evening Robin was waiting at her mother's home, where she often stayed when she took care of her sister's child, when Edna and Laurie arrived after getting off work. Rather than simply turn her niece over to her sister and leave, Robin remained at her mother's home to visit for a while, which was her custom. She was also waiting for her fiancé, Larron Francis Vitus Crowston, twenty-three, to meet her there when he got off work from his job. She and Larron, Robin told her mother, had made plans to meet some friends to go dancing at Baldy's Tavern later that evening. Baldy's was the only place close to where they both lived that featured live music, and that evening there was a country-rock band playing there. It would be the first time that they had gone dancing in several weeks, and both she and Larron were anxious to get started.

When Larron arrived a short time later, he came inside the house to see his "second family," just as he always did. Engaged to Robin two years earlier, on Christmas Day 1985, Larron had become very close to the Smith family. Even before his engagement to Robin, after he and Robin had met each other in 1982 through their friends and had begun dating, Larron had quickly gained the acceptance and friendship of the Smith family through the kindness that he had shown to Robin and out of his love and respect for her.

According to Edna, Robin hadn't given in sexually to Larron until after they had dated for a long time. And when she finally did become sexually active, it was always with Larron and Larron alone. It was obvious to Edna from the beginning that Larron and Robin's love for each other was genuine. They truly seemed made for each other and, in Edna's words, "theirs was a relationship born in Heaven."

Robin had been truly happy when she met Larron, according to Edna, and the period in which they had begun planning their future had been one of the most joyful times in Robin's life. Her primary goals at that juncture in her life were to get married, have children, and just be the basic housewife type. But she and Larron didn't want to rush into marriage. They wanted to do it right and not become stressed out financially as so many young couples do when they first start out, and that was the principal reason they had waited so long even to begin thinking about setting a wedding date. They were saving their money so that they could get off to a good beginning together.

Edna had certainly done her part by helping Robin and Larron obtain jobs in the quality-control section at Heath Tecna—which does work for Boeing, McDonnell Douglas and a number of other companies closely aligned to the aerospace industry— where Edna had worked for the past six years. Even though Robin had chosen not to stay at Heath Tecna, Larron had. He liked his job there, and he liked the company. But Robin, the homebody, liked to look after kids.

Looking at them that evening, sharing things like cigarettes and soda pop as they always did, and listening to them making their weekend plans as they got ready to leave and go out dancing, Edna knew that theirs was indeed a rare happiness. Their trust in each other was unusual, extraordinary, but it was a complete trust. Edna knew in her heart that if any couple could make it together nowadays, Larron and Robin could.

"Mom," Robin finally said as they stood up to leave, "Larron has plans to go fishing tomorrow. I don't want to spend the day by myself, so I might come back over tomorrow."

"Okay," Edna replied with her kind, motherly smile. "That's fine. It will be fun to have you." Edna meant it. She always enjoyed having Robin spend the day with her.

After they had pulled on their jackets, Edna walked Robin and Larron to the door. Robin and Edna kissed each other good-bye, and neither of them, not even for an instant, thought that they might not ever see each other again.

Robin Pamela Smith had everything to live for on that fateful evening. A loving family, plans to be married to a man who adored her, and a bright future with the only man she had ever truly loved. Tragically, none of those qualities and aspirations would be realized beyond that Friday night.

Endowed with an elegant natural beauty accentuated by her blond hair and blue eyes, Robin, petite and feisty-looking with her 5 foot 4 inch, 110 pound frame, typically turned a lot of heads without any effort on her part whenever she entered a room. Such was the case when she and Larron entered Baldy's Tavern late that evening. Ignoring the usual gawks, stares, and catcalls that go on in a crowded establishment like Baldy's when a good-looking woman walks through the front door, Robin and Larron made their way slowly through the smoke-filled tavern until they eventually found an unoccupied table near the dance floor. They ordered their first pitcher of beer that evening from a smiling, slender young woman named Mary.

When their beer came, Larron and Robin struck up a conversation with Mary. It didn't amount to much, mostly small talk regarding Larron and Robin's night out. But for some reason, perhaps because of the instant congeniality of the two women, Larron formed the distinct impression that Robin and Mary had met each other before that night. He would report later that he had thought that they were friends. But his assessment was wrong. Neither Robin or Mary had met each other before that night.

Larron and Robin drank their beer, danced, ordered more beer, and waited for their friends to arrive. However, as the minutes gave way to hours, they both realized that their friends were not going to show up. Nonetheless, Larron and Robin were in the mood to party and they stayed, and they danced.

Sometime between ten and eleven, Darren O'Neall walked into the tavern. Since there were no seats at the bar, where he preferred to sit, he took one of the few seats remaining at a table near the rear of the tavern. As usual, he was alone. O'Neall had stayed away from Baldy's for a few days prior because of the fighting and arguing that had been going on between himself and Mary. He really didn't want to see her any more than she wanted to see him, and it was naturally somewhat unsettling to Mary when he showed up and she realized that she had to serve him. Unknown to Mary and those around him, even though he again had that faraway look in his eyes, O'Neall had been fantasizing anew about finding the "perfect woman" that he could take into the mountains to live with him. As he glanced around the tavern that evening, he was certain that he had found her when he saw Robin Smith. But he also instantly understood that he had a problem: the man accompanying the pretty blonde.

As the evening wore on, the tavern became filled to the point that there was standing room only, typical for a Friday night. As a result, people eventually began to join O'Neall at his table. Some of them he knew from the tavern, others he didn't know at all. Most of them simply came and went for the next couple of hours, and no one person stayed with him throughout the few hours that he was there. O'Neall drank steadily as he watched Robin from across the room, until it was nearly closing time.

Shortly before 2:00 A.M. O'Neall called Mary over to his table. He put his best self forward, and appeared to be trying to make up with her for their earlier troubles. He told her that he was sorry that he had been so mean to her lately, but offered her no explanation for his actions. He quickly changed the subject and began talking about having an after-hours party at his apartment. Mary was hesitant at first, but she didn't disagree with him. She didn't dare.

"I think I'll invite a few of these people over this morning," O'Neall told Mary. "Will you be there, too, after you get off work?" He was making plans again, and was merely being manipulative in his encounter with Mary. He would use her while he still could, get her to do what he wanted.

"I don't know," she hesitated. "I guess so. A party will be okay. But don't go overboard. I don't even know some of these people that you want to invite. But okay, fine."

After gaining Mary's unneeded "approval" for the party and her assurance that she would be there, O'Neall pointed out Robin and Larron to her and asked her to go over to their table and invite them. Mary, who by now had become acquainted and was comfortable with them, agreed to O'Neall's request. He sat back and smiled to himself, satisfied that Mary would do his bidding as he watched her make her way through the crowd to Larron and Robin's table.

"Hey, we're getting ready to close," Mary said to Larron and Robin. "I'm gonna have a few people over to my place, just a little after-hours party. I live with a guy nearby. You two want to come?"

Feeling their beer, Larron and Robin looked at each other quizzically for a moment, then both of them agreed to go to the party, each apparently thinking that the other knew Mary better than either of them actually did. At least that was Larron's assessment of the situation in hindsight. Mary gave them the address, thought about it for a moment, and then told them that it would be easier if they just followed her over to the apartment after she closed up the tavern. They both agreed.

Chapter 3

People came and went throughout the night at the shabby complex of duplex apartments on Thirteenth Court East in the Edgewood area of Puyallup. It wasn't difficult for anyone to find the unit where the party was taking place. All they had to do was to follow the comings and goings of the revelers in the center of the complex, people who were staggering between the center units and the cars parked out front along the road. One by one the beer-drinking carousers entered the small, crowded, smoke-filled apartment where country and western music emanated with much distortion from a cheap clock radio tuned to an FM station that sat next to an equally cheap, dust-coated, small-screen television.

Darren O'Neall kept mostly to himself that morning, except during several instances in which he tried in vain to pick a fight with Mary. It was all that she could do to ignore his antagonistic and bellicose digs in which he viciously berated her verbally in front of the others, but she did. Instead of giving him what he wanted, namely a fight, she focused her attention on the guests, in particular a man, David Wells,* twenty-six, with whom she had become somewhat infatuated. Although O'Neall noticed that she was coming on to Wells throughout the morning, he really didn't care. His mind was elsewhere most of that time, far off in a fantasy that he would soon bring to life. He initiated very little conversation throughout the rest of the morning and spoke only when spoken to as he sat alone and drank beer after beer and chain-smoked Camel filters. He would occasionally get up from his perch on the sofa, from where he had been keeping a watchful eye on Robin Smith, and walk uneventfully down the hallway from the living room to the bathroom, where he alternated between relieving himself and injecting himself with cocaine, only to return to his spot revitalized, ready to resume his vigil with a fresh beer in his hand after an absence of only a few minutes.

Around three-thirty, in response to a guest's suggestions, the party at O'Neall's broke up and everyone drove to the home of Tony Sellers,* a suspected major drug dealer who lived in the Lake Tapps area just outside Tacoma near Sumner, off the road to Mount Rainier and Greenwater. Since Larron and Robin didn't know precisely where Sellers lived, they rode with their newly made acquaintance David Wells, introduced to them by Mary, in Wells's vehicle. Mary and O'Neall also rode along with them in the same car. Wells, who did not know Sellers personally, followed closely behind another acquaintance who knew where Sellers' house was located.

Sellers had thrown an after-hours party of his own, but much to everyone's dismay his party was winding down by the time the small caravan of cars arrived there from O'Neall's. Nonetheless there was a little life and lots of cocaine left in Sellers' party, and most of the new arrivals stayed for a couple of hours. It was near sunrise when that party eventually broke up, and the beer drinkers reluctantly moved back to O'Neall's apartment in Edgewood when Sellers finally threw them out. By then Larron realized that it was time for him to leave if he was to make it on time to his charter fishing appointment. He had one small problem, however. Robin wasn't ready to leave. Intoxicated, she was feeling her beer and was still having a good time. She wanted to stay a while longer.

"Let me stay, Larron," Robin begged. She looked over at Mary for support.

"Yeah, let her stay, Larron," echoed Mary, slurring her words. "I'll see that she gets home."

Larron thought about it for a few moments and, feeling the effects of the all-nighter that he had just participated in, reluctantly gave in. Besides, he knew from prior experience that it would not do any good to argue with Robin. She was headstrong, and when her mind was made up about something, there was little that anyone could say or do to make her change it.

"Okay," he said. "Under the condition that you, Mary, will bring Robin home in the next couple of hours or so."

"Oh, sure," Mary said. "No problem. One of us will get her home."

Larron and Robin embraced, kissed, and said their good-byes. He looked back and smiled at her as he left the apartment, followed outside by Mary.

"I've got to go and buy some more beer," Mary lied when she noticed Larron's inquiring eyes. Nothing else was said. They each climbed into their respective cars and left. Robin was alone inside the apartment with only O'Neall and David Wells. Larron wasn't worried, however. They had seemed harmless enough, and anyway Mary would be back soon from the store with more beer, or so he thought.

When Larron left Robin at O'Neall's apartment, he didn't know that during the course of the morning Wells and Mary had been coming on to each other. Mary, looking for a way to break away from O'Neall, had responded positively to Wells's advances and at one point indicated to him that she would like to meet him later. But they had to be careful, she had told him, to avoid angering O'Neall. She was afraid of O'Neall, and didn't want to become involved in another violent confrontation with him like the one that she had experienced earlier in the week. As a result, Mary and Wells formulated a plan in which Mary would leave the apartment on some pretext, such as making a beer run when the stores began selling alcoholic beverages again after 7:00 A.M.

Mary stuck to the plan and drove her gold Duster to the 7-Eleven store in Edgewood, where she parked and waited for Wells. Some twenty minutes later Wells announced to Robin and O'Neall that he, too, would be leaving. They were out of beer, and Mary hadn't yet made it back with more. Robin, not wanting to be left all alone with O'Neall, asked Wells for a ride to her home in Des Moines. Apologetically, Wells told Robin that Des Moines was in the opposite direction from where he was going and said that he couldn't take her home. Without giving too much thought about how Robin would get home, Wells left to keep his early morning rendezvous with Mary.

Everything had fallen conveniently into place for O'Neall. He had managed to separate Robin not only from her fiancé but from everyone else, and all with little or no effort on his part. It was amazing how well fate always treated him when it came down to finding a victim. Everything always seemed to happen just the way he wanted it to, and that morning had been no exception.

When Larron returned from his day-long fishing trip, one of the first things he noticed was that Robin, with whom he had lived for the past four years, was not at home. But there was no reason for him to worry, he told himself, at least not yet. Robin had said that she did not want to stay at home alone while Larron was gone on his fishing trip, and had indicated that she would likely spend the day at her mother's house. Larron, tired from the fishing trip and from staying up all night drinking beer, put the matter out of his mind and dozed off.

When he awoke a couple of hours later, it was

early evening and he still had not heard from Robin. Worry began to creep in, and Larron decided to call his good friend, James M. "Jim" Chaney, Jr., for advice. He related the story of the after-hours party, and the way that he explained it all to his friend, it seemed even to Jim as if Robin had known Mary before the evening of March 27.

"Hey, she's probably just having a good time with a girlfriend," Jim told Larron. "Don't worry about it. If the girl said she'd give Robin a ride home, she'll be home."

Though still somewhat troubled, what Jim had said did make sense to Larron. And he was so tired. His mind was probably playing tricks on him, causing him to worry for nothing. He decided that he would just go to bed and try to get some sleep, confident that Robin would show up at any time. But she didn't.

Neither Larron or Jim had any way of knowing what had really happened. They couldn't imagine that O'Neall, when left all alone with Robin, had come on to her sexually, that he had told her that he wanted to make her his woman and take her into the hills with him where the two of them could live out the rest of their lives and in the process make his survivalist mountain man fantasy become a reality. They couldn't know that when Robin had resisted his advances, he easily subdued her in her intoxicated state and, with his penchant for violent sex, had raped her in the apartment. No one could imagine how he had beaten her unconscious and then bound her hands and feet with extension cords that he ripped from the television, how he pushed a gag into her mouth to keep her quiet, then rolled her bleeding, naked body up inside a blanket. None of them ever would have envisioned how O'Neall, in his cruelty, had carried Robin outside in her weakened semi-conscious state and placed her inside the large, oversized trunk of the Chrysler New Yorker he was driving, alongside camping gear, food, and other supplies he felt they would need out in the woods. But he did all of these things and more, and there was nothing by that time that anybody could have done, even if they had known about his plans, to stop him.

When Mary returned to the apartment that she shared with O'Neall, she learned, much to her relief, that O'Neall was gone. The butterscotch-colored New Yorker was not in its usual parking space, and when she entered the apartment to begin packing up her own things, she quickly discovered that O'Neall had already moved out. Although some of his clothing was still there, much of it was missing from the apartment, as were two blankets that were normally kept on the bed. The camping gear that he always kept in the bedroom closet was also missing, and she guessed that he finally set out to fulfill his fantasy of living in the wilderness, independent of society. However, when she looked around some more, she discovered that he had left behind his sleeping bag and briefly wondered why. Had he left in such a hurry that he had merely forgotten it? Surely he would need it, she thought, if he had truly gone off to live in the wilderness. She quickly dismissed the thought and went about her own business of preparing to vacate the premises.

When she went into the kitchen, however, nagging thoughts of mild bewilderment surrounding the sudden departure of her former companion returned momentarily. One of the first things she noticed was that the kitchen had been cleaned up, thoroughly. That was strange, she thought, and so unlike Darren, especially after a party. He rarely cleaned up anything. To him, cleaning was a woman's work. Women, in Darren's mind, she recalled, were put on the earth to serve men, and they were rarely useful outside the kitchen and the bedroom. As she pondered O'Neall's absence, Mary turned to the refrigerator and saw that its handle had been broken off. It hadn't been broken when she left the day before, she reflected. The door could still be opened, but only by grasping its edge and pulling on it. When she looked inside, she found that O'Neall had apparently taken a large, frozen beef roast from the freezer compartment. As she was wondering how O'Neall had managed to break the refrigerator handle, she peered through the kitchen window and saw that O'Neall's German shepherd was still there, securely bound to a chain in the backyard. Although she wondered why he hadn't taken the dog with him, she quickly put it, too, out of her mind. Frankly, she didn't give a damn about any of those things, just as long as O'Neall was gone and out of her life for good.

* * *

When Larron Crowston awoke that Sunday morning and found that Robin still had not returned home, he flew into a panic. Pacing the floor and turning over in his mind all of the possibilities of what could have happened to Robin, Larron finally turned to the telephone and called Edna.

"Mom, can I talk to Robin?" Larron asked in a quavering voice when Edna answered, hoping desperately that she was there with her mother.

"Larron," Edna replied, "she's not here." Having detected apprehension, a distinct foreboding in Larron's voice, Edna suddenly did not feel right. After a few moments of silence she asked: "Larron, what's wrong?"

Suddenly realizing his agitated state and trying hard not to panic Edna, Larron explained that he hadn't seen Robin since early Saturday morning. He described the party, Mary and O'Neall, the circumstances of their parting, and said that he was concerned because from all appearances it did not look as though Robin had been home at all, not even during the day while he had been fishing. Apologetically, he said that he hadn't become too concerned until now because he thought that Robin had spent the day, and possibly the night, at Edna's.

"Let's get over to that house right now, Larron," Edna commanded. "We need to find her."

Larron picked up Edna, and they immediately drove to the apartment on Thirteenth Court East. Larron was hopeful that Robin might still be there, but he knew in his heart that she wouldn't be. He couldn't think of any reasonable reason for her to still be there. When they arrived, the only person that was there was Mary. She appeared busy, packing her belongings and preparing to move in with a friend in nearby Sumner, and acted like she didn't have time to talk to them.

Mary seemed nervous, somewhat shaken when she learned that they were there looking for Robin. She told Larron and Edna that she hadn't given Robin a ride home as she had promised, and explained that when she left the apartment on Saturday morning Robin was still there with a guy named David and O'Neall. She hadn't seen Robin or O'Neall since. When she returned home a short time before Larron and Edna arrived, she said, which was the first time that she had been home since leaving the party the morning before, she had discovered that O'Neall had apparently moved out. In response to their questions, Mary told Larron and Edna where O'Neall worked. She told them that she didn't know David's surname, which was true despite the fact that she had slept with him the night before.

When they arrived at Interior Form Tops a few minutes later, they were told that, yes, Darren O'Neall had worked there, but not any longer. He had come in two days earlier, on Friday, March 27, quit his job, and picked up his final paycheck. He was planning on going out of state somewhere, to Alaska, or so the manager thought. O'Neall had also talked about going back to Colorado, said the manager, where his parents lived. Sensing that something was very wrong, Edna grabbed Larron by the arm and led him out of the cabinet shop.

"Come on, Larron," Edna said. "We're going home. We're gonna get some friends and family and start looking for Robin. We need to get a hold of Jim right away."

Edna knew that something had happened to Robin, but she just didn't know what and she tried hard not to think of the worst. It wasn't like Robin to just disappear, and she knew that Robin wouldn't merely leave Larron like that, especially for an extended period of time. Even if she had been upset over Larron going fishing, Edna knew that Robin wouldn't have stayed away without calling. That was just not Robin. She wouldn't do something that she knew would cause any of her family to worry needlessly. Rather than waiting any longer for Robin to come home on her own, they picked up Robin's half brother, Robert "Bobby" Sharp, then drove directly to Jim Chaney's house.

Chaney, 34, a long-haired, bearded biker type, was a longtime loyal friend of the Smiths' and would become one of their strongest allies in their search for Robin. Normally a gentle soul with a heart of gold, Chaney became distraught and angry that Sunday morning when he was told of Robin's disappearance. When he learned of the circumstances, and feeling badly that he hadn't taken Larron's telephone call the evening before as a more serious warning that something was wrong, he didn't want to waste any more time. Hopeful that Mary might hold the key to what happened, the four of them returned to O'Neall's apartment to confront her again.

Mary repeated basically what she had told them earlier. However, recognizing the urgency of the situation, Mary eventually agreed to accompany Edna, Larron, Bobby, and Jim to the Pierce County Sheriff's Department to file a missing-person report on Robin. But when they arrived, they were met only with more frustration. The deputy on duty did not want to take the report.

"Go on back home," the deputy said after hearing the circumstances behind Robin's disappearance. "She'll turn up. If she doesn't, come back and we'll take a report." He calmly explained that it was departmental policy to wait 72 hours before filing a missing-person report, if there was no evidence of foul play, to allow the supposedly missing person sufficient time to return home on their own.

But that wasn't good enough. Not in this case. Angry and frustrated, Edna and her party became loud. They leaned across the desk and began yelling, and they had Mary repeat her version of what happened until they got the deputy's undivided attention. In order to calm them down, the deputy finally agreed to write up a report. It became report number 87-089-452.

Sadly, none of them knew that it was already too late for Robin. Although no one would ever be certain of the precise sequence of events that transpired after Robin had been left alone with O'Neall, investigators would eventually piece together what they believed happened based on the evidence they would discover. Much of what they would conclude, however, would be disputed by O'Neall, despite the fact that the he would ultimately claim that he could not recall many of the details due to his intense state of drug- and alcohol-induced intoxication during that period.

It would become apparent to the investigators, however, that on the day before, frustrated and nervous after having assaulted and raped her, O'Neall had driven with Robin still in the trunk of the Chrysler to a heavily wooded location near Mount Rainier and parked the car. Unknown to O'Neall, Robin, even though suffering from head wounds that O'Neall had inflicted with his fists at the apartment earlier, and later with a hammer during a brief stop at Frank Wilhelm's, when he had tried to borrow some money so that he could get out of town, had managed to undo her bindings after sobering up and regaining consciousness from having spent the past several hours in the Chrysler's trunk. When he unlocked the trunk and opened the lid Robin, without giving him any prior warning, jumped up and viciously attacked him with all of the energy and courage that she could invoke from her weakened state. Known as a fighter who would die trying to protect herself, Robin went for O'Neall's face and fiercely began hitting, clawing, and scratching him, ripping flesh and drawing blood. O'Neall, who had been alternating between swigging a bottle of Jack Daniel's and injecting cocaine and tar heroin, was in no shape to fend off the attack unaided. Angered and in a panic, he reached past Robin and picked up a claw hammer from inside the trunk. Swinging wildly, he began beating her savagely about the head and face. The blows were almost reflexive, at least at first. Robin's facial bones and skull cracked with each blow, and her blood sprayed and was slung onto the inside lid of the trunk. Although her screams of pain became more and more subdued with each blow and she eventually faded back into unconsciousness, he continued to beat her as her life blood spilled out of her head wounds and mushroomed onto the trunk's bottom surface. He watched with wild eyes as her otherwise lifeless body twitched and convulsed and involuntarily gasped for air, trying in vain to hang on to the final threads of life. Finally, she lay still.

O'Neall paced back and forth for a time, trying to figure out what to do with her body. He returned to the car and poked at her body with his hands, but there was no movement whatsoever. Certain that she was dead, O'Neall lifted her body up and out of the trunk, inadvertently allowing her blood-soaked hair to come into contact with the trunk's interior metal, leaving a brush stroke of sorts in crimson. Alone again in a silent forest, O'Neall carried Robin's ravaged corpse farther into the woods.

After removing approximately $120 and some change from her purse, O'Neall gathered up Robin's clothing and other belongings and carried them, too, into the forest. After neatly rolling them up, he attempted to hide the items beneath a rotting tree stump, not far from where he had dumped Robin's body, cold and naked, onto a damp bed of pine and Douglas fir needles. He walked to a nearby stream, where he disposed of the hammer and washed the blood, both his and Robin's, from his face and hands. Afterward, satisfied that she would not be quickly found, O'Neall injected himself again, drank what remained of the bottle of Jack Daniel's, and headed back down the road, destination unknown.

Chapter 4

At fifty years of age, Edna Smith had thought that the days and nights of worrying about her six children, now that she had them raised, were over. She was wrong. When Robin disappeared, she starkly realized that parenthood never ends, no matter what the age of the son or daughter. After filing the missing-person report on Robin that Sunday night, Edna began to think about the grim possibilities. For the first time in her life she found herself trying to come to grips with something that she felt she might never fully recover from. That Sunday night was such a sleepless night for her, unlike any that she had ever experienced before. It was far worse than when her kids had begun to come of age and had begun doing the things, like staying out late, that teenagers so often do. She had gotten through all those years, and for what? To have her worst nightmare come frighteningly to life? Emotionally drained, all Edna could do was think about what had become of her youngest daughter, unaware that that Saturday night was only the beginning of weeks, months, even years of sleepless nights. Unfortunately, no reasonable answers, or rather no comforting ones, came that evening to ease her pain of not knowing what had become of Robin.

The next morning, Monday, March 30, when Robin didn't show up to baby-sit for her sister Laurie, both Edna and Laurie, as well as other family members, grew even more concerned about her well-being. Robin had never missed showing up when she was supposed to, and if she had been going to miss on any given day she would have called her mother or sister the night before or, at the very least, early enough in the morning so that other arrangements could be made for the care of her sister's children. But nobody had heard from her all weekend long, and that was just not like Robin. She knew that she had to watch the kids on Monday morning. So what had happened to her? Edna wondered, worrying constantly as she sat on the sofa next to the telephone. Where was she? As each hour passed with no word from Robin, the dread in Edna's heart swelled.

Rather than sitting around and doing nothing, however, simply waiting for the police to begin looking for Robin, Edna decided that she had to do something, anything. Accompanied by Jim Chaney, her son Bobby, and son-in-law Mike Baker, who is married to Robin's sister, Brenda, Edna and her family began to search for answers on their own. They contacted Mary once again, this time making inquiries about any friends or acquaintances that O'Neall might have had in the area. Mary pondered the possibilities for a moment, but the only person that she could think of was Frank Wilhelm. Accompanied by Mary, the five of them drove to Wilhelm's house in East Tacoma, out of which he ran an automotive shop.

Wilhelm, who barely knew Mary, was hesitant to talk to anyone about O'Neall at first. He appeared to be busy, and seemed a bit tense by the presence of so many people asking questions. However, when Jim and Mike explained the circumstances of why they were there, Wilhelm eased up a bit and told them that he had last seen O'Neall on Saturday, March 28, at approximately 1:00 P.M. O'Neall had been there asking for money, Wilhelm said, supposedly to put down on a truck that he wanted to buy. But Wilhelm didn't believe that he had wanted the money to buy a truck. There was some other reason, Wilhelm felt, but he couldn't figure out what it was. His instinct kept telling him that O'Neall was in some kind of trouble.

When he realized that these people weren't going to leave without some answers, Wilhelm said that O'Neall had told him that he was going away for a while, and also asked him to look after his German shepherd puppy, which O'Neall had let out of the backseat of the car upon his arrival so that the pup could play with Wilhelm's dog. O'Neall never told Wilhelm why he was going away, and he hadn't pressed him for details. But there was something about O'Neall's demeanor that had disturbed Wilhelm.

"He seemed real nervous, like he was hiding something," Wilhelm told them, still cautious with the words he chose. "He parked his car across the street when there was plenty of parking right next to the building. I thought that was strange."

When asked if he knew where O'Neall had taken off to, Wilhelm said that he had no idea. When the subject of O'Neall's outdoors experience came up, Wilhelm merely laughed it off. When O'Neall had arrived at his place in November, Wilhelm had been making plans to go elk hunting with some friends. O'Neall had asked to go along and ended up accompanying them. However, Wilhelm said that O'Neall did not appear familiar with the outdoors at all.

"He only hiked into the woods one day," Wilhelm said of the hunting trip. "And one night he practically cried to get the keys to my truck. He said that he wanted to sleep in the cab and turn the heat on because he was cold."

Realizing that his visitors weren't satisfied with his answers yet, Wilhelm decided that he had to tell them more about O'Neall's visit. He hadn't wanted to get involved in any of O'Neall's troubles, but he was by now being dragged into it. He had no choice, he realized, and his voice became nervous as he continued to relate what happened.

Wilhelm explained that when O'Neall showed up on Saturday afternoon, he helped him rearrange things inside the shop. Afterward, O'Neall returned to his car and Wilhelm followed, his checkbook in hand. It was while they were talking about the money and the fact that Wilhelm could only write him a check that Wilhelm noticed something kicking persistently against the back seat from inside the trunk. O'Neall, aware that Wilhelm had noticed the commotion, appeared even more nervous and was anxious to leave.

"He told me he was having trouble with his dog, so he locked it in the trunk," explained Wilhelm. The dog in question would have been O'Neall's other dog, a full-grown German shepherd that, O'Neall had told him, had been misbehaving. He told Wilhelm that he had placed the dog in the trunk for punishment.

"I told him, 'That's sick. You don't put a dog in the trunk,'" Wilhelm continued. "Then I walked away without writing him the check and he drove off." After hearing the mysterious circumstances surrounding Robin's disappearance, Wilhelm added: "I never thought about it at the time. But now I'm totally convinced that someone was in the trunk. There was no barking, like there would have been if a dog had been back there."

While Wilhelm was relating to his unexpected visitors the details of his last encounter with O'Neall, a young man whom Edna, Bobby, Mike, and Jim would all describe later as a "space cadet" to the police came out of the shop. He seemed almost disoriented, and it was difficult for them to tell if he was currently high on drugs or if he was merely burned out from heavy prior drug use. He gave all the indications of being an acid head, that is, a user of LSD, the powerful hallucinogenic drug that was so popular among the all but forgotten hippies of the sixties but which has been making a comeback in recent years among our nation's youth. However, the young man, whether high or not, had apparently overheard portions of their discussion with Wilhelm, and according to what Jim, Mike, and Bobby would later report to the police, said: "Yeah, I remember that day. I was standing by the trunk when Darren opened it up because of a commotion, some noises. He grabbed a hammer and beat this naked blond girl in the head. All she was wearing was a pair of socks. They were white with purple trim, man."

While Jim, Mike, and Bobby were shocked, completely taken aback by the young man's unanticipated comments, Wilhelm purportedly blew up and said: "Shut your mouth! Get your ass back in the house!" He then turned to Jim: "Don't listen to him. He doesn't know what he's talking about. He invents things."

Now it was Mike who became enraged. What that young man had said about O'Neall's Saturday afternoon visit was very different from the version that Wilhelm had just told them. Did the kid simply invent things as Wilhelm had said? Or did he actually know something, perhaps at least some of the truth about what had happened to Robin? And if that was so, why had Wilhelm's version differed? Was he afraid to get involved, perhaps out of fear of retribution from O'Neall, if he had in fact either heard about or, worse, had himself witnessed O'Neall commit such a display of violence? Fearing that he wasn't going to get any more answers without some help, Mike sent Jim to call the police while he, Bobby, and Edna remained there with Wilhelm.

Due to a manpower shortage within the department and several other calls concerning crimes in progress coming in at a faster rate than deputies could handle, a sheriff's deputy was not able come out right away. When law officers eventually did intervene, however, they learned that the young man at Wilhelm's shop was enrolled in a drug-rehabilitation program in Pierce County. He was released during the day to work, but he had to go back to an institutional facility at night. Although the young man repeated some of what he had said to Edna and her family, Pierce County authorities quickly decided that they would not be able to use him as a reliable witness. Although specific on some points, he was vague on others and often seemed as if he was off in some sort of dream world.

"We can't use anything he's got to say because he's a space case," Edna said she was told by the deputy. "An attorney would chew him up in a minute on the witness stand, and anything that he had to say would be totally worthless in court."

Although it was a judicial blow against them, the first of many, Edna Smith and her family would eventually feel that the incident had been the closest that they would ever come to learning the true and most complete story of what had happened inside the trunk of Darren O'Neall's car that Saturday afternoon at Frank Wilhelm's house. Even though the story of the dog inside the trunk would be repeated many times, it was a story that they just never bought. Besides, they soon discovered that the dog in question was still tied up in the yard at O'Neall's apartment, and none of the neighbors reported seeing O'Neall return home that day and drop off the dog. If the dog had been with O'Neall at Wilhelm's home, and since O'Neall had not returned home after the visit with Wilhelm, simple logic dictated that the dog would likely still be with O'Neall, wherever he had gone. But since they knew that wasn't the case, it seemed reasonable to presume that if something had been kicking at the backseat of O'Neall's car from inside the trunk it had been Robin, who was by then sober and fearing for her life. It now seemed to Robin's family that her recurring nightmares of being held captive in a crowded, dark place had suddenly, and frighteningly, become a reality.

Later that same day, with nowhere else to turn in their endeavor to learn what had happened to Robin, Jim asked for Mary's permission to spend a few nights at the apartment she had shared with O'Neall. He wanted to be there just in case O'Neall decided to return, he said. Mary, who had not been able to move out yet because of the previous two days' events surrounding the search for Robin, readily agreed to Jim's request. She was happy to have Jim there because she certainly didn't want to be there by herself if O'Neall did, in fact, decide to return.

What she didn't realize was that Jim had other motives for wanting access to O'Neall's apartment. Sure, he would have paid good money to be there if O'Neall returned. At that point he would have liked nothing better than to take justice into his own hands. But he also wanted to search the premises to try to find clues that might shed some light on what had happened to Robin. Because she was scheduled to work the next couple of evenings at Baldy's, Mary postponed moving the rest of her belongings into her friend's home in Sumner until her next day off.

That evening, while Mary was at work, Bobby came over to help Jim with the search. Every room inside the apartment, they noted, was filthy, unkempt, a literal mess. Every room, that is, except for the kitchen. The kitchen was spotless, and that bothered both of them. A spotless kitchen with the rest of the apartment a complete mess just didn't fit. Something, they reasoned, must have happened to Robin in the kitchen. What other explanation could there be for it being so clean? Had Robin gone to the kitchen to try to find a knife or something else with which to defend herself from O'Neall? If so, had blood, either O'Neall's or Robin's, or both, been shed there? Somebody, probably O'Neall, they guessed, had cleaned up the kitchen before leaving because of something, likely violent, that had happened in there.

Jim and Bobby got down on the floor, on their hands and knees, and began searching for signs of violence, such as spots of blood. They crawled slowly, checking virtually every crevice in the tile, looking for anything that might help them discover what had occurred there that Saturday morning. But they never found anything that looked like blood. If anyone's blood had been spilled on the floor, it had been thoroughly cleaned up. And since they weren't cops, they didn't have the necessary equipment and chemicals, such as Luminol, at their disposal to properly search for mere traces of blood. They had only their eyes.

At one point Jim and Bobby, like Mary, noticed that the refrigerator's door handle had been knocked or torn off. Had Robin grabbed the handle, attempting to hold onto something firm to prevent herself from being dragged away by force? It was something that she used to do as a kid, according to Bobby. During play, whenever someone was pulling or trying to drag her away from something, it was always her custom to reach out and grab onto anything permanent or immovable that she could find. A strong girl, she would always hold on for dear life to whatever she could find to grasp in such situations. Was that what had happened here? It certainly seemed plausible, even likely. But how would they ever be able to prove it?

At another point Jim discovered a small bag of garbage beneath the kitchen sink. Inside it he found, among other things, pieces of broken glass. When he examined the glass more closely, he could see that the pieces had once been a beer glass, a schooner, the type used at taverns. Thinking that perhaps

Robin had used the beer glass in an attempt to fend off an attack from O'Neall and had perhaps struck him with it, he examined the pieces more closely for signs of blood. Finding none, and having none of the experience and skills of a trained evidence technician, he tossed the broken pieces back into the garbage bag and forgot about them. The bag was subsequently tossed out by someone, perhaps Mary or the apartment manager, and only later would Jim find himself wishing that he had kept the broken pieces of glass for the police to examine.

Using a flashlight, Jim continued his search of the cabinets beneath the kitchen sink. Interestingly, he soon found a large black candle in the shape of a human skull. Nearby he found another skull, but it was not a candle. It closely resembled a real human skull, about the size of a child's skull, and it had numbers painted on its various locations. Upon closer examination, it looked more like an imitation or reproduction of a skull than the real thing, something that might be used as a training device in a college anatomy and physiology class or medical school. He couldn't help but wonder what use O'Neall would have for such items. Jim considered that perhaps O'Neall had used them in some kind of satanic ritual. Since he had little knowledge about such things, the implications, especially with Robin missing, chilled him to the bone. He kept the items and later turned them over to investigators.

Before they were finished with their search, Jim and Bobby also found several pieces of identification bearing O'Neall's photograph but different names. It suddenly became clear to them that O'Neall had been going by a number of aliases. But for what reasons? They also found used hypodermic needles, a couple of spoons that had apparently been used to "cook" heroin or some other drug prior to injection, and several syringes. Someone, they realized, had been mainlining some heavy-duty drugs inside that apartment. Suddenly a frightening thought occurred to both of them. Had O'Neall injected Robin there? If so, it would had to have been against her will, by force. Given her conservative views on illicit drugs, they both knew that she would never have consented to such a thing. And if O'Neall had tried to inject her against her will, he would have had one hell of a fight on his hands.

Before giving up for the evening, Jim and Bobby found several paperback books, about thirty of them in all, scattered in various locations throughout the apartment. They were all westerns, and the majority of them had been written by Louis L'Amour. They collected them all and bagged them up for later scrutiny. Given O'Neall's background and fantasies of living in the outdoors, they reasoned that they and the police could go through the books in search of clues as to what O'Neall might do or where he might go to carry out such fantasies. They would pay particular attention to any pages that had been dog-eared, and would carefully study any passages that had been marked or underscored. Although the books would provide some insight into O'Neall's thought processes, they would not, unfortunately, provide the answers that they were looking for, and would ultimately serve only to deepen the mystery.

Tuesday, March 31, 1987
Pierce County Sheriff's Department
Tacoma, Washington

Detective Walter D. Stout, forty-nine, was sitting quietly at his desk in a small office on the second floor of the city-county building in downtown Tacoma when report number 87-089-452 reached his desk at 8:30 A.M. Stout, a twenty-four-year veteran of the department who was nearing retirement, had seen myriad missing-person reports during his career, and the one on Robin Smith didn't particularly stand out from many of the others, at least not at first. As he read through the sketchy details of the report, occasionally pulling at his dark beard and sipping his morning coffee, Stout figured that Robin would probably return home, and may have already done so as far as he knew, like so many of the people who are reported missing do. It wasn't until he studied the profile of Robin that had been provided by her family, which stressed aspects of her personality and habits and just how much out of character it would be for Robin to have merely left on her own, that his cop's instinct kicked in and began tugging at his gut. Before he had enough time to decide which avenue he would pursue first in the case, such as calling

Robin's family to see if they had heard from her yet, his telephone rang. The caller was Bobby Sharp, Robin's half brother, and he wanted to know what the sheriff's department was doing to find out what had happened to his sister.

"No one in the family has seen or heard from Robin since the early morning hours of March twenty-eighth," Bobby reported. "We think she's met with foul play, kidnapped or something, by this guy O'Neall. What are you guys doing about it?"

"We don't have a crime," Stout said, trying to be diplomatic and sympathetic while at the same time being realistic. "We have a missing person under suspicious circumstances, and the evidence indicates to us a high degree of possibility, not probability, that it was an abduction. We're going to check every available lead."

Stout assured Bobby that he and his partner, Detective Terry Wilson, would begin the investigation immediately and that they would report anything they learned to the family as soon as possible after they learned it. Stout promised that he would stay in touch in any event.

When they hung up, Stout contacted the Law Enforcement Support Agency (LESA) via the computer terminal at his desk and issued an all-points bulletin for O'Neall and the car he was believed to be driving. The sketchy description was all that he had for now, but he would update the APB as soon as any new information developed. He also included a description of Robin: 5 feet 4 inches tall, 110 to 115 pounds with blue eyes, blond hair parted in the middle, and a quarter-inch scar above her left eye. When last seen she had been wearing blue jeans, a pink and white shirt, a lavender jacket, and white tennis shoes.

Next, Stout began making telephone calls. One of his first contacts was with Gary Skinner, the owner of Interior Form Tops. He requested that Skinner provide him with a copy of Darren O'Neall's original job-application form, which he would use to begin researching O'Neall's background. Skinner agreed to Stout's request, and Stout indicated that he would send Detective Wilson over to pick it up. While they were still on the line, however, Skinner told Stout that O'Neall, while working at the company, had told other employees that he had connections in Montana. And on the day that he resigned, O'Neall had left instructions that his W-2 forms were to be sent to a post office box in Martindale, Montana, in care of the CYR Ranch. O'Neall had also talked of going to Alaska or back to Colorado, Skinner said.

Quick to follow up on the possible Montana connection, Stout called Agent Bill Duncan at the Criminal Investigation Bureau of the Montana Department of Justice, the state attorney general's office. He asked Duncan to run a check on Darren Dee O'Neall to determine if he had a criminal record in that state and if there were any motor vehicles registered in O'Neall's name there. He also requested that Duncan check with Meagher County, in which Martindale is located, to determine if a CYR Ranch was registered in that county.

It was 1:15 when Duncan called back. He informed Stout that he could find no records whatsoever on Darren O'Neall. Furthermore, said Duncan, after checking a number of sources, including the Department of Agriculture, he could find no listing for a CYR Ranch in Meagher County or anywhere else in Montana.

Later that afternoon, Stout received a telephone call from Frank Wilhelm. Aware that Wilhelm had already made statements to members of Robin's family about something or someone being inside the trunk of O'Neall's car on Saturday afternoon, Stout was more than happy to talk to him. Besides informing Stout that he had known O'Neall more than ten years ago when both had gone to school together in Louisiana and the fact that Wilhelm had heard very little from O'Neall until he unexpectedly showed up in the area in November, Wilhelm told Stout that he had heard that O'Neall was wanted on some type of crime in Colorado. Even though Wilhelm couldn't be more specific about the possible charges, his information did provide Stout yet another avenue to pursue in his quest for information about the elusive Darren O'Neall.

Because of what he had already heard about O'Neall's supposed interest in becoming a mountain man, Stout thought it would be best to disclose what information, though still scant, that he had on O'Neall to the U.S. Park Service at Mount Rainier

National Park and at other outdoor recreation areas in the Pacific Northwest. Although he didn't particularly expect any overnight results, he figured that it couldn't hurt. He spent much of the remainder of the day running computer checks on O'Neall, both locally and with other jurisdictions, but ultimately came up empty-handed.

Although it was Stout who had initially caught the assignment as the lead investigator in the Robin Smith disappearance, he would soon be assigned to another case, an unrelated homicide, that would take up much of his time. He would still spend a great deal of time working on the Smith case, but as a result of the new assignment his partner, Detective Wilson, would all but inherit the Smith case from him. It was frustrating for Edna and her family to have to begin dealing with another investigator so soon, but they quickly discovered that when dealing with an overworked and understaffed sheriff's department, they had little say in the matter.

Chapter 5

Terry L. Wilson was twenty-five when he decided to go into law enforcement. However, by his own admission, his impetus for becoming a cop was not as noble as many in his line of work often profess. In fact, it was almost an accident that he even entered police work, but it is a profession that he has grown to love and excel at. When that spark of interest in law enforcement first struck Wilson in the spring of 1970, when Darren O'Neall was only a 10-year-old boy in the fourth grade, Wilson was working as a draftsman in a shipyard. While he liked the work he was doing, he felt that it wasn't really the type of job he wanted to make his career. The business's solvency depended much too heavily upon gaining work order contracts, and at the time that industry, at least in the Pacific Northwest, was losing more contracts than it was procuring during the often shaky national economy under the Nixon Administration. It was, he felt, too unstable an industry. As a result, he began taking a half day off from work every Friday to look for other types of jobs. He never dreamed that his job searches would eventually lead to a position in which he'd have a suspected serial killer as a nemesis, an adversary hell-bent on rape and murder who would become one of the most hunted criminals in the country.

It all came about when Wilson, while in downtown Tacoma on one of those Fridays to take a test for a manager-trainee position at a local finance company, decided to stop by the city-county building to pay his electric bill. At that time that was where most people paid their electric bills. When he walked into the building he glanced at a public bulletin board and became sidetracked by a recruitment flyer that described an opening for the position of deputy sheriff for Pierce County. Back then he had little knowledge about what the duties of a deputy sheriff entailed. He knew that a deputy sheriff was a cop, but that didn't mean much to him because he hadn't had much contact with anyone in law enforcement. But as he read the job description, he skipped a good portion of the section that described the duties of the position and moved his eyes quickly down the page to the bottom, where the benefits section was located. Although he discovered that the benefits and pay were very similar to what he already had with his job at the shipyard, there was one sentence that really caught his eye. It basically stated that a deputy sheriff could retire after only twenty-five years of employment! He filled out the application, submitted it, and, after being placed on a list of thirty-three eligible people, ended up being the thirteenth person hired. He began his new vocation on July 1, 1970, long before the O'Neall family would move to Colorado Springs.

Shortly after Wilson received the congratulatory telephone call from the head of the county's personnel section, the reality of it all finally hit him. He sat in a chair, and his mind started going over all of the items that he'd skipped over on the job description when he applied. He suddenly began thinking about having to wear a uniform and a badge, carrying a gun, driving a police car, and arresting people. He began to ask himself if he really wanted to do all of those things. But then his mind went back to the retirement plan, and he quickly decided that it was something that he had been looking for anyway. He told himself that he could do the job, and much to his surprise, he discovered that he would do it well.

Wilson breezed through his police academy training, and by the time he completed his probationary period he found that he actually liked the job of being a lawman. He had decided right away that when anyone goes into police work, they're either going to like it or they're not; there simply was no middle ground. Fortunately, Wilson readily adapted to the often stern rank-and-file military aspects of police work. He started out in patrol, as most deputies do, where he spent seven years. He worked one year in corrections at the county jail, then moved into traffic for five years. However, his career goal was to become a detective, which he accomplished and had done for nearly four years when the Robin Smith missing-person assignment came his way.

One of the reasons he was able to adapt so well to police work was his military upbringing and background. It is interesting that Terry Wilson's and Darren O'Neall's early upbringing paralleled each other's so closely. Each, though more than a generation apart, came from a career military man's family. Like O'Neall, Wilson moved around a lot as a child, and was subject to a certain amount of the military discipline that goes with being a child of a career man, a lifer as they are commonly called. But that's where the similarity in their backgrounds ended. O'Neall's character took an abrupt and aberrant turn toward the side of lawlessness, while just the opposite happened to Wilson. Wilson worked hard, and always tried to do what was right. He became, quite simply, one of the good guys.

Though he was born in Omaha, Nebraska, Wilson never really lived there. Instead, he spent the first ten years of his life in Junction City, Kansas, just outside Fort Riley, where his father was stationed in the army. Due to his father's transfers, he went to Germany for two and a half years, came back to Kansas for a year, then moved on to Tacoma in May 1958, where he has been ever since, except for a three-year stint that he pulled in the army himself. Nine years after his discharge and after becoming a deputy sheriff, he joined the army reserves. According to Wilson, the reserves serves as a diversion from regular police life and provides, at least for him, a good mental break from the stresses of police work.

Wilson learned quickly that one of the required attributes of a good deputy is flexibility. It suddenly became necessary for him to start wearing a lot of different hats, so to speak, something that he had never had to do before. One minute, he found, there might be a little old lady who had been burglarized and had lost some family heirlooms, irreplaceable things, and all of a sudden it was his job not only to take the report but to try to comfort her as well. Then the next minute there might be a call to go and quell a bar fight somewhere. And after that there might be a car accident in which somebody has been badly mangled or even killed. And there was, of course, the occasional distraught mother whose daughter had disappeared, as in the case of Edna Smith. It was all of those types of cases and more, Wilson discovered, that required such flexibility. It also became necessary, he realized, to keep his own emotions in check in order for him to be able to properly do the job that was required of him.

He quickly found that emotions, if allowed to go unchecked, often tugged him in a number of different directions and actually impeded his ability to handle a given investigation properly. After a while, he learned, in order to maintain the highest degree of law enforcement professionalism, his emotions somehow had to be suppressed. It wasn't that he didn't have feelings or was not sympathetic to people facing difficult problems. Quite the contrary. He would never lose that part of police work, the benevolence of it all and one of the primary reasons that makes the work so rewarding.

"On the other hand," Wilson said, "you've got to keep your emotions under control. If you don't you're going to be in trouble. You often hear stories about hard, callous cops, unfeeling people. But it has always been my experience that these unfeeling cops once were, more times than not, the 'Officer Friendlys,' the nicest people you'd ever want to meet. But what happened was, every time they went out on an emotional-type call, they became emotionally involved in the case. As a result their emotions were taken away slowly, a little bit here, a little bit there, and pretty soon they've got nothing left to give. They become hard, and after a while they begin to experience real difficulty in a job like this. They have trouble separating their emotions from their professionalism, and it eats them up.

"In this job," he continued, "you see a lot of good things and meet a lot of good people. On the other hand, however, you meet a lot of ugly folks. Personality-wise, just plain evil people, bad folks. You see lot of bad stuff. In the years that I've been on this job, I've seen probably as many dead bodies as someone in combat may have seen, but I've seen them all up close, personally, where I'm sitting or standing there at a crime scene trying to figure out what happened. But you don't dwell on those things. I have a very effective memory-suppression system. Don't get me wrong. I don't forget. It's back there, all right. But I can suppress a lot of what I see in the line of duty. I can recall it if I want to, remember it like it happened yesterday, in living color. But I leave it back there, and it leaves me alone. That's how you survive this job emotionally."

Detective Wilson kept his emotions in check when he met with Robin Smith's sister Laurie at noon on March 31, in the parking lot of the Secoma Bowling Lanes in Federal Way, a community located halfway between Tacoma and Seattle. He had arranged to meet Laurie there in order to obtain photos of Robin, and he knew ahead of time, from speaking with her on the telephone, that it was going to be an emotional meeting.

Laurie was, naturally, very distraught over her sister's unexplained disappearance. After obtaining two photos of Robin from her, Wilson questioned her regarding Robin's habits and personality, knowing that his questions would bring forth tears. Often sobbing uncontrollably, Laurie related how Robin had been living with her boyfriend, Larron Crowston, for the past four years, and described their relationship as a good one. She told Wilson of Robin's quiet nature, and explained how her sister was afraid of the dark and not very trusting of strangers. However, she stressed that Robin was very strong for her size, and would have put up quite a fight for anyone trying to abduct her if she had not somehow been first subdued. Laurie explained all of the events, at least as she knew them, that had led up to Robin's disappearance, but all of her information was secondhand, as would become the rule in this difficult case. Wilson thanked Laurie for her help and offered her enough kind words of encouragement to keep her hope alive, but not enough to instill a false hope that everything would turn out fine. Somehow, he felt in his gut, it would not.

That afternoon, while Detective Stout continued to run computer checks and make telephone calls from his office, Wilson contacted Mary Barnes at the residence she had shared with O'Neall. When Wilson first met her, he had the feeling that Mary didn't particularly like speaking to a police officer. However, as the interview progressed, Mary loosened up a bit and told Wilson what he wanted to know.

She explained how the idea of the after-hours party had originated, as well as the circumstances that had led to Larron and Robin being invited. A large quantity of beer had been consumed that morning by those in attendance, and the general mood among everyone had been congenial. The only obvious discord between anyone had been between Mary and O'Neall. They had spent a good deal of time bickering with each other over mostly petty things, and he had tried his damnedest to hurt her with cruel words in front of the others. O'Neall, she said, had also ranted and raved again about his desire to go into the mountains to live. She described how the party had moved to the Lake Tapps home of Tony Sellers later that morning.

"David was driving," she said.

"Who's David?" Wilson asked.

"A guy who was at the party."

"Do you know his last name?"

"Uh, no, I don't," she responded. "But I think he was driving a green Camaro."

"Okay, go on," Wilson urged.

"Okay. Well, let's see. David was driving, and it was me, Darren, Robin, and her boyfriend who went to Lake Tapps."

"About what time was that?" Wilson asked.

"Probably about three-thirty, I'd say," Mary responded. Mary, Wilson reflected as he eyed his witness, could easily have passed for the fictional television character of Peg Bundy on Fox's *Married With Children* if she was a little taller and considerably more buxom. Many of that ditsy character's other traits, such as flightiness and the ease with which she became confused, were certainly present in his witness. He realized that he might have trouble sorting out the useful information she was providing from the not so useful.

"What time did you get back to Darren's house?"

"We stayed at Lake Tapps for a while. I think we got back . . ." Mary trailed off, as if she was having difficulty remembering the details of that morning. Finally she said: "I'm not too sure. It was early morning when we got back."

"Did you have any conversation with Robin and her boyfriend during this time?"

"Oh, sure. I talked to them both pretty much, and to Robin, you know, I talked to her a lot."

Mary explained how she had sensed that Robin hadn't liked O'Neall very much. While at Tony Sellers' home, she said, Robin and O'Neall got into an argument with each other.

"I didn't hear it all," Mary offered. "But it was like some kind of disagreement."

"Don't you know what it was about?" Wilson pushed.

"Not really. Uh-uh. 'Cause I didn't want to get into it." Mary explained her prior altercation with O'Neall, the one that had scared her so, and indicated that she had not wanted to give him a reason to attack her again.

"But they still agreed to go back to the house after they left Sellers' place?" Wilson asked.

"Well, yeah, they were gonna come with us to our house," Mary said.

"Now, at some point in time here, Robin's boyfriend had to leave. Is that correct?"

"Yeah. He said he had to go on a chartered fishing trip on the Sound. It was already planned and paid for or something like that, so he had to go."

"Where were all of you when he said this?" Wilson asked. "Were you still at Lake Tapps or at Darren's house?"

"It was back at Darren's, uh, our house."

"And then what did Robin do?"

"Well, let's see. She wanted to stay and party. He wanted to go, and she didn't. He wanted to know if somebody could give Robin a ride home if he left without her. And I says, you know, I guess so, one of us will. I told him I'm not too sure what I'm going to be doing 'cause I was supposed to be delivering some clothes to a girlfriend, which was a lie because I just felt I had to get out of there. I just didn't want to be around Darren no more."

"And who was left at the house at that time?" Wilson asked.

"It was just me, Darren, Robin, and David."

Mary explained that at one point that morning she had gone into the bathroom, and Darren had followed her. He noticed that she was preparing to leave, and he wanted to know where it was that she was going.

"I told him that I was gonna take some clothes to a girlfriend," Mary said, " 'cause she took off with another guy from the party. It was a lie, like I said, just to get out of there. But he suddenly got real pissed off, like he was gonna blow up again. He wanted to know if he could go with me, and I told him no. I said, 'You invited people to this party. Don't you think you had better stay and entertain 'em?' I told him that he wouldn't miss anything anyway, that it was just going to be woman talk and that he wouldn't want to be around anyway. He just got more pissed off."

"What did he say to you?"

"I can't remember. I tend to block things like that out when people yell at me. But I do remember that he said, 'Fine. How come I can't go with you?' He went on and on about it, just ranting and raving, and then pouting like a little kid. It was as if he knew I was takin' off to leave him."

"And what was Robin doing during all of this?" Wilson asked.

"She was out in the living room."

"Her and the other guy? David?"

"Yeah, and Larron, too."

"Now, were they still drinking at this time?"

"Yeah. Everybody's drinking, everybody had . . . some drugs." She hesitated for a moment, as if trying to decide whether she should tell a cop about their use of drugs that night. Finally, after apparently considering the severity of what Wilson was investigating, she added: "Basically everybody pitched in, bought drugs from the guy at the party up at Lake Tapps."

"Did you see Robin using any of the drugs?"

"Yeah. She had a few lines. It was coke."

"Now, you say a few lines. You're talking about coke?"

"Yeah, it was coke."

Wilson had trouble envisioning Robin doing cocaine. From everything that he had so far heard about her, it seemed to be too much out of character for her. It was one thing for her to get mixed up with a tavern crowd and go to an after-hours party, but it didn't fit that she would do coke. Her family and friends had characterized her to Wilson and Stout as someone who was dead set against using illicit drugs. Wilson considered that it was possible that Robin had become so drunk that she had momentarily let her inhibitions down to the point that she decided to experiment or perhaps had simply given in to pressure from the others. At any rate Wilson had to go on the presumption, at least for now, that what Mary was telling him she believed to be true even if it was not totally accurate.

"All right. Did she act like she knew what she was doing?" Wilson asked.

"In a sense, yeah. But she was maybe not as aware as most people would be who had been using it for a while."

Mary told Wilson that Robin seemed somewhat naive about drugs in general, but that she had followed what she had seen some of the other people doing that evening. The drug taking had occurred several times over the course of the night and, she said, everyone who was present had participated at one point or another. Darren usually had prepared the cocaine by laying it out on a mirror, after which he would crunch its already small white powdery crystals into an even finer powder by repeatedly tapping a single-edged razor blade into it. He liked to "play" with it in this manner for quite some time before eventually dividing it into narrow lines of about two to three inches in length on the mirror. Afterward, those who wanted to join in would sniff one of the lines into each nostril, using a small three-inch long segment that had been cut from a plastic straw. When Wilson asked if Larron had participated as well, she first answered yes, he had, and then went into deep thought again, as if she was becoming confused. After a few moments she indicated that she wasn't really certain if Larron had participated or not.

Mary explained that she had not remained at the duplex for very long that morning after they returned from Lake Tapps. Because Darren had suspected that she was lying about taking some clothes to a girlfriend that morning, Mary said she made up the plan about going out for more beer. By that time, she said, she had already made the plans to meet David at the 7-Eleven in Edgewood. She and Larron had left simultaneously, she said, and had driven away in opposite directions. She told Wilson that she had not returned to the duplex until the following morning. Everyone was gone, she said, including O'Neall, and she noticed that most of O'Neall's clothing was gone.

"Can you describe the clothing that he took with him?" Wilson asked.

Mary thought about this for a moment, then told Wilson that O'Neall had taken a brown leather coat, a black-and-red-checkered wool shirt, a pair of cowboy boots, a pair of brown hiking boots with red laces, a heavy tan coat, and two blankets. One of the blankets, she said, was thin with small blue and green flower patterns, and the other had orange and yellow zigzag lines that ran across its width. She also said that he had taken a backpack with him when he left.

"Do you recall the color of the backpack?" Wilson asked.

"Yeah, it was green. Dark green. But he left the

sleeping bag." She wondered aloud why he would have wanted to take the backpack and not the sleeping bag.

"Anything else of his missing? Or of yours?"

"Yeah. He took a pair of my black patent leather shoes. Nothing else was mine. But he did take two extension cords to the television."

"What color were the extension cords?" Wilson asked.

"They were brown." She thought for a moment, then added: "He also took a green leather dog leash and a frozen pot roast out of the icebox." Nothing else appeared to be missing, she said.

"Is there anything else that you want to tell me about Darren? Such as his habits, his demeanor, and so forth?" Wilson probed.

Mary explained for Wilson's benefit how O'Neall constantly read westerns and fantasized about living in the wilderness. She described O'Neall as a cold person, someone with little emotion. She emphasized that while their relationship had been largely of a sexual nature during the short time that they were together, especially at first, they never really developed a closeness to each other. She described O'Neall's declining interest in sex, and she told Wilson again in vivid detail about her frightening and violent encounter with O'Neall the week before. She ended her statement by telling Wilson that she was in the process of moving and provided him with a telephone number where she could be reached. Wilson left her a business card and told her to call him when she had a new address.

Later that afternoon, Wilson drove to Frank Wilhelm's residence and place of business. Wilson informed Wilhelm that he was aware of O'Neall's contact with him on the previous Saturday afternoon, and asked him to recount the episode for him so that he could get it in a statement format.

"Can you describe for me what took place that day?" Wilson asked as he placed his tape recorder on the table in front of them.

"Okay," Wilhelm responded. "But I think I had better start a few days before that."

"That's fine," Wilson agreed.

"That day, which was Saturday, March twenty-eighth," Wilhelm said, "was the day that I finally talked with O'Neall. But a week or two prior to that, every day in a row for about a week, I was getting a telephone call from Darren O'Neall. I happened to not be in the office at the times when the calls came, and they were either picked up by my answering service or by my phone-recorded message, my answering machine. But on approximately Thursday of that week, which would have been about the twenty-sixth of March, I happened to be in the neighborhood where O'Neall lived. I didn't know exactly where his house was, but I knew where it was within about a two-block vicinity, so I drove around until I saw his car. I pulled in front of his house and parked, got out and walked up and knocked on the door for a while, but no one answered it. So I just started to leave. I got out to my car, and I believe I even got inside and got it started when all of a sudden Mr. O'Neall opened his door. So I shut my car off, went back to the house, and asked him why he had been calling me."

O'Neall, according to Wilhelm, had been calling him to obtain money for some tools that he had left at Wilhelm's house when he had stayed there in November. Wilhelm told him that the tools were probably only worth twenty to thirty dollars, but to come by his place on the following Saturday and he would see what he could do for him. O'Neall agreed, and showed up that Saturday at approximately one o'clock.

"Was O'Neall driving that older Chrysler at that time?" Wilson asked.

"Chrysler New Yorker," Wilhelm responded, nodding affirmatively.

When O'Neall arrived, Wilhelm explained, he had parked his car across the street from Wilhelm's driveway, next to an abandoned house with an overgrown driveway into which he had backed his car with the front end pointing toward Wilhelm's house. Wilhelm told Wilson that he had thought that this was strange because his own driveway has room for about four or five cars and his shop parking area could easily handle over a dozen cars. When O'Neall arrived, there were only two cars there, and he seemed nervous. He told Wilhelm that he wanted to borrow $50 to put with the $1,150 that he said he already had, money that he said he was going to use to purchase a four-wheel-drive truck from a car dealer called Jet Chevrolet.

"I was working out in the shop," Wilhelm said. "I don't remember what I was doing. I had a helper there. We were cleaning up, I think, when O'Neall came in and asked me about the money."

Wilhelm said that he agreed to give O'Neall the money for the tools if he helped them out for a while. O'Neall helped Wilhelm and another man move heavy items around the shop for approximately forty-five minutes.

"Then a customer came along," Wilhelm continued. "He was wanting to talk to me about a job or something, and I was talking with him for about fifteen minutes outside my shop. Then O'Neall came up and interrupted, and said that he was in kind of a hurry. He wanted to leave, and said that he would just come back later. I told him to just hold on, that I'd be done in a few minutes. So O'Neall walked over to his car that was parked across the street, and ten or twelve minutes later, when I was done with the customer, I walked over there, too. He was sitting inside the front seat. He looked really strange, just staring straight ahead. It was like he wouldn't turn his head sideways and look at me. Again he asked for the money, and I said that I didn't have any cash but that I would write him a check. He said that he didn't have any identification to cash the check. I think I had a hundred-dollar bill on me, but I wasn't about to trust him with a hundred-dollar bill, so I told him that I would write him a check. He told me to just forget it, that he would come back later or something. It was while I was talking to him at the driver's side door that I saw the backseat move."

"Now, we're talking about the backrest portion of the rear seat of the car?" Wilson clarified.

"That's correct," Wilhelm responded. Wilhelm repeated the story about the dog for Wilson's benefit and how he had chastised O'Neall for putting a dog in the trunk. "He looked, you know, pretty guilty about something. His face was all red, and he was just staring straight ahead . . . moments later he just sped off down the road and that was it."

"Have you seen him since?" Wilson asked.

"No," Wilhelm responded.

"Has he called you since?"

"No, he hasn't."

Wilhelm told Wilson that he had driven over to O'Neall's residence the following day, and he noticed that O'Neall's other dog, the one that had supposedly been inside the trunk of the Chrysler on Saturday afternoon, was still at the duplex.

"Now, when you say the backrest or the back portion of that rear seat of his Chrysler was moving, it was definitely a movement from the inside of the trunk pushing out?"

"Yes."

Wilhelm explained that the seat was being pushed out only a little, only enough so that it was noticeable, first in the middle and then on the driver's side and then in the middle again.

"So you could see the seat move out into the passenger area?"

"Right, there's no mistake about that," Wilhelm answered.

It seemed highly improbable to Wilson that the dog in question had ever been inside O'Neall's trunk. Mary Barnes had told Wilson that the larger of O'Neall's two dogs had not been away from the residence at any time during the weekend, at least not to her knowledge. And Wilhelm had said that he saw the dog the following day, on Sunday, after O'Neall and Robin had disappeared. If all of that was true, Wilson wondered, how could that dog have been in the trunk of O'Neall's car on Saturday? Had he returned it home before leaving the area? Wilson didn't think so. It also seemed highly improbable to Wilson that a dog, any dog, could have pushed against the seat back in two different places at almost the same time. It seemed far more likely that a person locked in the trunk of the car with their mouth gagged to prevent them from calling out for help, kicking the backseat with both legs in an attempt to escape or attract attention from people whose voices were audible, would have been responsible for making the seat move.

Chapter 6

At 8:20 A.M. the next day, Wednesday, April 1, Detective Walter Stout checked out Frank Wilhelm's tip about O'Neall possibly being wanted in Colorado. Having since learned that O'Neall had lived in Colorado Springs for a time, Stout contacted Detective Dave Spencer of that city's police department. During his conversation with Spencer, Stout was informed that there was an outstanding felony warrant, a bench warrant, that had been issued out of El Paso County District Court charging Darren O'Neall with second-degree rape. The charge, said Spencer, stemmed from a sexual assault on a cousin's girlfriend in June 1986.

The woman in question, Spencer explained, was a prostitute. O'Neall allegedly had solicited her services, and then had pulled a knife on her while she was sitting inside his car. Another hooker, a "lookout" who was watching from a car parked nearby, had seen the knife and flashed the headlight beams of the car she was in into O'Neall's car. It had been enough to distract him long enough to allow the woman he was trying to hold captive to escape. The two prostitutes remembered the license plate numbers of the car that O'Neall had driven away in, and police quickly traced it back to him. He was promptly arrested, but was released on $15,000 bail, ten percent of which someone put up for him.

When he failed to show up in court later, a judge issued a bench warrant for his arrest, and the bail money that had been paid was forfeited. O'Neall's family, according to Spencer, had more or less disowned him after that because of the scandal that he had caused. Spencer also told Stout that he had obtained a fairly recent color photograph of O'Neall, which he promised to send to Stout along with the warrant information and any other criminal records on O'Neall that he might be able to dig up. Spencer said that there was a note attached to the warrant that indicated that Colorado would extradite O'Neall if he was apprehended. Because of O'Neall's disfavor at home, Stout doubted that O'Neall would seek help from any of his family members.

Later that morning, at ten-thirty, Stout received another telephone call from Bobby Sharp. Sharp told Stout that he had obtained several telephone numbers from Mary Barnes, and thought that they might provide some connection with Darren O'Neall or perhaps a clue to his whereabouts. He gave the numbers to Stout, who assured Bobby that he would make every effort to obtain subscriber information on the numbers and would check each one out individually.

When the telephone numbers came back that afternoon with names and addresses attached to them, Stout soon determined that they belonged to several of the people who had attended the after-hours party at O'Neall's apartment and at the Lake Tapps home of Tony Sellers. Stout quickly checked out all of the numbers except for one, that one being the number of a person who was not at home when he called. Unfortunately, none of the people that he was able to reach had anything significant to add to what had already been told to the investigators about the after-hours parties and, similarly, none of those people had seen or heard from O'Neall since early that Saturday morning.

That afternoon, Jim Chaney called Stout and told him that he had found some items at O'Neall's duplex that might be of interest to the investigators. Stout dropped what he was doing and drove to Thirteenth Court East in Edgewood, where Chaney was still maintaining his vigil. Chaney showed him all of the items that he had found during his searches.

"Where did you get all of this?" Stout asked, his anger rising. Realizing that a potential crime scene had been compromised, unknowingly contaminated by people who were inexperienced in evidence-gathering techniques, Stout chastised Chaney for taking it upon himself to do the search. Chaney similarly rebuked Stout and basically told him that he wouldn't have had to do the search on his own if the sheriff's department had taken a greater interest in Robin's disappearance from the outset. Stout knew that Chaney was right, up to a point at least, and after the detective had calmed down a bit, he reminded Chaney that no one really knew what had happened there. When Robin disappeared all they really had was a missing person under suspicious circumstances. Stout reminded Chaney that there were no initial signs of foul play, and in defending his department's actions, he opined that the department should not be unfairly blamed for merely following routine procedure in the case.

Interestingly, in addition to all of the other items that Chaney had found, he turned over to Stout three handwritten sheets of paper. The handwriting would eventually be determined by experts to be O'Neall's. Stout read with interest the following undated sheet, replete with misspellings and other errors:

My Future—Plans & Ultimate Goal (Outline)
To live in the wilderness w/minnimum assistance from the outside!
Regoin—Suskatuwan Rockies West
Place—Vally w/high mountain, year round running watter
Home—Cabbin-Hidden, *secluded?* w/same grazing & farm range.
Needs—House; seed; 10 horses; 10–15 cows; 2–5 bulls; farm equip, ie., plow, traises, spaides (& other implements.) Grain & feed seed. Vegitable seeds. Horse tack, breeding stock (for riding & packing). Home sted & or land permits for Sasquatuan (or the lamb or squatters prasces). Pork-beeves-floure-med.-

books; Books—Black Stock, Assopoglees, Bible, Louis L'Amour (Sacketts—all).
Acheiving prosec—1) Steddy job; 2) save money; 3) Accumulate nessesities; 4) Nalledge of terraine & local laws.

The next sheet was a letter that he had begun, dated Friday, November 21, 1986:

> Dear Kathy,
> I hope you are well!
> I've been thinking about you alot in the last year. There are many things I would like to say to you, but as you know I'm spending most of my time running from the law. I'm not the man I would like to be. I hurt inside so deeply I can not put it in words. I won't tell you about me, being in jail or how I got out, but I'm working now under an assumed name & making some money. Before I broke jail I heard about you and the kids being hit by a car. I'm so sorry for

The letter ended abruptly, and was not signed. Although written in a sloppy hand, as sloppy as the first sheet, Stout noticed that not a single word had been misspelled! What did this mean? Stout wondered. Did O'Neall's fantasy of living in the wilderness transcend certain psychological boundaries to the degree that he was actually able to form a specific, yet unconscious, mindset that somehow compelled him to write and spell like a frontiersman? The mere thought of such a possibility was chilling, and prompted Stout to reflect on just what kind of mind he was dealing with here.

The third and final sheet simply contained the name and address of a Kathy, presumably the same Kathy that he had started writing the letter to in Pennsylvania. There was no discernable indication of the nature of the relationship between Kathy and Darren O'Neall anywhere in the letter, but Stout sensed that she might have been a girlfriend. Because he felt O'Neall might possibly seek her out for assistance, Stout made a note to himself to find out who this woman was and what she had meant, if anything, to O'Neall.

Interestingly, there was also a medical card among the papers. The card had been issued by the Mercy Medical Center in Nampa, Idaho, and was imprinted with a patient name of Zebulan J. Macranahan. It was also imprinted with a chart number and a date of issue of October 28, 1986. Stout considered the possibilities for a moment, and then decided that Macranahan was probably an alias used by O'Neall. He kept the card with the papers, and would check out its significance to O'Neall later.

Despite the fact that the scene had been contaminated, Stout decided to make a walk-through of the premises after he finished reading the materials that Chaney had handed him. He walked through the kitchen, looked around, went through the living room, into the bedroom, down the hall and into the bathroom, and finally exited out the front door. Finding nothing that would obviously suggest that foul play had occurred there, coupled with the fact that if anything had happened there the evidence was by now likely lost or had been rendered useless, Stout drove back to his office. There was no reason now, he felt, to bring a crime-scene unit out to the duplex.

Later that day, Stout contacted Christa O'Neall, Darren's mother, by telephone at her home in Colorado Springs. Mrs. O'Neall, although not particularly pleased to be speaking to a detective about her son, told Stout that she and her husband, Darrell, believed that Darren suffered from mental and emotional problems. She implied that Darren's mental illness was the result of excessive alcohol and/or drug consumption. She stated that she and her husband had gained legal custody of Darren's five-year-old son, Christopher, due to his lifestyle and problems. Christopher, Stout learned, had been born when O'Neall was married to a woman named June Hodges. Mrs. O'Neall said that Darren had been in the army for approximately a year in 1982, which, Stout noted to himself, was in direct conflict with the information that O'Neall had been including on his job applications. He had been saying that he had been in the army for a full four-year hitch in the Ranger Company. Mrs. O'Neall told Stout that neither she nor her husband had seen Darren for several months, not since he had suddenly taken off the previous autumn.

The fact that O'Neall had been married to a woman named June Hodges certainly explained the tattoo across the knuckles of his left hand, but it also opened yet another avenue to investigate. Stout wanted to talk to June to see if O'Neall had been in touch with her recently, and also to learn any additional background on O'Neall that June might be able to provide. Unfortunately, no one knew where June currently resided, and Stout was faced with the task of having to track her down.

Meanwhile, before the day was out, Jim Chaney, for some inexplicable reason, suddenly wanted to travel to an area near Greenwater, Washington, to search for Robin. Greenwater was a small community about an hour due east of Tacoma, situated just off Highway 410 on the outer perimeter of the northeast sector of Mount Rainier National Park. He conceded, as much to himself as to the Smith family, that there was no rhyme or reason for him to want to go to Greenwater. It was just something that he couldn't get out of his mind. Perhaps it was because he, Larron, and Robin had gone camping in that area in the past, or perhaps it was something about O'Neall's fascination with the rugged outdoors that compelled him to want to search there. Everybody else wanted to conduct searches initially in the area around where O'Neall had lived. But Jim insisted on Greenwater as a place of significance, and he and Mike Baker drove up there in Mike's small, white four-wheel-drive Toyota pickup. As a matter of caution they took their guns, just in case they ran into O'Neall or some other undesirable up there in the vast forests.

They drove through the area around Greenwater, taking many different roads, some of which took them through areas where mountain cabins were nestled among dense clusters of Douglas fir. It was as if he was merely feeling his way along, waiting for a sign of some sort to tell him which way to go. Their meandering went on for some time, and eventually began to seem aimless. However, shortly after passing through Greenwater, Jim told Mike to slow down. To this day he's not sure why he did it, but he picked a narrow, nearly impassable dirt and gravel road that turned to the right off Highway 410, known as both Huckleberry Creek Road and Forest Service Road #73, and instructed Mike to take it. It was strictly a gut hunch on Jim's part. He, Larron, and Robin had driven down that same road a year or so earlier looking for a campsite, and both Robin and Larron had protested. They had said, "No way, not here," and Jim had gotten that same feeling. It was just too eerie a place to want to spend the night in the outdoors. As a result, they had found another location, one that wasn't so isolated, to set up camp. Now, a year later, here he was again, on that same eerie road searching for his missing friend, not really knowing why he had been compelled to return there.

Right after Mike had turned onto the road, Jim instructed him to take the first fork to the right. They drove down the road perhaps a half mile, then pulled over and parked at what appeared to be a fairly fresh campsite. When they got out of the truck, for some reason the fact that the campsite had recently been used and the eeriness of the forest frightened them both. It scared them so much that the hair stood up on their arms, almost as if being drawn outward by static electricity. They quickly decided, or perhaps just hoped, that it was only the intense quietude that was bothering them. It was so quiet that it seemed unearthly, so still that it, paradoxically, seemed noisy to them, like dead silence had suddenly become loud. They looked quizzically at each other, each obviously as frightened as the other.

"Jim, I don't know how you're feeling, but something is going on here," Mike said, suddenly breaking the silence. "Something has happened here."

Jim agreed. They loaded their guns and walked down the road a few yards, trying to keep a watchful eye in every direction. But their feeling of discomfort continued to grow in intensity, until it suddenly felt as if there were fifty people with guns out there, watching their every movement from behind the bushes and trees. Were they really being watched? They wondered. Was O'Neall out there, hiding and watching them? Had O'Neall driven Robin down that very road, perhaps even assaulted her there before moving on to yet another area? Or were their imaginations simply getting the best of them? All either of them knew for certain was that they were terrified and that they had to get out of there. They walked hurriedly back to the truck, climbed inside, and drove on down the road. To Mike's and Jim's relief, the farther they distanced themselves from that location, the better they began to feel. Although neither one of them possessed any known psychic abilities, they would later decide that Robin had been assaulted, perhaps was even killed, at that location, and some kind of inexplicable phenomenon was trying to let them know it.

At another section of that same road they found another campsite and pulled over. Mike dropped Jim off at the campsite, located at a parking space that was merely two ruts in the ground the width of a car where people had repeatedly backed their vehicles a few feet off the road into the forest. As Jim began to explore the area, Mike drove down the road, perhaps twenty yards, across a large mound of dirt that would have made the road impassable to most passenger cars. If O'Neall had driven the New Yorker down that road, he wouldn't have been able to drive beyond the campsite where Mike had dropped Jim off.

Still trying to shake that eerie feeling, Jim searched the campsite that was located toward the rear of the parking spot. Finding nothing of significance, he then crossed the road and walked down the trail to a narrow river. He would learn later that its name was the White River. From there he took another trail, but it went nowhere and eventually just disappeared. He walked back toward the road, changed direction, and headed toward a quietly running stream, Boundary Creek. From there he walked out of a small clearing and into the woods, several yards in each direction, then came back out of the woods and into the clearing. Mike was there by then.

Jim stood next to him, and stared at an almost imperceptible trail that led into a dense patch of forest.

"Do you think I should go down that trail over there?" Jim asked Mike.

"Nah," Mike said after glancing at the trail. They decided that it was probably just an animal trail, one that was rarely used.

Without looking back at Mike, Jim continued to stare into that section of woods for another thirty seconds or more, but didn't know why at that time. It was as if there was something, a heavy presence of sorts, coming out of the woods at them, a signal of some kind. He told Mike about the feeling he was getting, but they eventually brushed it off as "inexplicable" and drove on home.

Jim spent that evening with Mike and Brenda, and ended up staying overnight at their house. With no history of nightmares, that night Jim had what he termed "the nightmare of all nightmares."

In his dream he was standing on that road again where he and Mike had been, and he was again staring into that same section of woods. He suddenly saw a man, a huge, muscular white male. In place of a human head this "man" had a steer's head and horns. Without warning he came charging at Jim at lightning speed, through the woods, up over the trees, and through the bushes. Suddenly Jim awakened and jumped out of bed, his body covered with a cold sweat. He had just had the living daylights scared out of him and he didn't know why. He felt, *knew*, really, that the nightmare had something to do with Robin, but he didn't know what. He brushed such thoughts aside for the time being, with no way of knowing that what he had just experienced would be nothing compared to what he and Robin's family would eventually discover. In the weeks ahead he would learn that Robin's nude body had lain in the section of woods that he had been so compelled to stare at, rapidly decomposing, and her remains were being eaten and scattered by wild animals as he and Mike had looked on, wondering what to do next. They had been so close to Robin's body that had the wind been blowing in their direction that day in the woods, they likely would have been able to smell the distinct odor of putrefaction. In more ways than not, Jim and Robin's family members would consider it a blessing that he and Mike had not stumbled onto her body at that time. If they had, they might not have been able to recover from the horror that they would have seen.

Mike's and Jim's frightening ordeal in the woods near Mount Rainier and Jim's subsequent nightmare would be but the first of several bizarre incidents related to Robin's disappearance that would be experienced by Jim and the Smith family in the days and weeks to come, experiences which, they would all come to believe, served to help them put two and two together and ultimately brought them closer to discovering what had become of Robin.

Chapter 7

Robin and Larron, like all young people, were always on the go, looking for something to do no matter how humdrum or commonplace their activities seemed to others. It didn't matter what they did together just as long as they were together. It was just along those lines that, a couple of years before Robin disappeared, she and Larron had ended up going to a Sunday swap meet near Tacoma. Of course, it wasn't anything too exciting, nor had they expected it to be. But before the afternoon was over, they had stopped at a booth out of which a man was dipping small souvenirs, trinkets, charms, and so forth, virtually anything that people would bring him, into a pot containing a molten mixture of a gold-like substance, all for a price, of course. Since the mixture he was using contained a certain amount of real gold, the price he charged depended upon the size of the particular item to be dipped. Larron merely took a dime out of his pocket and paid the man a few bucks to dip it into the gold mixture. Afterward, Larron gave the dime to Robin and it became her lucky charm.

She loved it, and she showed it to everybody. All of her friends, including a close friend named Angie, knew that she had it. Despite the simplicity of it all, the gift of the gold dime had been the highlight of their day together and would play a part in the mystery surrounding Robin's disappearance.

One day not long after Robin vanished, her friend Angie, following her usual routine, walked to a convenience store located across the street from her home to buy a morning newspaper. She also picked up a few other items that particular morning, took them to the counter, and paid the cashier for them. The cashier handed her back the change, which she placed in her jacket pocket without looking at it. When she returned home, Angie laid the newspaper and the small sack of other items on the kitchen table. Unconsciously, she took the change out of her jacket pocket and dropped it, too, on the table. When she glanced down for no particular reason, something shiny caught her eye. Mixed in with her change was a gold dime, just like Robin's.

Angie, already distraught over the fact that her friend was missing, literally freaked out when she saw the dime. She immediately called Edna and told her about it, and Edna, herself rankled and upset, in turn called Jim Chaney and sent him over to calm Angie down and to get what information he could from her about the dime. When Jim arrived, Angie was still trembling and shaking. With unsteady hands she gave him the dime.

"Where did you get this?" he asked, recognizing it as being just like Robin's.

"Over there," she said weakly, pointing her finger. "Across the street."

Jim looked out the window at the store on the other side of the boulevard, and instantly went weak in his knees. The sign on the store read O'NEILL'S MARKET. The spelling of the store's name was not the same as that of Darren O'Neall's surname, but Jim and Robin's family could not help but wonder if he had stopped there because of the name and had spent the dime, mixed in with other money, hoping that someone would notice it and make the connection between Robin's dime and the name O'Neill. They wondered if he had done it in his arrogance to taunt the family or the police, or perhaps both, or if he had spent the dime merely by accident and that its turning up in Angie's change had actually been a sign of some kind from Robin to her family.

While it certainly added a touch of drama and another riddle to be considered to the steadily deepening mystery, to the Pierce County investigators the dime was simply a coincidence and nothing more. The investigators just couldn't buy into the spiritual phenomenon idea that Angie, Chaney, and the Smiths embraced. The nature of their work required that they take a more methodical and analytical approach to the newly found evidence, if it was in fact evidence. There likely were, they reasoned, other gold dimes floating around, and to them the fact that one had turned up in the change of Robin Smith's friend did not prove anything one way or the other. And even if O'Neall had spent the dime in question at the store across from Angie's home, they reasoned that he likely hadn't done so with the idea of taunting anyone. On the lam and in his unstable state of mind, they felt that O'Neall probably never even realized that he had the dime in his possession—if in fact it was, of course, Robin's gold dime. But to the Smith family the finding of the dime would be only one of several spiritual signals from Robin indicating that they were on the right track in their search for her and that they should not give up.

Meanwhile, in his continuing effort to locate David Wells, Detective Walt Stout made contact with a man named Mike Thomas.* When Mary Barnes had related to Detective Wilson how she had arranged to go off and meet a man named David from the party on the morning that Robin disappeared, she had not provided him with a last name. She had not known it, she said. As a result, Stout and Wilson would have to track him down by interviewing anyone named David who was associated, even remotely, with the party at O'Neall's.

The purpose of Stout's contact with Mike Thomas, of course, was that the subject still known to them only as David may have been one of the last persons to have left O'Neall's party prior to Robin's disappearance and, as such, may have been one of the last people besides O'Neall to have seen her. Second, Thomas's telephone number had been one of those given to Stout by Robin's brother Bobby, who had obtained several numbers from Mary. Stout met with Thomas at the home of his mother in Puyallup.

In response to Stout's questions, Thomas stated that he had not been at Baldy's Tavern, O'Neall's apartment, or at the party at Tony Sellers' home near Lake Tapps. Employed at a local bingo parlor, Thomas said that he had worked on the Friday night in question. He said that he had arrived home by 2:00 A.M., which his mother confirmed. Thomas suggested that Stout contact Larry Ross,* a relative of Thomas's who had been at both of the parties in question.

Stout subsequently located Ross at his home in the community of Fife, just outside Tacoma. Ross promptly confirmed that he had indeed been at Baldy's Tavern on the evening of March 27, and that he had gone to the party at O'Neall's as well as to the party at Lake Tapps. After leaving the Lake Tapps party, Ross said, he returned to O'Neall's apartment only for the purpose of picking up his car, which he had parked there earlier. He did not go inside O'Neall's apartment a second time that morning, and he did not notice who or what cars were still parked in front of O'Neall's residence when he left. By the time Stout finished his interview with Ross, he realized that he was not any closer to finding out who the mystery man David really was.

However, all that changed a short time later when Stout received a telephone call from Edna Smith, who had by now taken even more of the responsibility for finding out what had happened to her daughter into her own hands. Edna and members of her family, she said, had spoken with Mary Barnes again and had obtained an address in Sumner that might shed some light on the identity of their mystery man. Her son Bobby had been surveilling an address on 52nd Street East, and had reported seeing a Camaro parked in front of the residence. Stout promptly drove out to the location, found the Camaro, and ran a license plate check on it through the Motor Vehicles Division. As a result he learned that the car was registered to a David Wells.

Though several attempts to make contact with the twenty-six-year-old Wells ended in failure, Stout eventually found him at home a couple of days later. Wells, an assembly-line worker at a Seattle truck-manufacturing company, confirmed that he had been at the parties in question. He explained that he would have come forward on his own had he known about Robin's disappearance sooner. He said that he had only recently learned some of the details from Mary Barnes, but did not know that the sheriff's department was looking for him.

Wells confirmed much of what everybody else had told Stout and Wilson about the parties, including the fact that Robin and Larron had attended them. He also told Stout about having made the plans to meet Mary Barnes on the morning of March 28, and for that reason had not wanted to take the responsibility for driving Robin home when she had asked him for a ride.

"During the night or early morning hours," Stout asked, "did you see any action between Darren O'Neall and Robin?"

"No," Wells responded. "Not really, no."

"Was he coming on to her?"

"No," Wells said. "Darren and Mary were arguing, but as far as him approaching Robin, I never noticed anything."

"Did you ever see her trying to come on to him?"

"No. I didn't see her coming on to anybody . . . I was rather infatuated with her myself, but I didn't see her coming on at all."

When Stout finished questioning Wells, he drove back to his office and called Edna Smith. He explained how he had finally located Wells, and that Wells had confirmed that he had left Robin and O'Neall alone together at O'Neall's apartment. Wells had said that he had not known O'Neall prior to meeting him at the party.

"He said that nothing seemed wrong at the time," Stout told Edna. "He said there wasn't anything unusual about it. There was no problem at the time. Now, of course, he feels bad, that maybe he should have done something. But he took no responsibility for Robin's safety or for getting her home."

Edna, now more certain than ever that whatever had happened to Robin had been done to her by O'Neall, began making plans with her family and Jim Chaney about what to do next. Despite the urging of

Pierce County authorities for her to leave the investigation to them, Edna had decided early on that they couldn't just sit around and wait. They had to do something to find Robin.

A short time later, at eight-thirty on the evening of April 4, Stout learned that information about a possible encounter with O'Neall had been received at the Pierce County Sheriff's Department from the staff at Auburn General Hospital. Staff members there reported that they believed that Darren O'Neall had been treated in the hospital's emergency room on Saturday night, March 28. The information was generated and subsequently called in to the department, Stout learned, after an information poster that Edna Smith had created on Robin's disappearance had been distributed throughout the area. One of the posters had made it in to Auburn General Hospital through Larron's mother, Judy Crowston, who worked there, and emergency room personnel had subsequently seen it. Having recognized the description of O'Neall from the poster, one of the employees had phoned in the tip. Though it was late, Stout knew that the information couldn't wait until the next day. He immediately drove from his home in Puyallup out to Auburn.

Upon his arrival at the hospital, Stout contacted two maintenance men, both of whom had been working on the night in question. John Horner and Mike McBreen had been summoned that Saturday evening by emergency room nurses because of a man who had come in with a number of facial cuts, scrapes, and bruises. The man was acting in an erratic manner, which had caused some concern for the nurses. Although Horner and McBreen were not security officers at the hospital, they often provided security for the female employees during unusual situations such as this one.

Both Horner and McBreen recalled that the man had shown up alone at the hospital at approximately 8:00 P.M., and had told the emergency room nurses that he had received the cuts and scratches during a fight. He had not described the fight, however, and he had not identified the person with whom he had been fighting. McBreen said that the first thing he had noticed about the man were the letters J-U-N-E tattooed across the knuckles of his left hand. McBreen said that his birth date was in the month of June, and that was why he remembered the tattoo so clearly. McBreen also recalled that there was a star or some other small tattoo-like mark on the man's cheekbone, just beneath his left eye. Before finishing his account of the incident with the man, McBreen told Stout that he remembered the man's car as well. The man had parked his car, a somewhat tan or cream-colored early seventies model Chrysler, in the emergency entrance area. Since that was an unauthorized area for parking, McBreen had asked the man to move it. That was when he noticed that the car had out-of-state plates on it.

After interviewing Horner and McBreen, Stout was convinced that the man in question had been

Darren O'Neall. When he checked the hospital's emergency room log for the evening and night of March 28, he discovered that the man had been treated under the name of "Mark O'Neil." That didn't surprise Stout. Based on what he was learning about his suspect, Stout figured that O'Neall would have used a name other than his own. But he also figured that O'Neall would have been more clever with his use of an alias. He brushed it off, reasoning that O'Neall probably had been stressed out over whatever had happened between him and Robin, or that his resourcefulness was at an all-time low due to his mind being clouded with alcohol and drugs from the party the night before.

Shortly after the television and print news media finally latched on to the story of Robin's disappearance, reported sightings of O'Neall began pouring in to the Pierce County Sheriff's Department, as well as to law enforcement agencies in other outlying jurisdictions, from all over the Puget Sound area. One of those alleged sightings occurred on the morning after the incident at the emergency room of Auburn General Hospital.

According to an account received by Stout, a man matching O'Neall's description had walked into a Safeway grocery store in Enumclaw on Sunday morning, March 29. He purchased pastry, cigarettes, and Black Label beer, and then left quietly. Although the clerk recalled that the man's face had cuts and abrasions, she did not notice what type of car he had gotten into when he left. But then, she said, there would have been no reason for her to notice his car. She did not routinely follow customers outside, nor did she watch them from the windows in the front of the store when they left.

Meanwhile, at noon on April 9, Stout received information that a person had come into the sheriff's office to report having seen who he believed to be Darren O'Neall. The person was a flagman, and he had been working at a road construction site on the Crystal Mountain road near Mount Rainier, just off Highway 410, the road that passes through Greenwater. Stout knew the location. It was near a popular ski resort.

The flagman believed that it had been on Monday, March 30, when he noticed an older, somewhat tan Chrysler with Montana license plates being driven up to the construction site located between Enumclaw and Crystal Mountain by a man who appeared to be alone. The car, he said, was the second in a line of cars waiting to get past the road work.

The flagman told Stout that the car had drawn his attention because it had been the only one in a long line of cars that was not carrying any skis. Furthermore, he said that the driver was the only driver who failed to acknowledge him as he passed. The driver parked in a nearby turnaround area, where he sat and watched the construction and the traffic for approximately twenty minutes. He then pulled back onto Crystal Mountain Road and headed back toward Highway 410, the direction from which he had come.

Later that day the flagman, on his way home from work, stopped at a Chevron gas station on Highway 410 at Greenwater, where he saw the same Chrysler with the same driver behind the wheel. Stout showed the flagman a series of photographs, one of which included a photo of Darren O'Neall.

"That's him," he said after a few seconds. "I know that's him." He pointed at the photo of O'Neall.

After Robin disappeared, no one in Edna Smith's family was able to eat or sleep much. Their minds were running constantly by this time, and no matter what they did, they couldn't shut off their thoughts about Robin. All they could do was take cat naps, a half hour to an hour at a time, while they waited for some word about Robin.

They began working in shifts as they waited and surveilled O'Neall's duplex, an effort that turned out to be in vain. Within days after Mary moved out, the apartment was rented to another tenant, and everyone realized that O'Neall wasn't coming back. When they weren't contacting Wilson or Stout seeking information or turning over new leads, they were busy making plans as to what they would do next. Soon Edna's sister flew out from Connecticut so that she could be with Edna and help in any way she could. But even though they tried to keep busy, they all felt so helpless, as if none of their efforts would ever pay off.

Nonetheless, Edna remained convinced that if they were going to obtain clues and find out what had happened to Robin, they had to get the word out to the general public. That not-so-easy task, she knew, could come about only by utilizing the print and broadcast media, something that she hadn't wanted to do. Once she had gotten the attention of the media, however, Edna, looking tired and haggard, made an impassioned public plea for anyone holding Robin to please let her go:

"Release her in the parking lot at Albertson's [a nearby grocery store] or someplace before something bad happens, and give us a call. We'll go pick her up," Edna pleaded. "She just happened to be in the wrong place at the wrong time, and we just want her back."

The hope in Edna's plea was grievous and heartbreaking. While Wilson and Stout had all but given Robin up for dead, here was a mother whose daughter had been missing for more than two weeks making an impassioned plea for her daughter's release and holding out hope that Robin might walk through the door of her home at any time.

After appearing several times in the local newspapers and on the nightly news, family members realized that in addition to bringing out the well-wishers and those wanting to help, all of the attention had also brought out some of the nut cases, psychotic cranks who had seen them on television. Mike Baker, Robin's brother-in-law, reported two incidents to the police in which he had been followed by someone who wanted to find out where he and Brenda lived. Although it had taken considerable effort, he had managed to shake off the persons pursuing him. He later found it necessary to borrow a relative's vehicle just so he wouldn't be as easily recognizable by those who wanted to follow him. The incidents only added to the agony that they were all going through.

"It's so hard to let people know how we were feeling," Jim Chaney said. "The only way to relate it to somebody so that they could even begin to understand is to say something like, 'Okay, you got any kids? I'm gonna come over tonight and take one of your kids while you are asleep. And I'll keep it for a long period of time, and not tell you anything about it. It's just going to suddenly be gone.' Now, what that person would experience is what all of us have gone through."

"It's a nightmare," Edna agreed. "I would never want anybody to go through it. But yet I know it's happening on a daily basis to a lot of people. It happens to somebody else every day. And somebody else gets to go through what we went through. Believe me, my heart goes out to these people. It's torture."

"Oh, yeah," Jim said. "You can't sit and watch television after experiencing something like this. You watch the news and hear about something like this. They're always flashing something about some little girl or some little boy's photo, or a prostitute, or a mother or daughter who has disappeared. And we instantly go through it all over again. It doesn't even have to be somebody you know."

As for finding Robin alive, Jim added: "In the back of everybody's heads, I think everyone thought, 'Well, she's been killed.' But we couldn't come out and admit it. That was something that would not come out of our mouths. It just stayed in the back of our heads while we went looking, and hoping, and praying that we could find her and that those thoughts would not be true. We just couldn't give up."

Having a somewhat religious background, Edna Smith and her family had begun praying for Robin's safe return right after she disappeared. When it became evident that Robin was not going to be returning home, the family began praying for signs to her whereabouts. Right after Robin vanished, Robin's sister Brenda had a dream, a "vision" as she called it, of a place where she believed Robin, or her body, could be found.

In relating the details of her dream to the others, Brenda described how she had seen Robin walking slowly down a forest path. She had appeared calm, serene, and wasn't crying, and she had not appeared to be afraid of anything. Brenda said that as soon as she realized that she was looking at an image of her sister, she bolted upright in her bed.

"Where are you?" Brenda said she had asked the image of Robin.

"I'm coming home," Robin responded.

Brenda, although upset, called everyone together

after the dream. Larron, Jim, Edna, and several other family members tried to calm her down as she related what had just happened to her. She was trembling, in part because she *knew* that she hadn't been sleeping when Robin's image appeared to her. Brenda, who hadn't seen Robin since the Wednesday of the week before she disappeared, described the clothing that Robin was wearing in her dream. Larron, who was sitting next to Edna, was stunned. His eyes widened in disbelief, and his mouth dropped open, yet he uttered not a sound. Brenda, who hadn't talked to anyone about the actual clothes Robin was wearing the night she disappeared, had just described exactly what Robin had worn on the evening that she and Larron had gone out dancing. Brenda also described the area that she saw as having an abundance of tall trees and scattered campsites.

"That sounds like Greenwater," exclaimed Bobby's girlfriend, Trina.

Jim Chaney, in complete agreement, suggested that they return to the Greenwater area and focus most of their attention there, especially after what had happened the day that he and Mike had gone there to search for Robin. In reality the area that Brenda had described in her dream could have been anywhere west of the Cascades. But for some reason that none of them fully understood, they were all but consumed with thoughts of the Greenwater area.

Edna's family and a few of their friends spent the next few days searching the isolated roads and trails around Greenwater, to no avail. There was just so much land and water up there, literally hundreds of square miles, in which Robin's body could have been discarded. It was all so discouraging. Brenda, five months pregnant, was fast becoming disheartened, in part because she was worried about her health as well as that of her unborn baby. She wasn't eating or sleeping well, and the search was clearly beginning to take its toll on her. But she, like the others, refused to give up.

Every night, upon returning home after a day of searching, Brenda kept praying, asking for a sign of some kind so that they would know whether they were even searching in the right area or not. It soon became a ritual of sorts with her, but it offered her encouragement and hope. In fact, the night before yet another planned trip to Greenwater, Brenda prayed especially long and hard. For whatever reason, whether it was a divine sign from God, a spiritual message from her sister, or just a macabre nightmare, Brenda had another dream.

That night Brenda fell asleep and dreamed about a dog with no head. It was there, in the forest somewhere, all alone and without the presence of any people or other animals. Despite the intensely disturbing nature of the dream, Brenda described it to everyone the next morning just before they set out on another search of the Greenwater area. The dog, she said, was gold in color.

Shortly after commencing the search in the woods that day, tramping through a soft cover of freshly fallen snow in a small clearing, Brenda, her husband, Mike, Jim, and another family friend stopped dead in their tracks. There in front of them was a dog, its coat golden-blond in color, just like the dog in Brenda's dream. It was attached to a leash, but when they approached it, the dog remained motionless. It looked strange, as though its head was burrowed into the ground with its body protruding outward. When they walked all the way up to it, they suddenly realized that its head was missing.

The dog, they noticed, had been dead for only a couple of days at most. They searched for the dog's head, but could not find it. They did find a portion of a newspaper with blood on it, and this initially concerned them. However, it was later determined that the blood wasn't of human origin.

Their new, grotesque discovery was indeed chilling, and it frightened all of them. It wasn't just another coincidence, as the police would call it, at least not in their minds. And they didn't buy the police theory that the animal had been decapitated as some sort of sick cult ritual, perhaps satanic. They viewed it instead as an assurance from Robin that they were searching for her in the right area. They had already heard about the flagman's sighting of O'Neall nearby, and after putting two and two together, they were convinced they should concentrate their efforts even more diligently in that area in the days and weeks ahead.

Chapter 8

Reported sightings of Darren O'Neall continued to flow into the Pierce County Sheriff's Department daily from throughout the Puget Sound area, largely because of all the media exposure that the case was receiving. Because there were so many presumed sightings, detectives Walt Stout and Terry Wilson had no choice but to pore over the reports in a process of elimination to determine which sightings were most likely the real thing. There were just too many suspected sightings and not enough hours in the day, which, of course, made it impossible for the two men, even with help from uniformed deputies, to physically show up and take a report every time somebody called in to say that they had seen O'Neall. As a result, they tended to focus their attention on those reports that provided the best physical descriptions of their suspect.

One of those sightings occurred at a convenience store in Bonney Lake, located on Highway 410, the road to Greenwater and Mount Rainier. A cashier at the store called in to report that she had seen a man who fit O'Neall's description, right down to the knuckle tattoos and a small "mark on the cheekbone below the left eye." The cashier reported that the man had come into the store on two, possibly three occasions over the weekend of March 28–29. The convenience store was only a few miles from the Safeway store in Enumclaw where O'Neall had been seen on March 29.

As far as Stout and Wilson were concerned, the sightings meant that O'Neall had remained in the area for a while after abducting Robin Smith. And for that weekend at least, because of the reported sightings, they believed that O'Neall had traveled extensively between Federal Way and Crystal Mountain. They theorized that he had tried to lay low by hiding in the forests, but had been forced to come out and travel to town for food, cigarettes, and other items. They reasoned that they might get lucky and spot him during one of his excursions from the wilderness, and as such assigned additional road deputies to the area. But they doubted that he would be foolish enough to continue such a risky routine for long, and in all likelihood he had already left the area.

Another report of a possible sighting soon came in from a concerned citizen who had seen a person resembling the "mountain man" description that was by now circulating via posters and word of mouth throughout the area. The "mountain man" in that report had been walking a black and tan German shepherd on a leash near Puyallup. The man had a scraggly beard, was wearing jeans, and was carrying a 10-inch knife in a sheath on his left side. Stout and Wilson filed this one as a "maybe," but they didn't really believe that the man was O'Neall. For one thing, they doubted that O'Neall would have remained that close to Puyallup. It was much too close to home, and there was way too much heat on there at the moment, which would make a criminal with any sense at all on the run from the law want to stay out of there at all costs. For another, O'Neall had left his German shepherd behind at the apartment, and they doubted that he had gotten another dog so soon. He had too many other things to worry about, they figured, like staying warm, eating, and keeping himself one step ahead of the law.

Yet another possible sighting of O'Neall early in the investigation involved a woman who reported having seen a man who closely fit O'Neall's description reading a poster that had been placed outside a Kingston drugstore. When the woman went over to read the poster, too, she noted that it was one of the posters that Edna Smith had put together about Robin's disappearance and featured a roughly sketched drawing of O'Neall's likeness. The woman turned to the man and told him that he looked like the person on the poster. The man didn't look at her, nor did he answer her. He simply left, and the woman didn't know if he was on foot or driving a vehicle. Stout and Wilson noted that Kingston was about 45 miles north of Tacoma, near Bremerton. If that sighting had in fact been O'Neall, they reasoned, their suspect was now heading north.

And so it went. Sighting after sighting of a person or persons believed to be Darren O'Neall. Some of the sightings were undoubtedly of O'Neall. Others may or may not have been him. One thing appeared certain to Stout and Wilson, though: Darren O'Neall was on the move. But what were his plans? And where was he going? The two detectives didn't have a clue, and neither would venture a guess at this point.

On Wednesday, April 8, seeing that Edna Smith's posters had brought forth such prompt and frequent reports from the public, Stout and Wilson put together their own special poster/bulletin. It included a photograph of Robin Smith, another of Darren O'Neall, which they had received from the Colorado Springs Police Department, and a front, side, and back view illustration of a 1972 Chrysler New Yorker. They had 300 copies of the poster printed up, and these were distributed to law enforcement agencies throughout western Washington. Stout also sent another teletype, this time to all western states law enforcement jurisdictions to ensure a wider distribution of the information than the first teletype had covered. He also entered what little else he knew about Darren O'Neall and the Chrysler New Yorker he was believed driving into the National Crime Information Center (NCIC) and the LESA data banks.

* * *

Meanwhile, Mike Baker, Jim Chaney, and Bobby Sharp had expanded their own investigation into Robin's disappearance. By now another of Robin's brothers, Albert Smith II, had become involved in the search. Al, as he likes to be called, was serving in the Marine Corps at the time Robin disappeared, but managed to come home on emergency leave. Together they pursued every clue, and their efforts would ultimately link Darren O'Neall to another missing-person investigation in a different jurisdiction.

Because they had learned from a number of people that O'Neall and others had purchased cocaine and possibly other drugs from individuals attending the party at Tony Sellers' home, and because people had told them that Sellers was a major drug dealer in the area, Mike, Jim, Bobby, and Al began staking out Sellers' $250,000 house, set right on a lake. They watched the comings and goings from a distance at first, taking note of the license numbers and the makes and models of the cars that came and went from Sellers' house. Their reasoning was that perhaps O'Neall would show up there himself to make a purchase. Or perhaps some of the people that they were watching, many of whom were "mules" for Sellers, would come across O'Neall eventually, especially if he needed a fix and contacted one or more of them wanting to buy some drugs. They figured that if they followed these mules long enough, O'Neall might show up to make a score if he was still in the area.

As time went on, they became even more daunt-less, and no longer seemed to care if anyone noticed that they were watching the comings and goings at Sellers' house. On one occasion, when Sellers' drive-way was full of expensive sports cars and pickup trucks, they decided that they would approach his house. Someone came out and met them with a shotgun, however, and refused to answer any of their questions. Not wanting to get shot, they didn't per-sist and backed off even though they were by then packing their own firearms.

Nonetheless, they continued to follow the drug dealers that they had identified. They watched the dealers make drug pickups and deliveries, switch cars, steal license plates, and so forth. As a result it wasn't long before Mike, Jim, Bobby, and Al began to notice that they were being followed, too. They also began receiving unsettling telephone calls in the middle of the night. Some of the calls were merely hang-ups, while others were of a threatening nature. No matter what was said, or even if nothing at all was said, the message was crystal clear: they were to back off and mind their own business before some-one ended up getting hurt.

Although they did recede a bit, they certainly didn't quit. They just changed their tactics, and kept a little more distance between themselves and the drug dealers. Nonetheless, they continued to make new contacts and persisted in getting the answers to their questions. Before long they learned from an as-sociate of Sellers' about a party that had occurred at his house approximately two weeks before Robin disappeared. The party had possibly occurred on Monday, March 9, or Tuesday, March 10. The witness wasn't certain about the date. O'Neall had attended that party, however, said their new witness, of that she was certain. But he had taken off early and was gone all night, and did not return until very late the next evening. Shortly after he did return, the witness said that she and a friend borrowed O'Neall's car to go to the store, and while they were gone they had heard noises, occasional thumping sounds, coming from inside the trunk. Neither of them, however, opened the trunk to see what was causing the noise. They had been afraid to, fearful not only of what they might find but fearing what O'Neall might do if he discovered that they had been snooping around where they had no business.

At first the story didn't mean much to Mike, Jim, Bobby, and Al. It was simply an earlier but equally frightening and similar in nature version of what had occurred at Frank Wilhelm's house the day Robin disappeared. Except in this instance there had been no noticeable kicking at the backseat, only the thumping sounds that had come from inside the trunk. But when they related the story to Edna and talked about it among themselves some more, they recalled having read news stories about a young girl, 18-year-old Kimberley Kersey, who had disappeared on her way home from school near Vancouver, Washington. Kimberley, they soon learned, had vanished on Wednesday afternoon, March 11, and hadn't been

seen or heard from since. If the party at Sellers'
home had occurred on Tuesday, March 10 and not
on the day before, March 9, they reasoned, O'Neall
would have had ample time to make the two-and-a-
half-hour drive from Pierce County to Vancouver and
spend the rest of that night and most of the next day
hunting for a victim before returning to Pierce
County. Because the time frame and the suspicious
noises heard in the trunk of O'Neall's car were simply too much for them to brush off as mere coincidence, Edna and her family contacted the Clark
County Sheriff's Department in Vancouver to make
certain that they were aware of the similarities in the
cases of Robin and Kimberley. In part because of
their contact, Clark County detectives Dave Trimble
and Steve Nelson would look very closely at Darren
O'Neall as a suspect in *their* very mysterious disappearance case, and would share their information
with Stout and Wilson.

As they followed up on the Clark County missing-
person case, Stout and Wilson eventually learned
that Kimberley Kersey, a senior at Mountain View
High School in Vancouver, had been last seen at approximately two o'clock at her school locker. It was
believed that she was on her way home at that time,
but she never made it. Normally, according to members of her family, she would have obtained a ride
home from school. On other occasions, however, she
would take a shortcut, a trail that led from her
school through a wooded area and eventually ended

near the street where she lived. If she had taken the trail, the walk home should have taken her only a half hour. Taking her usual route, she would have crossed busy Mill Plain Boulevard at Northeast 136th Avenue, on which she would have headed north. She would have left 136th Avenue, which was also a busy road, and cut over onto a path in a heavily wooded and largely undeveloped area. The path, had she not been abducted from it, would have brought her out of the wooded area a short time later near the apartment complex where she lived on Northeast 18th Street.

Shortly after she disappeared and the search for her began, a notebook belonging to Kimberley was found in the wooded area just off the trail that she would have taken. Several of its pages had been torn out and scattered about. Stout and Wilson read from the information shared by their Clark County colleagues that additional school books belonging to a girl had also been found nearby. It was clear that a struggle had occurred between Kimberley and the person who abducted her.

An exhaustive search of the wooded area by more than 35 members of the sheriff's office, as well as by members from the Silver Star Search and Rescue and the Clark County Search and Rescue, had failed to turn up any sign of the girl, and the mystery only deepened when they brought in bloodhounds. The dogs had picked up Kimberley's scent, then quickly lost it, unable to find her trail out of the wooded area. There was an unexplained 70-foot gap from the point where the bloodhounds lost Kimberley's scent and where her books were found. It was almost as if someone had been waiting along the trail, saw her coming, somehow disabled her, wrapped her up in something, and carried her out of the woods, discarding her books along the way. When last seen, she had been wearing sneakers, white socks, light blue denim pants, and a white sweatshirt bearing the words "University of Paris" printed in pink, blue, and yellow letters.

Like Robin Smith, Kimberley was just a little bit of a thing. At only 5 foot 2 and 100 pounds, she wouldn't have been able to put up much of a fight against anyone, especially a drug-crazed man. The detectives, as well as the Smith family, noted that a side-by-side comparison of Robin's and Kimberley's photographs revealed an uncanny, almost haunting resemblance to each other. But the similarities, physical and otherwise, didn't end there. Kimberley had shoulder-length blond hair and blue eyes. And like Robin, Kimberley was described as a quiet person—a little headstrong but someone who never caused any major problems at home. She never failed to call home whenever she was going to be late, even if only a few minutes. It was also totally out of character for her to just go off anywhere without telling someone where she was going. She was too close to her family and friends to simply leave of her own volition without saying good-bye, even though she was 18.

Like Robin, Kimberley was engaged to be married to a young man living in the Puget Sound area. She had recently purchased, but had not yet picked up, an Amtrak ticket to Seattle for a trip that she would have made on Saturday, March 16. She was planning to attend a Mountain View boys' basketball playoff game, then spend the rest of the weekend with her fiancé and his mother. Excited about making the trip, Kimberley had already packed half of the things she was planning to take with her.

Shortly after her disappearance, the Clark County detectives were contacted by a mother-son team who claimed to be psychics. They had read news reports of Kimberley's disappearance and wanted to offer their help. Although skeptical, the investigators conceded that psychics had been correct in other missing-person, homicide, and similar investigations, so they felt compelled to give them a chance in their case. Besides, they reasoned, if they didn't allow the psychics to help, it wouldn't show much compassion on their part for Kimberley's family.

When the psychics arrived, they asked a few questions about the case, visited Kimberley's home, examined some of her belongings, and went to the wooded area from which she had disappeared. Afterward, they directed the investigators to an area along the Columbia River, just upriver from where the Interstate 5 bridge links Oregon and Washington, and pointed out where they believed Kimberley's body would be found. However, after an hour-long dive in a 30-by-50 foot area of the river, nothing but a couple of old bank deposit bags, locked but slashed open and their contents removed, were found.

By early April, Kimberley, like Robin, remained missing. She had simply vanished without a trace. And, as in Robin's case, there was no direct evidence of foul play, only a strong suspicion that something horrible had happened to her. But the detectives from both counties felt that the two cases could be linked not only by their similarities but by a single suspect. They just lacked the evidence to prove it.

On April 9 at 11:20 A.M., Stout received a telephone call from Nick Lawson,* a man who claimed to know Darren O'Neall. Naturally, Stout wanted to hear what he had to say.

"I saw O'Neall's photograph in the paper this morning," Lawson said, "and I read the information about him."

"Go on," Stout urged.

"I got to know him at Baldy's Tavern, but I never knew his name," Lawson continued. "But we talked sometimes, just casual conversation. Sometimes we talked about Montana at great length."

Lawson explained that he occasionally traveled to Montana, and said that he and O'Neall had talked about a place known as Spire Rock in the Gallatin Gateway area, located along U.S. Highway 191 south of Bozeman.

"O'Neall knew that area," Lawson said. "He talked about it in such a way that I could tell he was familiar with it. He must have been there before to know as much about it as he did."

Damn, just what he needed. Another Montana

connection to pin down. The others hadn't panned out yet, and Stout had his doubts about this one, too. So what if O'Neall had been there before? It didn't necessarily mean that he was going back there. Or did it? Stout couldn't just ignore it. He had to cover all the bases, so to speak. He couldn't take any chances on letting O'Neall slip by.

Stout promptly contacted Lieutenant Bob Christie of the Gallatin County Sheriff's Department in Bozeman and informed him about the case and the tip that he had just received from Nick Lawson. Before he hung up, Stout told the lieutenant that he would send over some of the bulletins that he had made up. Christie assured Stout that he would distribute them when they arrived, and in the meantime would make the information available to his department so that patrol units would be on the lookout for O'Neall and his car.

Before the day was over, Stout received another telephone call from a woman in Marysville, near Everett, about an hour's drive north from Pierce County. The woman, a dress shop owner, claimed to have seen a man fitting O'Neall's description walk past her shop. She said that she had had the impression that he was heading toward a nearby bus stop, from which the bus would take him to Everett. She described his skin as smooth and well tanned, as if he had spent the past couple of weeks going to a tanning salon every day or, perhaps, someone who had spent a good deal of time in recent days in the outdoors. She said that he had a strong jaw line and his hair was brown with auburn highlights and that it lay in soft, natural curls. When she arrived home that day and read her copy of the *Seattle Times,* she saw O'Neall's photo and recognized it as the man she saw walk past her shop.

"I never forget a face," she said.

Well, if it was O'Neall, Stout thought, he was still in the state and had not headed toward Montana. At least not yet. But where the hell was he going? Stout, at that point, didn't yet have enough information to enable him to make an educated guess. Although he didn't know it yet, O'Neall's route out of the area would not take him through Montana. When all was said and done, Stout and Wilson would realize that the supposed Montana connection did not exist except in O'Neall's mind. He had been there in the past, all right. But he had made no plans to return there, and all of the information coming in about Montana only served to send the investigators on a wild goose chase for a murderer who was headed in a different direction.

Chapter 9

It was a few minutes after 5:00 P.M. on Friday, April 10, when Detective Terry Wilson reached his partner by telephone and informed him that the 1972 Chrysler New Yorker driven by O'Neall finally had been located. The car, Wilson told him, had been abandoned at a rest area near Marysville in Snohomish County. Recognizing this as possibly the first real break they had received in the case, Stout was naturally elated at the news. He promptly called the Snohomish County Communications Center and spoke with an operator, Kathy Titerness, who filled him in on what she knew about the car's discovery.

According to Titerness, Washington State Patrol Trooper Dan Schei had found the abandoned Chrysler on Monday, March 30, at a rest stop on the northbound side of Interstate 5, approximately 12 miles north of Everett, while out on routine patrol. He tagged the car, and when he checked again the next day he found that it was still there. At that point he called Kazen Towing Company, located in nearby Arlington, to come and impound the vehicle.

Titerness informed Stout that the car in question, bearing Montana license plates 4-148307, had been reported stolen on November 2, 1986, out of Nampa, Idaho, but that there had been some difficulty in obtaining that information. When he pressed her for more information, she explained that she did not yet know all of the details herself. Stout, wondering why the hell it had taken so long for the vehicle to turn up listed as stolen on their fancy and expensive computer systems, wanted some answers, and fast. He first, however, contacted the Tacoma Towing Company and requested that they send a tow truck to Kazen Towing in Arlington to pick up the Chrysler and bring it to a storage facility at the Pierce County Sheriff's Department's West Precinct in Lakewood.

As he pondered the possibilities surrounding the problems associated with the stolen Chrysler, the city of Nampa, Idaho, suddenly rang a bell in Stout's mind. When he thought about it, he soon found himself wondering why the alarm in his head hadn't sounded earlier. He recalled the medical card from Mercy Medical Center in Nampa, the one that Jim Chaney had found inside O'Neall's duplex apartment, made out in the name of Zebulan J. Macranahan. Stout promptly called the Nampa Police Department and spoke to Officer Chris Klein, who provided the detective with information about the stolen Chrysler and Stout's mystery man.

According to Klein, a subject calling himself none other than Zebulan J. Macranahan had befriended a Nampa resident, Barry Fenwick.* The two first had met sometime toward the end of September, "about two months ago," according to what Fenwick had reported to the police. Macranahan had been hitchhiking, and Fenwick had picked him up. Macranahan had needed a place to stay while in Nampa, and Fenwick, being a person of a trusting nature, allowed him to stay with him at his home. There had been no trouble until the third week in October, when Macranahan showed up late one night at the emergency room of Mercy Medical Center, the apparent victim of a stabbing. The medical records indicated that he had been stabbed in the abdomen, but that the wounds hadn't been serious. He was treated against a possible onset of infection, stitched up, and promptly released.

As with all reported incidents of violence, Macranahan's stabbing, even though it hadn't been all that serious from a medical point of view, was investigated by a detective from the Nampa Police Department. During the detective's inquiry Macranahan told him that he didn't know who had stabbed him, and the description that he provided of his assailant was sketchy at best. Macranahan further told the detective that he was originally from the Coeur d'Alene, Idaho, area, but subsequent checks with the Coeur d'Alene Police Department failed to turn up any information on a Zebulan J. Macranahan. Similar inquiries with the Idaho Department of Motor Vehicles and the state's law enforcement data system proved fruitless. There was simply no one, criminal or good citizen, on record in the state of Idaho by the name of Zebulan J. Macranahan.

Then, on Sunday, November 2, 1986, Fenwick, a long-haul truck driver, had left Nampa during the early morning hours on a job that would take him to Portland, Oregon, and back. Prior to leaving, Fenwick had entrusted Macranahan with $150, which he had asked him to deposit into the bank for him when the bank opened on Monday morning. Fenwick also told Macranahan that he could use his Chrysler New Yorker to take the money to the bank and to drive around town while he was gone.

The same day that Fenwick left, Macranahan took the car out for a spin. Before long, however, he was stopped at Ninth Avenue and Second Street North in Nampa by Lieutenant Rick Wiley, who was working traffic that day, because the driver looked like a "suspicious" character. Macranahan, who had no driver's license and no proof of insurance, explained that he had borrowed the car from a friend for use around town. He provided Fenwick's name, and explained that he was staying with Fenwick. When Wiley called the information in, he found that the car was indeed registered to Fenwick, and no information surfaced on Macranahan. Wiley, with no reason to hold him, issued Macranahan a citation for not having a driver's license or insurance. He also issued him a stern warning to take the car back to Fenwick's house and to leave it parked there until he obtained his license and insurance. Macranahan promised Wiley that he would.

However, when Fenwick returned on Tuesday, November 4, he discovered that Macranahan and his Chrysler were gone. When he checked around his home, he also discovered that a box of new tools had been taken, along with his Ruger .357 Magnum revolver. When Fenwick checked with his bank, he discovered that his checking account was nearly to the point of being overdrawn. He also discovered that several blank checks were missing from his home, and a bank employee told him that there was no record of a deposit in the amount of $150 having been made.

When Fenwick reported the stolen car and the theft of the money and other items to the police, he told them that during the time that he had known Macranahan, he had never seen any identification or other proof of his identity. He had merely taken Macranahan at his word. He said, however, that he had heard Macranahan refer to himself as "Jim" and "Larry Sackett" to other people, but he had not questioned him about it.

Officer Klein told Stout that Macranahan had since been charged with grand theft, that Fenwick's car had been entered into the NCIC computers, and that a statewide alert had been issued for it. However, the car had not been seen since it was reported stolen by Fenwick, and the Nampa Police Department had no idea where one "Zeb Macranahan" might have fled.

Stout, recognizing that "Sackett" was the name of a frontier family in a popular series of Louis L'Amour novels, immediately ordered that all of the L'Amour novels seized from O'Neall's apartment be carefully read and studied, something that they had been planning to do anyway, to determine if they contained any clues to where O'Neall might have fled after abducting Robin Smith. It was becoming ever clearer to Stout and Wilson that the earlier reports about O'Neall's fantasies of becoming a mountain man and survivalist from Mary Barnes and others were beginning to bear more credence, especially now that he knew that O'Neall had used at least one alias drawn from a L'Amour book.

The next morning at eight-thirty, Saturday, April 11, Stout called Chief Criminal Deputy Prosecuting Attorney Tom Felnagle to bring him up to date on the investigation and to inform him that the missing Chrysler had been located. Because the car was in fact stolen, said Felnagle, and because it had been driven by O'Neall and was not his own vehicle, coupled with the fact that the car had been abandoned and subsequently impounded by the Washington State Patrol, the car could be searched in relation to the Robin Smith missing-person investigation. O'Neall, furthermore, could not expect any rights to privacy regarding the stolen vehicle that he had abandoned.

At 10:40, Stout and Wilson drove to the storage facility at West Precinct. Because it was a weekend and the wheels of nearly every level of bureaucracy had come to a screeching halt at five on Friday, a full examination would not be conducted at that time in the presence of identification officers and criminalists from the Washington State Patrol Crime Lab. Instead, Stout and Wilson would go over the car in a preliminary fashion.

The keys were still in the ignition, just as they had been when Trooper Schei had found the car, prompting the detectives to wonder why. Had O'Neall been frightened by something, such as the presence of a police officer and, not wanting to be seen with the stolen car and recognized in connection with the Robin Smith case, had fled? Or was there another reason?

As they examined the car's interior they noted that it was filthy, with a large amount of garbage, paper sacks, blankets, food wrappers, and empty beer cans strewn about virtually every inch of it. A paperback copy of Jean Auel's *The Mammoth Hunters* lay open on the front seat, and there was even more of the outdoor and survival-oriented reading material that O'Neall seemed to prefer beneath the seats. From all appearances, the car looked as though it had been used by somebody who both didn't care about cleanliness and who had obviously been living inside it for a while.

Using one of the keys attached to the key ring that dangled from the ignition lock on the steering wheel column, Stout opened the car's truck. Inside he found a sleeping bag, a fishing pole, a backpack, a hunting knife inside a leather sheath, other outdoor equipment, and several articles of dirty clothing.

However, both Stout's and Wilson's attention was quickly drawn to a large quantity of blood inside the trunk, now dried. Much of the blood had soaked into the left side of the trunk's inner cardboard panel and into the carpet covering the panel. But they also noticed that there were significant blood spatters on the interior underside of the trunk lid. The spatters, they noted, appeared to be of low to medium velocity in origin, consistent with those that might have been caused by a downward and side-to-side flinging motion of something heavy, perhaps while held in someone's hand.

As they carefully examined some of the trunk's contents, not wishing to disturb or otherwise destroy any evidence that might be present, their attention was soon drawn to a lavender ski jacket that appeared to match the description of the one reportedly worn by Robin Smith when she was last seen. The jacket, which was small and appeared to be of the type that a young female would wear, was also stained heavily with blood. Because of the severity of what they had found, neither Stout or Wilson examined the contents of the trunk any further.

Instead, they focused their attention back to the interior of the car. Within minutes they found a receipt on the floorboard near the front passenger seat. It had been issued by a cashier who worked at a Safeway store in Enumclaw, and was dated March 29, at 8:10 A.M., the day after Robin had been last seen. The receipt suddenly became very significant to both of the detectives because its information coincided with the reported sightings of Darren O'Neall and the Chrysler in the east part of Pierce County, near Greenwater and Crystal Mountain, on the weekend that Robin disappeared. The receipt also verified the reported sighting of O'Neall from the Safeway clerk who had reported serving him that weekend.

At one-thirty that afternoon Stout had the bleak duty of informing Edna Smith, along with other members of her family, that the missing Chrysler had been found. Worse, he found that it was necessary to disclose the details of the blood and what was believed to be Robin's jacket found inside the trunk.

"It looked like the quantity of blood was such that a person had bled severely inside that trunk," Stout told Edna and her family. "Someone received very serious injuries." He paused a moment, trying to be considerate, then added: "Do any of you know, or have access to, Robin's blood type?"

"I have no idea what her blood type is," Edna said.

"Do you know whether Robin has been treated locally by a doctor or hospital for anything that might have necessitated the typing of her blood?" Stout asked, pushing for the answer.

"No, I don't," Edna responded slowly, dragging out her words as she mulled over the grim possibilities. "As far as I know, Robin hasn't been treated by any doctor that would require blood work. She did have surgery once, but that was when she was an infant at a hospital in Southington, Connecticut."

Edna explained that she and her family had lived in New Britain, Connecticut, for a number of years, and that they had also lived in Meriden until Robin was twelve, at which time she moved her family to Washington. The surgery, she explained, had been done when Robin was a little more than a year old to correct a hernia condition.

Because it didn't take much of an imagination for Edna and her family to begin speculating that the blood inside the trunk of the Chrysler was most likely Robin's, Stout saw little reason not to persuade them gently to begin preparing themselves for the worst. He explained that if Robin was still alive after having lost as much blood as he and Wilson had found inside the trunk of the car, her condition would have to be very critical. Before leaving, Stout requested that Edna and the other family members safeguard any items, either in the residence that Robin had shared with Larron or in the Smith residence, items such as combs, brushes, head bands, and so forth, anything that might reasonably be expected to contain samples of Robin's hair.

At 1:50 P.M. on Monday, April 13, Stout eventually reached Washington State Patrol Trooper Dan Schei with the assistance of the Marysville Police Department, in whose patrolling area Schei was working that morning. Schei briefly explained how he had first noticed the car parked at the rest area at approximately 6:10 A.M. on Monday, March 30, and how it appeared to him to have been abandoned. It had been parked in the last parking stall on the north end of the area, near a brushy and wooded area that surrounds the rest stop. Schei explained that it was normal procedure to leave a suspected abandoned vehicle at its location for at least twenty-four hours and then recheck it. If it still has not been moved and no registered owner could be located, proper procedure is to have such cars impounded. There are statutes, he explained, that regulate the length of time a vehicle can occupy a space at a rest area.

When Schei rechecked the car again on the morning of March 31, he found that it had not been moved. Strangely, he said, the keys were in the ignition, something that he had not noticed the day before. Unaware that the car was wanted in connection with a criminal investigation, Schei said that he tested it to determine if it would start. It readily started, he said, and appeared to have only a small amount of fuel left in the tank. He said that he did not examine the car further.

However, Schei said that he did run the license plate through the system, but for some reason it had not came back through the NCIC as a reported stolen car, nor was he able to come up with any registered owner information. Baffled as to why he hadn't gotten a hit on the vehicle as stolen, Schei said that he followed procedure and had it towed from the rest area.

After he got off the telephone with Schei, Stout drove to the rest area near Marysville so that he could take a look around himself. The last stall, just as Trooper Schei had said, was next to a brushy area that led off to the east from the asphalt and into a

wooded area. Stout observed that there were approximately fifty feet of trees and low brush between the
paved area and the freeway. The paved area and the
freeway were separated by cyclone fencing. There
were a number of trails through the area, most of
which led from the space where the Chrysler had
been parked. The trails were used, Stout observed,
by people who had stopped at the rest area for a
number of reasons. Some locked their doors and
slept for a short time, and later stretched their legs
by walking along the trail before moving on. Others
studied their maps and ate packaged food from vend-
ing machines, many of whom also took a short walk.
Stout noticed that some, after using the indoor rest
rooms and having a complimentary cup of coffee,
walked their dogs along the trails for exercise and to
provide their pets a "rest" stop of their own. He
walked all of the trails and through some of the
brushy, tree-covered areas to see if he could find any
signs of Robin or other evidence that O'Neall might
have discarded while at the site. However, after having spent considerable time in the area, he found
nothing of significance.

But why, he kept asking himself, had O'Neall
abandoned the car at that location? And even more
baffling to Stout was why he had left those damned
keys in the ignition. Then, suddenly, as he stood
back and looked at the spot where O'Neall had
parked the car, it struck him. O'Neall had most likely
abandoned the car near the trail heads and left the
keys in the ignition in the hope that someone would

come along and steal it. That way, if and when the car was ever stopped by the police—and O'Neall was certainly intelligent enough to know that the police would eventually be on the lookout for it—it would not be in his possession. Moreover, the evidence linking O'Neall to the car, if stolen from the rest area, would be contaminated by the presence of additional fingerprints left by the new thief, which conceivably could make matters even more confusing and ultimately more difficult to prosecute. The move, if it had been successful, might have even served to throw the police further off track, and it certainly would have provided more time for the evidence inside the trunk to deteriorate. Whatever O'Neall had been thinking, his actions, at the very least, would have forced the cops onto another avenue of investigation and thus slowed them down in their pursuit of O'Neall. But the plan hadn't worked, at least not entirely. No one had chosen to steal the car, which was a miracle in itself considering the location where O'Neall had abandoned it. All his actions had done was to delay the cops in drawing any conclusions about what had become of Robin, and allowed him to move about a little more freely.

Stout was still curious about how the stolen Chrysler had slipped past the National Crime Information Center and other law enforcement computerized information data systems. Because those systems were the normal route to finding out about a stolen vehicle and thus locating it, he wanted to know how the car had been identified as stolen without the help of the NCIC and why it had taken so long to make the identification. The car, after all, had been towed from the rest area on March 31. Yet it had taken from March 31 until April 10 for his department to be notified of its discovery. Why? By the time he had finished his inquiry, he had all of the answers to his questions, but he was not happy about it.

For starters, he learned, it was a mere fluke that the Chrysler had even been identified as being wanted in connection with the disappearance of Robin Smith and the search for Darren O'Neall. As it turned out, the tow truck operator and owner of his own towing business, Don Kazen, 62, who had impounded the vehicle from the rest area 11 days earlier, had been reading a newspaper story about Robin's disappearance. As he read the description of the car, he suddenly realized that it was stored on his lot, being prepared to be auctioned off as an abandoned vehicle the following weekend. After it had "clicked" in his mind, Kazen contacted the Snohomish County Sheriff's Department, and they, too, wanted to know why the car hadn't surfaced in their multimillion-dollar computerized equipment. As they launched an investigation of their own, they in turn had notified the Pierce County Sheriff's Department of the car's discovery rather than hold them up in their investigation.

One of the things that had gone wrong and had been turned up by the Snohomish County investigation was that a state police communications officer

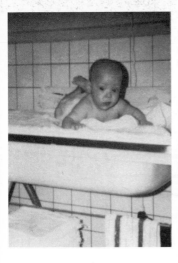

Robin Pamela Smith,
age 5 months.
(PHOTO BY EDNA SMITH)

Robin in 1968.
(PHOTO BY EDNA SMITH)

Robin, age 11.
(PHOTO BY EDNA SMITH)

Robin in 1982.

POLICE DEPARTMENT
COLORADO SPRINGS

8·7·0·2·2 ·0·3·1·2·82

POLICE DEPARTMENT
COLORADO SPRINGS

8·7·0·2·2 ·1·0·31·

O'NEALL, Darren L. 10-26-60

O'NEALL, Darren

POLICE DEPARTMENT
COLORADO SPRINGS

8·3·0·2·2 ·07·31·86·

POLICE DEPARTMENT
COLORADO SPRINGS

8·7·0·2·2 ·07·31·86·

ONEALL, DARREN LEE 000 02-26-60

ONEALL, DARREN LEE 000

The many faces of Darren Dee O'Neall: *top left:* Colorado Springs, 1982; *center left:* Colorado Springs, 1985; *bottom left:* Colorado Springs, 1986; *top right:* Metairie, Louisiana, 1987; *bottom right:* Multnomah County, Oregon, 1989—before being sentenced to 27 years and 9 months in a Washington prison for the murder of Robin Smith and 135 years for kidnapping and numerous counts of rape and sexual abuse.

Edna Smith, Robin Smith's mother.

James M. Chaney, Jr., leader of a civilian search for Robin Smith's body, at the site where her remains were found.

Detective Walter D. Stout, Pierce County, Washington, Sheriff's Department, was initally assigned to Robin Smith's case and began an investigation of O'Neall. (PHOTO COURTESY PIERCE COUNTY SHERIFF'S DEPT.)

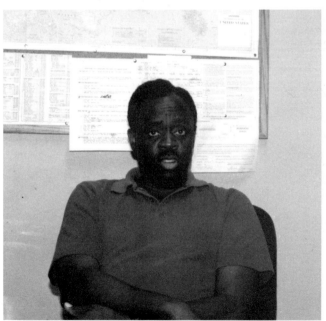

Detective Terry L. Wilson, Pierce County, Washington, Sheriff's Department, inherited the Smith case from Detective Stout and headed the Washington state investigation of O'Neall.

Kimberly Kersey, age 18. She has been missing since 1987. (PHOTO COURTESY PIERCE COUNTY SHERIFF'S DEPT.)

Wendy L. Aughe, age 29, missing mother of two. She disappeared from her Bellingham, Washington, home and is believed dead. (PHOTO COURTESY PIERCE COUNTY SHERIFF'S DEPT.)

The Chrysler that O'Neall stole in Idaho and reportedly used to transport Robin Smith's body. The car was found abandoned. (PHOTO COURTESY PIERCE COUNTY SHERIFF'S DEPT.)

Robin Smith's heavily blood-stained jacket after it was removed from the Chrysler's trunk.

Bones believed to be Robin Smith's found at a forest site near Mount Rainier, Washington.

Larron Crowston and Robin, right after Larron proposed
marriage and Robin accepted.

Larron and Robin's grave site.

had failed to correctly enter the information from the car when it was impounded, according to Bill Burkett, public information officer at the Washington State Patrol. The communications officer, who was new on the job, should have taken the information and entered it into the computer exactly as Trooper Schei had radioed it in to headquarters in Olympia. And the same should have been done later, after Schei wrote up his report and impound order and sent it in. However, in both instances the communications officer incorrectly entered the state abbreviation for Missouri, which is MO, when she should have entered MT for Montana, the correct issuing state for the license plates that the car bore. As a result, when the Washington State Patrol's computer in Olympia linked up with the National Crime Information Center's computer, nothing turned up because it was looking for a stolen Chrysler with Missouri plates, not Montana plates.

"It was an error of newness on the job and not having assimilated all the details," Burkett reported. "There's no question but that it was a mistake on the operator's part. She'll be counseled."

If the communications officer had entered all of the information correctly, law enforcement agencies would have quickly discovered that the car had been reported stolen the previous November from Nampa, Idaho, Burkett said.

But that wasn't all, Stout learned. On April 1, radio operators at the Law Enforcement Support Agency, one of the communications arms that handles information for the Pierce County Sheriff's Department, had mistakenly broadcast to only a handful of agencies the information and descriptions concerning O'Neall and the Chrysler, information that both Stout and Wilson had entered into the system. Stout's request for help should have gone out to agencies across the state. However, the alerts were sent out only to the Washington State Gambling Commission, the Port Angeles Police Department, and the Bremerton office of the Washington State Patrol.

It was indeed an unfortunate set of circumstances, Stout conceded. If everyone had performed their jobs correctly right down the line, Pierce County might have learned about the abandoned Chrysler as early as March 31 and they could have been closer to nabbing O'Neall. But eleven days had passed since the car had been impounded from the Interstate 5 rest area, enough time to allow O'Neall's trail to get cold and certainly ample time for him to have fled the state.

At 1:55 that same afternoon, Detective Terry Wilson arrived at the vehicle storage cage of the West Precinct in Lakewood, where he met criminalists H. W. "Skip" Johnson and Larry Hebert, both from the Washington State Patrol Crime Laboratory. They were there to process the Chrysler New Yorker for evidence.

Johnson carefully photographed the car in general, from angles that showed both the interior and exterior portions. He also photographed the interior to show the driver and passenger sides in both the front and back seats. Afterward, when he was certain that he had captured every detail of the car's interior on film, he moved to the trunk, where he photographed it and its contents just as thoroughly.

Johnson also took photographs during the subsequent search of the trunk as items were seized and marked as evidence by Hebert. He took several photos of the lavender jacket that depicted the locations of the bloodstains, and afterward promptly transferred the jacket to a freezer to better preserve the blood evidence it held. He then photographed what appeared to be several hair "swipes" in the large portion of blood on the cardboard panel that covered the left rear wheel well.

Next, he took pictures of blood on the inside of the trunk lid, most of which was visible on the left-hand portion in a "splatter" pattern. He also took close-up shots of what appeared to be fresh marks or gouges in the metal, within the areas of the blood spatter, which could have been made by someone wielding a heavy instrument, such as a claw hammer, and had inadvertently hit the interior of the trunk lid while striking a subdued victim directly beneath it. Similar marks or gouges that exposed the metal beneath the paint were also found on the right portion of the interior trunk lid. As they removed the evidence, they found additional blood on the inside of the trunk near the opening, in the area nearest the taillights, on both the left and right sides.

Wilson found and bagged as evidence an athletic or crew sock, similar in appearance to the socks that Robin was described by Larron and her family as wearing on the day she disappeared. The sock was also similar to that described by the person on drug rehabilitation who claimed to have seen O'Neall striking the "naked blond girl in the head" when O'Neall was parked across the street from Frank Wilhelm's home and place of business. The sock, Wilson noted, had bloodstains on it as well as what looked like a bone fragment.

On the car's exterior, they noted damage to the left rear quarter panel. There was considerable dirt in that same area, as if the car had been driven and bounced across some rough, muddy terrain. There was also a large amount of dirt in the driver-side doorjamb. Samples of the dirt from both sections were recovered by Hebert.

Johnson found two human teeth and a possible bone chip on a heavily bloodstained section of the carpet inside the trunk. He photographed the items before removing them, and again afterward. He also removed a sample of the bloodstained carpet, as well as a control sample that did not appear to be stained. He repeated the process during the removal of the bloodstained cardboard panel.

As they went through the car and removed evidence, they found a number of beer cans and bottles, mostly Black Label but also Budweiser, Schmidt, Rainier, and Schaeffer's. They also found an empty pastry package that had contained Mrs.

Wright's Danish Butterhorns, and empty boxes of Camel filters. They also recovered a black patent leather woman's shoe, size seven, a red plaid "Timber Topper" large-size shirt, the paperback by Jean Auel and considered by the investigators as too literary for O'Neall's tastes, a stocking cap, a pair of blue shorts, a Zerex antifreeze bottle, and a number of envelopes.

After they had removed all of the large items, they focused on the smaller, even microscopic, items. These included a silver earring, an earring backing for post-type earrings, the Safeway sales receipt, a number of hair and fiber strands, and soil samples. The car was also carefully processed for latent fingerprints, of which many were located and recovered.

Later, Johnson compared latent fingerprints from two of the Black Label beer cans found inside the Chrysler with the inked prints of Darren O'Neall that had been provided by authorities in Colorado. Not surprisingly, he determined them to be O'Neall's.

A short time later Stout and Wilson delivered the two teeth that had been recovered from the trunk of the Chrysler to Dr. Peter Hampl, a forensic dentist, at his office in Tacoma. Both teeth, a maxillary right incisor and maxillary right lateral incisor, appeared to have been recently fractured. Based on the information that the dentist provided them, including the angle of the fracture and other minute detail, it appeared to the detectives that the teeth had been violently knocked or broken out of the victim's mouth by someone wielding a heavy, blunt instrument.

Chapter 10

Soon after finding the stolen Chrysler and collecting the evidence from it, Stout and Wilson traced its owner, Barry Fenwick, to Portland, Oregon, where Fenwick had recently traveled on another driving job. They wanted to inform him that they had located his car, and they needed to know if Fenwick could identify "Macranahan" from a photo throw-down. He said that he was certain he could pick him out if his picture was among those shown to him. The detectives arranged to meet with Fenwick, and he picked the photograph of Darren O'Neall out of a photo throw-down that consisted of six photographs of similar individuals.

Fenwick recounted a lot of the details of his association with O'Neall for Stout and Wilson, things that they had already learned from the Nampa Police Department, including how he had come to meet up with him when he knew him only as Zeb Macranahan. But he also told the Pierce County detectives of O'Neall's captivation by Louis L'Amour novels. Not only did he sometimes call himself by the names of some of L'Amour's characters, he had written to the author a number of times. Fenwick thought that L'Amour had responded twice, possibly more. At least that's what his house guest had told him.

Armed with this new bit of information, Stout and Wilson decided that it was time they contacted Louis L'Amour's publisher, or even the author himself, regarding the letters that O'Neall had purportedly written to L'Amour. They got on the phone together and soon found through L'Amour's publicist that the author was traveling and could not immediately be reached, so they settled for calling L'Amour's publisher, Bantam Books. Their call was transferred to Stuart Applebaum, a vice president at Bantam Books and L'Amour's editor.

The detectives explained that they were looking for any letters that O'Neall might have written to L'Amour. If he had written to the author, they said, the letters might provide some insight into O'Neall's planning and thinking. But Applebaum quickly dashed any hopes they held.

"You have to realize," said Applebaum, "you're talking about a person who gets hundreds of letters a week. I don't know how we'd be able to find the ones you're looking for." As to O'Neall's actions, Applebaum added: "This sounds like a code of behavior that would not be sanctioned in any way by L'Amour. If indeed this alleged perpetrator is taking his ideas from a Louis L'Amour book, he's chronically taking them out of context and what it means to be a man. Having spoken to Louis on many occasions, I know he'd absolutely deplore this as totally misunderstanding the concept of manhood."

Stout contacted Applebaum again a few days later, after the editor had had a chance to speak with L'Amour, one of the world's most popular authors. Unfortunately, Applebaum said that L'Amour could not recall having received any correspondence from a Darren O'Neall or a Zebulan J. Macranahan.

"If this alleged perpetrator is a L'Amour reader," Applebaum said, "he has tragically misunderstood and misappropriated the frontier ethic that Louis puts forth in his novels, because in no way does L'Amour ever advocate breaking the law or doing any harm to your fellow man. If L'Amour's characters violate the law, they pay a debt to society."

Applebaum said that it was L'Amour's hope that O'Neall would turn himself in to the police.

Meanwhile, frustrated in the face of growing adversity and doubt at not being able to positively find out what had happened to Robin, Edna Smith and her family did not give up. Edna, recalling how psychics had volunteered their time and energy in the Kimberley Kersey case, began mulling over the idea of finding a psychic herself. Even though the psychics in Kimberley's case had not achieved any significant results, Edna held out the hope that it might be different in Robin's case. But where would she find a psychic, especially one that would not simply be out to make what money she could from Edna's tragic plight? Someone recommended that she check with the University of Washington in Seattle for assistance, and she did. At the university's suggestion, Edna consulted with a known psychic who did not wish to be publicly identified but agreed to help her free of charge.

Edna and her family took the psychic to O'Neall's apartment in Edgewood, and upon entering, she immediately began receiving what she termed "bad vibes." She began to have visions of where she believed O'Neall was, or possibly had been, in the mountain forests. She suddenly picked up images of Robin, and was getting a peaceful feeling about it all. She told Edna that Robin was in an area near Mount Rainier, that she was near running or dripping water, but she wasn't sure which. Edna, at that time, took the peaceful feeling that the psychic was receiving to mean that Robin was either in a coma or drugged. She refused to believe that the peaceful feeling could have meant that Robin was dead.

At that point Edna really didn't know what to think. She didn't know whether to believe that Robin was being held hostage by O'Neall or whether she lay dying on some cold forest ground from the severe bleeding wounds that nearly everyone else associated with the case was certain that she had sustained. But one thing was certain: it was all beginning to add up. O'Neall's fixation with the outdoors. The sightings of O'Neall by the clerk at the Safeway store in Enumclaw, by the clerk at the convenience store in Bonney Lake, and by the flagger on the road to Crystal Mountain. Jim's and Mike's bad vibes in the forest. The blood, teeth, bone fragments and Robin's bloodstained jacket in the trunk of the Chrysler. And now the psychic's direction to a mountainous forest area near running or dripping water. They were on the right track. They had to be. There was nothing else for them to believe.

"She could still be alive," Edna said, hanging on to the thin thread of hope. "The psychic said that it's very possible that the feeling she gets of total peace could mean that Robin could be in a coma. Or she could be so drugged up that she can't respond to anything." After a moment of silent reflection she finally said, for the first time: "The other possibility is that she could be dead."

Despite the unrealistic odds of finding Robin alive, there was a part of Edna and her family that still refused to give her up for dead. Instead, they began making plans for a large-scale search of the Greenwater area, a search that was largely organized by Jim Chaney.

But they also held out for one other possibility, namely that O'Neall, holding Robin hostage, was fleeing across the country. They were hoping against hope that Robin was still alive and had her wits about her, that she was somehow trying to con O'Neall into driving east, hopefully to Connecticut. It was only painful wishful thinking, nothing more, and each of them knew that to be true in their hearts. But it gave them something to hang on to.

Stout and Wilson, however, being realistic because of past experiences in such cases, told Edna and her family that they were no longer holding out much hope for Robin. In the slim chance that she was still alive, they said, her chances of surviving with the massive blood loss that had occurred in the trunk of the Chrysler diminished severely with each day.

To sum up the case at that point, Stout and Wilson knew that they had no body yet, and their only suspect was a modern-day outlaw who was as elusive as his fantasy of surviving in the great outdoors. Stout and Wilson didn't believe that his trail had gone cold; they knew that it simply no longer existed. The only other thing that they knew for certain was that O'Neall was out there somewhere, and would likely continue his deadly course of maiming and destruction unless he was somehow stopped.

Chapter 11

Admittedly reaching for leads to O'Neall's whereabouts, Stout and Wilson, as well as a number of road deputies, began examining several vacation cabins in the Greenwater area. They found that many of the cabins, though not often used, were kept well stocked with food and other supplies by their owners. Even though they didn't expect O'Neall to still be at one of these cabins, the detectives theorized that he might have holed up in one or more of them in the days immediately following Robin's disappearance and, if so, he may have left important clues as to what had happened to Robin and quite possibly his plans for the future. Much to their dismay, however, no one in the area had reported any burglaries and in-person checks of the vacation dwellings showed no signs of forced entry.

In the meantime, additional background on Darren O'Neall began to come in from a number of law enforcement agencies, including the FBI, the Colorado Springs Police Department, and the Fremont County, Colorado, Sheriff's Department. The

FBI had by now become involved due to an unlawful flight to avoid prosecution warrant that had been issued in connection with the June 1986 second-degree rape/felony sexual assault charges he had allegedly committed against the Colorado Springs prostitute, and they were also interested in him for investigation of interstate transportation of a stolen vehicle. The other agencies also provided information about crimes they suspected O'Neall of committing in their jurisdictions.

As Stout and Wilson pored over the reports they received, they learned a great deal about O'Neall's past, which naturally provided them with significant insight into what kind of person they were most likely dealing with. They already had learned that he had a penchant for violent sex, was capable of kidnapping, and, after having found the Chrysler and the revealing evidence in its trunk, knew that he was capable of much worse, probably murder. The stacks of reports also helped them to develop a time line on O'Neall, which would enable them to track more easily his past movements and, they hoped, establish certain patterns that might help them predict his future activities. Although hard or conclusive evidence that O'Neall might be a serial killer hadn't yet surfaced, Wilson and Stout were beginning to consider such a possibility from the information they were learning. It was a thought that they kept to themselves, however, at least for the time being.

* * *

Darren Dee O'Neall, they learned, was born on February 26, 1960, in Albuquerque, New Mexico. His parents, Darrell and Christa O'Neall, raised three other children besides Darren, who was next to the youngest. Michael and Kevin were both older than their brother, and Kristen, Darren's sister, was younger. O'Neall's father was somewhat of a disciplinarian due to his military background, but not harshly so. The O'Neall's reared their children lovingly, and both parents cared about what went on in each of their children's lives. Although military life was often disruptive and kept them on the move, the O'Nealls taught their children responsibility and to respect others, always emphasizing the golden rule. Much to their dismay, however, Darren had more difficulty adhering to such a concept than did his siblings, especially as he grew older.

When Darren was old enough, he joined the Cub Scouts. He came home from school one day after hearing a pack leader give a recruitment speech, and both his parents encouraged him to join. Darren, as best that the Pierce County investigators could determine, got along well with the other boys in his group, and went on to become a Boy Scout. Throughout his youth, perhaps as a result of his Cub and Boy Scout affiliations, he participated in nearly all sports, though he could be classified only as a fair athlete. He greatly enjoyed the time he spent in the outdoors, especially the time he spent participating in snow activities such as skiing. He particularly enjoyed hunting, fishing, and camping, and taught himself how to recognize birds, animals, and plants, which he often sketched for his own amusement and education. His grades in school reflected only an average student, but scholastic tests indicated that he had much greater potential. He just never chose to apply himself, nor did he aspire for any more than a two-point grade point average.

By his own later admission, he experimented with marijuana as a teenager, which proved to be a great disappointment to his parents, and later tried opiated hashish. But his illicit drug use was considered typical in the seventies, when it was somewhat fashionable to do so. What he really liked to do, however, especially in high school, was to drink beer, much more so than taking the drugs at that time in his life. He was known to be able to finish off a case of beer in a single night, and the heavy drug abuse would not come until later. Despite his affinity for drinking, he never got into any trouble that involved the police until after he entered his twenties. The only problems that he had as an adolescent, at least those that could be determined by the authorities, was that he was self-absorbed and had a temper that often became a rage that he could not control. In that vein he began fighting with his parents and his brothers, often physically breaking things and punching holes in the walls at home. But his rage soon accelerated to the point that he began threatening to kill people, such as his brothers, and there was at least one documented incident in which he actually attempted to shoot one of his brothers.

When Darren was 16, his father was transferred to Fort Polk, Louisiana, just outside of Leesville, following a tour of duty in Germany. It was there that he met and began dating June Hodges while attending the same high school. June, who also came from a military family, got along well with Darren's family. However, their time together was short.

In June 1979, Darren and June, both 19, moved to Colorado Springs, Colorado, when Darren's father, due to be transferred to Korea for what would be his final tour of duty prior to retirement, moved the rest of his family there. June enlisted in the air force the following year, after which she and Darren were married by a chaplain at Fort Carson, located just outside of Colorado Springs. Following six weeks of basic training at Lackland Air Force Base in San Antonio, Texas, June was transferred to Fairchild Air Force Base near Spokane, Washington. O'Neall spent half of his time with June in an off-base apartment in Spokane, and the rest of his time in Colorado Springs.

One day in February 1981, during one of the few occasions when he felt that he wanted to do something more with his life than merely loaf, drink beer, hang out with the guys and let June take care of him, O'Neall walked into a downtown Spokane recruiting office and joined the army. It was an impulse decision, one that he would soon regret.

He was promptly sent to Fort Benning, Georgia, for his basic training, and in spite of his military upbringing he soon began wondering what he had gotten himself into. Following basic training, in which his performance was rated as only average, he was sent to Fort Polk, Louisiana, for a short time before being transferred to an army base in Bremerhaven, Germany, despite all of the choices of other duty locations he had requested on the army's "dream sheet." Upon his arrival in Germany, he was assigned to a job as an office clerk. June, in the meantime, pregnant with O'Neall's son, left the air force in May of that year and moved back to Leesville, Louisiana, where she could be near her own family when the baby was born. She gave birth to Christopher O'Neall on November 20, 1981.

O'Neall, unhappy with army life and strongly disliking his assignment in Germany, began looking for ways to obtain a discharge. But getting out of the service, he discovered, was a lot more difficult than getting in. Nonetheless, he did his research and soon found his way out on a "hardship" discharge when he talked June into what started out as a phony separation. According to O'Neall's crafty plan, June agreed to grant him custody of their son, after which O'Neall applied for a single-parent discharge. The plan worked, and O'Neall was sent back to Leesville, where he picked up Christopher. He was then honorably discharged on February 28, 1982. However, instead of reuniting with June, O'Neall took the boy and returned to Colorado Springs, where he soon began his *known* criminal history. Having legal custody of the boy and choosing not to revert custody back to June as previously agreed, O'Neall instead eventually granted custody of the child to his parents when he found that he was incapable of raising the boy himself.

From reading official police records out of Colorado, the Pierce County investigators learned that O'Neall, drunk and disorderly, was arrested on March 12, 1982, for disturbing the peace. In September 1982, they also learned, he was cited for damaging private property and for committing a third-degree assault against another man that stemmed from a drunken brawl. The following month he was cited for drinking in public, and over the next year and a half he would be charged and investigated for crimes that ranged from interfering with police, drunken driving, eluding police, urinating and defecating in public, receiving stolen property, and theft of money, liquor, and motor vehicles. Despite all of the investigations related to those charges, however, he spent little time behind bars because of the state's inability to obtain convictions for a combination of reasons including lack of physical evidence and witnesses who were unwilling to testify against him, either because they feared retribution or because they had their own problems with the law.

O'Neall's whereabouts went unaccounted for between March 1983 and October 1984.

In November 1984, however, O'Neall was charged with the knife assault and robbery of a Colorado Springs prostitute. As Wilson and Stout studied that case, they soon realized that it was the first such charge of that type against O'Neall and that it had occurred nearly two years prior to the second-degree rape charge that he had skipped bail on. The charge initially was listed as first-degree sexual assault but was later reduced to aggravated robbery. However, the charges were ultimately dropped because the victim, a prostitute who had been found in possession of cocaine, had fled the state and could no longer be located to testify against O'Neall.

Between January and August 1985, O'Neall spent a good deal of time in Pennsylvania. Little was known about his activities there except for the fact that he had developed a relationship with a woman named Kathleen. Although not legally divorced from June, his relationship with Kathleen was such that she, by law, had become his common-law wife. A son, Jason, was born from that relationship, and had continued to live with his mother. During that same time frame, according to information developed from contact with Kathleen and others, O'Neall roamed around New Jersey and Delaware. No one, however, knew the purpose of his roaming or what he had been up to, or whether his activities had been lawful or unlawful, during this period.

O'Neall was known to have returned to Colorado Springs in October 1985, but his whereabouts were again largely unaccounted for between November 1985 and June 1986, the month in which he allegedly committed the second-degree rape against the Colorado Springs prostitute.

On a night in September 1986, O'Neall became

the prime suspect in the burglary of a business in Chaffee, Colorado. By that time he had injured his back while working as a tree trimmer and had undergone surgery to correct the problem. He had, however, become addicted to a powerful painkiller, Percodan, a synthetic drug similar in its effect to morphine, and had begun abusing it. When his doctor refused to renew the prescription, he turned to alcohol and illicit drugs. He blamed his unlawful activities at the time on his "addiction," and would continue to use his drug-abuse habits as excuses for his behavior. Shortly after the Chaffee burglary, however, on September 12, his parents, tired of his declining behavior and accelerated physical and verbal abuse of family members, threw him out of their home.

The following evening, September 13, he was suspected of stealing money and a motor home from his employer, a tree-trimming company. It was believed at the time that it had been his need for money to pay for his drug and alcohol addiction, coupled with the need for a place to stay, that had prompted the incident involving the alleged thefts. In that case O'Neall had left his car behind in a locked facility on his employer's grounds, a senseless blunder or an act in which he had simply not cared about the consequences that made it easy for the police to focus on him as their primary suspect. The motor home was subsequently discovered on September 20, abandoned in a gully near Salida, west of Colorado

Springs. By that time O'Neall had apparently left the area before authorities could arrest him.

Before fleeing the state, however, O'Neall attended a party in rural Fremont County. He was accompanied to the party by an attractive woman who was virtually unknown in the area, someone that investigators from the Fremont County Sheriff's Department believe he brought with him from another county or perhaps even from a different state. A few months later, at about the same time that O'Neall disappeared from his own party in Washington state with Robin Smith, a decomposed female body was discovered by two hikers northeast of Canon City, Colorado, near the end of a trail in a rugged mountainous area. The remains, discarded about two-hundred feet off a little used mountain road near U.S. Highway 50, was partially covered with rocks.

The body, according to Sergeant Bert Battu of the Fremont County Sheriff's Department, was clearly a homicide victim. Her hands were bound together, and her jacket was soaked with blood and other bodily fluids, such as urine and semen. Investigators said that it was almost a certainty that she had been sexually assaulted, but due to the severity of the decomposition it was impossible to make a definite determination.

According to Battu, a key was found in the victim's clothes. It was later determined that the key had been made in Colorado Springs, and Battu said that he and investigators from his office had attempted to tie the key in with places where O'Neall was known to have lived, to no avail.

"We know he had a girl up to his parents' house and she fits the general description of this girl," Battu said. "O'Neall's MO fits this body almost to a T."

Wilson and Stout recalled that O'Neall's method of operation was simply to contact women in bars and/or at parties, then separate them from others. It was beginning to look more and more like some of the women seen with O'Neall were not seen again— alive. Other aspects of his MO were that he transports his victims in vehicles; abandons vehicles; uses restraints on his victims; and leaves a bloody crime scene, as in the trunk of the Chrysler, indicating foul play.

The location where the Colorado woman's body was found, said Battu, was very near where the authorities alleged that O'Neall abandoned the stolen motor home.

"He very easily could have come down the dirt road where the body was found by hikers," Battu said.

"He's a serial killer and this fits into the pattern," agreed Captain Dave Reed, also of the Fremont County Sheriff's Department.

Although the victim closely matched the description of the woman seen with O'Neall at the party several months earlier, Wilson and Stout read that she remained unidentified. She is, however, believed to have been between twenty-five and thirty-five years old at the time of her death. Because of the severe decomposition and the resulting lack of evidence, the Fremont County coroner, Dr. Henry C. Grabow, was unable to determine the date and cause of the woman's death. As a result, O'Neall has never been charged with her death.

Interestingly, if not for the inquiries about O'Neall from the Pierce County detectives in connection with the disappearance of Robin Smith, the Fremont County, Colorado, investigators might never have linked their mysterious homicide victim to O'Neall. Because of Wilson's and Stout's inquiries, Colorado authorities had been able to publicize their case as well as provide details of the disappearance of Robin Smith. Due to the similarities in both cases, witnesses who recognized O'Neall's photograph came forward and told them about the unnamed woman seen with O'Neall at the Fremont County party. Unfortunately, no one knew the woman's identity. It was only a few days after the Fremont County party that O'Neall showed up in Nampa, Idaho, going by the name of Zebulan J. Macranahan.

It was a lot of information to digest. However, by the time Stout and Wilson finished reading the background on O'Neall and his possible connection to other crimes, particularly homicides and mysterious disappearances, they officially considered for the first time that they might be dealing with something much bigger than they had initially thought and began discussing such a possibility with their colleagues. He liked violent sex, seemed to dislike women, and had an unusual, almost abnormal affinity for knives. He traveled a great deal and always put a lot of miles between himself and the locations where he was suspected of committing crimes, and he frequently lived under aliases. From everything they were learning, it now seemed very likely to Stout and Wilson that O'Neall was a serial killer. But would they ever be able to prove it?

Chapter 12

It wasn't until Saturday, April 18, that the "big" search, as it came to be called, of the Greenwater area got underway. Jim Chaney had worked all week organizing the search at a time when the weather was clear and relatively mild. He held high hopes, as did Edna and Robin's sisters, that the effort would be successful. However, late on the night before the search, the temperature dropped below freezing and it began snowing in higher elevations. By Saturday morning a fresh blanket of snow, six inches deep in places, covered the area around Greenwater. Although Chaney conceded that it was going to be a bad day to search and felt like canceling the effort, he decided at the last minute to press on with it and see how it turned out.

Up until that point, while the case was still in the early stages, Edna Smith and her family had felt like they were all alone, and at times it seemed as if they were the only ones trying to get something done in the search for Robin. However, they were overcome with emotion on that Saturday morning, literally brought to tears as they watched people arrive in large numbers at the search location. These were complete strangers, young and old alike, high school and college students, people from all walks of life who had become emotionally involved in the Smith family's plight and who had volunteered to help locate Robin despite the overnight snowfall and the overwhelming odds against finding her in the vast wilderness that they were about to search. People arrived by the car load, many even bringing their children, and parked at the makeshift headquarters next to the Natches Tavern in Greenwater. One person even brought their motor home along, out of which they served coffee, hot chocolate, and sandwiches to the searchers.

Before the search got underway that morning, Detective Walt Stout also showed up, accompanied by deputies. Stout was clearly not happy about the search when he approached Jim Chaney and issued him a stern warning.

"Okay, you're puttin' on this search," Stout said. "Now, here's reality, bud. If anybody gets hurt, it's your butt. If somebody gets in a car wreck, falls off a tree or a boulder, it's your rear end. Yours alone, not mine, because you arranged this."

Chaney, more angry than shaken by Stout's warning, decided to continue with the search. Chaney, along with Robin's brother Bobby and sisters Brenda and Laurie, and Brenda's husband, Mike, organized the searchers into groups of twos and threes and sent them out into the wooded areas along Highway 410. They handed out hand-drawn maps of the areas to be searched, including the snow-covered side roads. All in all, the areas to be searched stretched from several miles southeast of Greenwater to the northwest toward Enumclaw.

Brenda, six months pregnant with her second child and dressed in rain gear and hiking boots, carried a long, straight stick and headed off into the woods with her husband and a friend to search their chosen area. She and Mike pushed aside fallen logs and brush, and poked with the stick into snowdrifts as they looked for any sign of Robin or her body. Many others wanting to help out in any way they could searched nearby areas in a similar fashion. Still others organized their own searches, and many went off on their own cruising the roads, walking along the perimeter of the forest and poking around with sticks. Following the instructions laid out by Chaney, the volunteers tied yellow ribbons everywhere they searched, marking areas that they had been through so that other people wouldn't search that same area again. When they ran out of yellow ribbons, they began marking off the areas they had searched with rocks. The setting for the search could easily have come out of one of the Louis L'Amour novels that O'Neall constantly read, but this wasn't western, outdoor fiction. It was all too real.

Other people chose to search from the road, and they set off areas between one mile marker and another to search. Paired off, one person would look on the right side of the road while another would search the left side, checking ditches and peering into the dense forest for any signs of unusual activity, such as footprints or trampled brush, that might have recently occurred.

"In my heart I believe she's still alive," Bobby said during the search effort. "My mom believes it, and all my brothers and sisters believe it. We believe it because my sister is a strong girl. I don't give up. I can never give up. If you give up, then you might as well give up hope. And I ain't gonna give up hope. O'Neall will be found, and my sister will be found, too."

In reality, however, their doubts about Robin being alive were ever present by this point. They merely clung to a thread of hope because it gave them strength in the face of adversity, and helped them to face the task at hand in the forest.

Despite the hopefulness of Robin's family and the searchers, and despite the efforts of Pierce County sheriff's deputies, who had covered miles of woods with four teams of German shepherds, by day's end there still were no signs of Robin, her purse, or clothing. The search effort had been made up of good intentions by everyone concerned, but it had proved futile. It now seemed that Robin would never be found.

After the big search Chaney and Robin's family left Greenwater alone for a while and searched other areas. They walked for many square miles along mountain logging roads that they couldn't drive on because they had been blocked off for one reason or another or were otherwise impassable by car or on-road trucks. They chose many roads that they thought O'Neall might have taken when he left his apartment, and they searched the backwoods in many rural communities. Buckley. Sumner. Out towards Mount Rainier on highways other than the road to Greenwater. Up toward Redmond, Everett, Bothel, Monroe, and so forth, all random searches because they didn't know where else to look. Something, however, in the weeks ahead, would continue to steer them back toward Greenwater.

The same weekend that the big search was conducted, Detective Terry Wilson, accompanied by several deputies and three dog handlers, left from the West Precinct to conduct their own search of an area near the west fork of the White River. Their reasoning was that if Robin was still alive, there was a chance that the dogs would pick up her scent. If she was dead, however, there was little chance that the dogs would be successful because search dogs typically are trained from an early age to ignore the scent of the dead. Wilson directed the deputies and dog handlers to search along Evans Creek Road, just off Highway 165. Seven and a half miles from the Carbon River Ranger Station Road, it was in a very remote area near where a man fitting O'Neall's description had been seen camping in the forest and had been reported to the authorities.

The dog units and their handlers searched down the dirt road and continued all the way to where the road ended. From there they headed into the woods and underbrush and continued toward Evans Creek until the brush became too thick to traverse. It was very rugged terrain, and included steep slopes as they neared the creek. The snow, which had continued falling sporadically throughout the weekend and was by then more than six inches deep, also hampered their efforts. By nightfall, however, they had found no sign of Darren O'Neall or Robin Smith. The search effort, for now, was called off. They knew that the chances of finding Robin alive were practically nonexistent by this time, and they decided to proceed with the investigation as if the worst had happened.

Wilson, back at his desk on Monday morning and again working the case mostly by himself, traced June Hodges to Jacksonville, Florida, where he spoke to her by telephone. She hadn't seen O'Neall recently, not since 1983, but did not seem particularly surprised to learn of the crimes O'Neall was suspected of committing. Throughout the conversation she referred to O'Neall as "Buppy," a nickname, she said, given to him by his mother.

"Buppy liked going up in the mountains," she said. "He always talked about that." She explained that she learned about the trouble O'Neall had gotten into when her mother sent her newspaper clippings about what had happened. "I knew he got into fights with guys like everybody else, but I never thought of him doing something like this to a girl. He was a gentleman when he wanted to be."

June explained that when she first met O'Neall, he had a strong interest in football, liked skiing and other outdoor sports, and enjoyed photography as a hobby. He especially liked photographing outdoor scenes.

"He had brains, but he didn't apply himself," June said. "He didn't read much in school. Instead, he enjoyed playing with knives and hatchets. He would toss them around and open and close them like you do real quick. He also liked to play with nunchucks."

Nunchucks, Wilson knew, was a martial-arts weapon that consisted of two sticks made of a hardwood and attached together on the ends by a chain. If used correctly, they could be deadly.

"Did Darren always have a fascination with Louis L'Amour's western novels?" Wilson asked.

"No, not really," June replied. "He didn't get into Louis L'Amour until we got to Colorado."

"Why did you decide to leave Darren?"

"I was tired of supporting him," June said. "He was lazy. And he had his friends over all the time, which I didn't like. He was drinking all the time and using drugs, mostly marijuana. He would do acid every once in a while, and speed. But really, he's done it all at one time or another. He drank about a case of beer every night since he was in high school."

June told Wilson that she first became aware that O'Neall was a compulsive liar about the time that they were married at Fort Carson. She said that she tried to ignore it but couldn't. She said that it was her decision to split up with O'Neall and that although she had filed for a divorce, she hadn't followed up on it and was legally still married to him. She said that O'Neall had seemed upset when she decided to leave him.

"But I don't know if he really was," she said. "He always had to tell people things that weren't true to make himself look better. I hope he's caught soon and put behind bars."

When Wilson finished his long-distance telephone interview with June, he called the Royal Canadian Mounted Police in British Columbia. Because O'Neall's car had been found abandoned at a rest stop in Marysville, less than two hours by car from the Canadian border, Wilson suspected that he might have been headed to Canada. Wilson decided to alert Canadian authorities about such a possibility. Much to his dismay, however, an investigator for the mounties told Wilson that O'Neall had not been spotted north of the border.

Although Wilson had no way of knowing it yet, Darren O'Neall had headed north, all right. But he had stopped along the way in the town of Bellingham, a small, picturesque city situated on the northern shores of Puget Sound. He had come into town on April 2, leaving behind the chaos that he had created in Pierce County, and had been staying at the Lighthouse Mission in downtown Bellingham under the name of Mike Johnson ever since.

Darren Dee O'Neall. Also known as Zebulan J.

Macranahan, Larry Sackett, "Buppy" and "Zeb." Wilson would soon add the name of Mike J. Johnson to the growing list of aliases used by the fugitive, but not before yet another woman turned up missing under mysterious and violent circumstances after meeting up with Darren O'Neall.

Chapter 13

Several people were waiting at the main entrance to City Hall when the Bellingham, Washington, police department opened its doors on Wednesday morning, April 29, 1987. Two friends and two relatives of Wendy L. Aughe, 29, were there to file a formal missing-person report on the attractive, bubbly woman who had not been seen since the early morning hours of the previous Saturday. Although they had spoken to the police already by telephone, they had been advised to wait for a few days, which they had done, to see if Wendy returned on her own. It was standard procedure, of course, in cases involving adults who went missing or otherwise became unaccounted for. Standard procedure or not, it could have been a replay of how Robin Smith's case was handled at the outset. The missing-person report would become Case Number 87B10189.

After being asked to huddle around a desk in a small cubicle barely large enough to handle one person, let alone six, Wendy's friends and relatives described her to the two veteran detectives who caught the assignment, Carlotta Jarratt and Fred Nolte. Wendy was 5 feet 6 inches tall, 105 pounds, with hazel eyes and brown shoulder-length hair, they said in worried, hushed monotones, each taking their turn and offering a detail or two that one of the others had inadvertently left out. A divorced mother of two young girls, Wendy had gone on a date with a man, Mike Johnson, on Friday night, April 24, said one of her friends. She had left her two children with a baby-sitter, but had not returned to pick them up, offered a family member. Instead, the baby-sitter had notified Wendy's relatives early that Saturday morning, who promptly came and took the girls. Wendy's car, a 1972 two-door Ford Gran Torino with a red body and black vinyl top, bearing Washington license plates HNB 826, was also missing. Nolte took the description of Wendy and the information on her car and promptly entered them both into the NCIC system, and additional alerts were sent by teletype to specific police agencies up and down the West Coast. It was immediately apparent to Jarratt and Nolte that they were dealing with something very serious, which resulted in their taking action promptly. Still, like the Pierce County detectives, they found themselves wishing in hindsight that their department had taken action sooner on the missing woman, but it was too late now. They resigned themselves simply to run with what they had and hope that the case could be resolved quickly.

When they were finished interviewing Wendy's friends and relatives and were confident that they had obtained sufficient information with which to get started, they realized that they also had more than sufficient reason to conduct an in-person welfare check on the presumably missing woman. They promptly drove to Wendy's home, accompanied by family members, who were required to remain outside.

Upon entering Wendy's small, single-level white house at 2223 H Street near downtown Bellingham, detectives Jarratt and Nolte knew instinctively that something was wrong. Perhaps it was the slight odor of the days-old garbage emanating from the kitchen, or the acrid fetor of decaying blood that assaulted their olfactory lobes and wrenched at their guts. Both smells they were all too familiar with in their line of work. Their grim feelings were confirmed when they entered Wendy's bedroom and saw all of the blood. If there had been any doubt up until that point, there was no longer any question that something violent, something terrible, had happened there. Now it was their job to sort out the pieces to find out what.

The blood, and there was lots of it, had pooled and then soaked through the sheets and into the mattress in two large areas near the head of the bed. Their attention was also drawn to two sets of blood spatters and smears on the headboard, where strands of blond hair adhered to one section. Jarratt and Nolte looked at each other momentarily, each realizing that the hair could not be Wendy's. She had dark brown hair, they recalled. There were other, though smaller, blood spatters on the walls near the head-board and a number of other locations, all of which suggested to the detectives that somebody, probably Wendy, had been severely beaten and perhaps stabbed or cut while on the bed. Strangely, there were no blankets on the bed, and an inventory of the house later revealed that three blankets were missing.

There were also other bodily fluids, now dried like the blood, that stained the sheets. The two detectives recognized the stains as "peter tracks," or semen, and they had no doubt that some kind of sexual encounter, most likely an unwilling one, had occurred there. Because it was obvious that a crime had been committed in that bedroom, Jarratt and Nolte promptly sealed off the house and posted police officers as sentries to prevent unauthorized entry to ward off the possible contamination or destruction of evidence by unwanted or untrained people.

When they brought in the lab technicians from the Washington State Patrol Crime Laboratory, several pubic hairs were collected from the bed sheets. At this point they didn't know whether the hairs had come from Wendy or her assailant, and since they had no control standards with which to compare those found, it would likely be some time before that determination could be made. They knew that they either had to find Wendy's body or capture her assailant to obtain the needed hair strands.

As they continued their search for clues, they soon found two broken artificial fingernails—one ripped in half—in the bedroom, one on the bed and the other on the floor. The fact that the fingernails were broken and ripped indicated that a violent struggle had occurred there. The bedroom as well as the rest of the house was also processed thoroughly for latent fingerprints, which would have to be checked in a tedious process of elimination against people known to have been inside Wendy's house.

Meanwhile, Jarratt and Nolte learned that Wendy had been close to graduating from McDonald's School of Cosmetology at the time of her disappearance. From the looks of things, going to school had caused her to have money problems at times. Trying to raise two little girls on meager wages and tips at today's prices was at times a monumental task for Wendy. But, said family members, her financial situation recently had been improving. She had been working more hours as a cocktail waitress at a couple of Bellingham lounges, and the additional hours also brought in more tips. Even though she was in debt to the beauty school, most of the costs she had incurred there didn't have to be paid back until after graduation. To make matters even easier for her, some of those costs had been picked up by federal and state grant programs earmarked for education for those in low-income brackets. Now, however, the prospect of her being able to graduate and enjoy the fruits of her labor looked bleak at best.

The detectives were told that her failure to pick up her daughters from a baby-sitter and the fact that she had not shown up for cosmetology classes since

Friday, April 24, were both unusual and atypical of Wendy's behavior. She was much too responsible for that, said her classmates and instructors. The fact that she loved her children dearly and had been looking forward to working full-time as a cosmetologist after graduation were factors that, in addition to all of the physical evidence found inside her house, made her disappearance look more and more like an abduction or, sadly, something much worse.

One of Wendy's classmates told the detectives that Wendy had gone to lunch at the La Paloma Restaurant, across the street from the beauty school, on Friday, April 24, where many of the school's students often ate lunch and gathered in the eatery's bar after school, especially on Fridays. When she returned to class from lunch an hour or so later, she was excited about a date that she had made for that evening with a good-looking guy who had introduced himself as Mike. He was new there, she had said, and she had described him as being a nice guy. None of Wendy's classmates, however, had seen him yet, and were unable to characterize him firsthand for the detectives.

"She was really flattered that a guy who she thought was nice would ask her out," said one of her friends at the beauty school. Seeing how eager she was to go on the date, several of her classmates helped her get ready by doing her hair and makeup that afternoon. Her classmates last saw Wendy when she left the school late that afternoon and headed toward the La Paloma to meet "Mike" for their date.

According to what the restaurant's owner, Loretta

Lindquist, told the detectives, a man calling himself Mike Johnson had been interviewed and hired as a waiter and bartender only a day earlier. They had been short-handed and needed someone fast, and Lindquist had hired Johnson on the spot based on the recommendation of another bartender there. She said that he had worked a nine-to-five shift that Friday, his first day there and the same day he met Wendy.

"I've known Wendy since she was a little girl," Lindquist told the investigators. "I feel very bitter about this whole thing."

Lindquist and the other bartender, Doug Cherry, had soon begun to wonder about Johnson. He talked a lot, and the stories he told just hadn't struck them as being truthful. As a result, an element of distrust had quickly made its way into the back of each of their minds. Even though Lindquist had hired him, both she and Cherry had agreed that they would have to keep their eyes on Johnson, at least until he had proven himself worthy of their trust. When the detectives pushed Lindquist and Cherry to be more specific about what it was that had bothered them about Johnson, they said it was because he had spoken mostly about his stint in the army. But when they tried to get more personal with him, Johnson had suddenly become evasive, as if he didn't want anything about himself revealed unless it was in the form of one of his "old army stories." Although his evasiveness had initially raised their doubts about him, Lindquist and Cherry had decided to leave well enough alone for the time being. After all, they had needed the help, they said, and it was always possible that they could have been wrong about him.

At the end of his shift that Friday, Johnson met Wendy and they had drinks together in the restaurant's bar and were served by Cherry. A little later on they were joined by a bar regular, Tom Lewis,* who began talking about having recently moved to Burlington, a small town located about thirty miles south of Bellingham just off Interstate 5. At six-thirty the three of them left together, apparently to go to Lewis's new home after Wendy agreed to give him a ride there. Lewis drove Wendy's car since he knew the way and she didn't, but stopped briefly at the Lighthouse Mission so that Johnson could change out of his work clothes and into something more comfortable for their date. A few hours later, the detectives were told, Johnson and Wendy dropped Lewis back at the La Paloma's bar. Neither Lewis nor Cherry knew where Johnson and Wendy were going after they dropped Lewis off.

However, it wasn't long before Jarratt and Nolte learned that Wendy and her date had gone to another bar in Bellingham. She had called her close friend, Lugene Warner, from the bar, and Warner tearfully recounted to the detectives how Wendy had wanted to introduce her new friend to her. Although it was late, Warner, wanting the company, had told them to come on over. As a result, Wendy and Johnson arrived at Warner's home at approximately midnight, but they had not stayed there very long.

Warner did not know for certain where they were going when they left her home, but she said that she had suspected that they were going to Wendy's house to spend the rest of the night together.

As they continued to piece the story together by interviewing witnesses, Jarratt and Nolte soon learned that Johnson showed up for work again the next morning, but had stayed for only fifteen minutes. Johnson introduced himself to Jim Evans, the La Paloma's former cook, served a few customers, did a little work behind the bar, and then disappeared. Evans, after being unable to locate Johnson, had called Loretta Lindquist and informed her that Johnson was gone and that customers were angry about not being served. When Lindquist arrived a short time later to take over Johnson's shift, she discovered that the money in the cash register was gone and a bottle of Jack Daniels was missing from the bar.

When Johnson applied for the job at the La Paloma, they recently had run out of standard application forms and hadn't yet purchased a replacement pad. As a result Johnson had used one of the restaurant's paper place mats on which he had scribbled his personal and prior employment information. One of Lindquist's employees searched and found the place mat that Johnson had used and turned it over to the investigators. When they returned to their offices and ran the information from the place mat on the computer, they soon discovered that the Social Security number Johnson had provided was invalid.

They sent the place mat, sealed in plastic, to the identification section, where it would be examined for latent fingerprints. It was always possible, they reasoned, that Johnson was wanted by the law and had left one or more of his fingerprints on the place mat.

When Jarratt and Nolte drove to the Lighthouse Mission, they were informed that Mike James Johnson had stayed there once before, but for only one night on Friday, February 20, 1987. He had been there this time, however, for more than three weeks, prompting the detectives to wonder where he had been staying during the interim. He was characterized by mission employees and transient residents as quiet and as having stayed mostly to himself, and had not caused any problems during his stay. He was always quoting the Bible, though, which some of the homeless shelter's guests found strange and annoying. In an occasional match of Bible verse wits, nobody could outdo him. He knew the Bible thoroughly, as if someone had taught it to him all of his life.

Tracie Goodnight, an employee there, told the detectives that when Johnson had come in on Friday evening, April 24, to change his clothes, he stopped as he climbed the stairs to his room on the second floor and told her about having just met a woman. He told her that he was excited about meeting the woman and that they seemed attracted to each other. He had not, however, mentioned her name.

"I liked him real well," Goodnight recalled. "He

came across right away as a young southern gentleman . . . his whole manner was gentle and quiet. He put in a little flattering word here and there."

Another mission employee, Bill Palmer, who worked the desk as a night clerk, told Jarratt and Nolte that he had loaned Johnson a black coat and tie to wear to his new job as a bartender. Like Lindquist and Cherry, Palmer characterized Johnson as someone who did not appear truthful. At approximately seven-thirty Saturday morning, just as Palmer was getting off work, he observed Johnson leaving the mission with a duffel bag. When he casually inquired about where he was going, Johnson told him that he was moving into the home of a woman he had met a day earlier.

"He said that the woman was in the car, waiting for him," Palmer said. However, Palmer had watched as Johnson drove away from the mission in a red car. He was alone.

The last person to see Wendy, the detectives learned, was Reana Witter, who observed Wendy shortly before six on Saturday morning walking near Haggen's grocery store on Meridian Street, near Wendy's home. Wendy had been carrying a small package or a purse, Witter said, but she wasn't sure which. The detectives recalled that neither a purse nor any identification belonging to Wendy had been found inside her house. Witter didn't even speculate about why Wendy had been out so early that morning, and the detectives didn't venture any guesses, either.

Jarratt and Nolte theorized that whatever had happened to the Bellingham woman—provided, of course, that Johnson was in fact responsible for her disappearance—had occurred either between 5:45 to 6:00 A.M. and the time Johnson showed up for work, or right after Johnson abruptly left work that morning. It seemed most likely, however, that the violence in Wendy's bedroom occurred before Johnson had gone to work and had prompted him, nervous and shaken over what he had done, to steal the money and the bottle of whiskey from the restaurant before fleeing.

Laboratory tests conducted on the bloodstains found on and around the bed, mattress, and sheets were determined to be type B. Much to their vexation, however, they learned that Wendy's blood type was type AB. Why weren't they of the same type? It was perplexing to the point of being maddening, and Jarratt and Nolte had to know the reason for the incongruity. When the detectives pushed the issue with the lab technicians, they were told that it was possible that the blood had deteriorated from the passage of time, between the time when Wendy disappeared and the discovery of the carnage inside her house. Such a passage of time, said the blood experts, might have resulted in a faulty identification of the blood type. The blood experts explained that in type AB blood, the A appears to a lesser extent than the B and the blood's deterioration might have caused the A to disappear. Such a contradiction in blood evidence isn't common, but it does happen occasionally. Theoretically, it was still possible, even likely, the detectives were told, that the blood was indeed Wendy's.

As they had expected, tests with acid phosphatase revealed the presence of semen on the mattress and bed sheets.

A few days later, after the all-points bulletin on Wendy Aughe's car had been received by law enforcement agencies from Canada to California, an astute United States customs agent, Bob Castro, was busy comparing records of border crossings between the United States and Canada against records of suspicious vehicles from his stack of APBs. When he found the record on Wendy's car, he stopped and stared at it for a few seconds. It rang a bell, but he wasn't sure why. But when he read the log, he saw that her Ford Torino had crossed into the United States via Oroville, Washington, located in the center of the state's northern border, at 9:58 P.M. on Sunday, April 26, 1987, after having exited Canada from Osooyus, British Columbia. The car had been photographed as it entered the United States customs sector, and its driver, the vehicle's sole occupant, was a male. Having had no reason yet to detain the car, a customs agent had let it pass through without incident after the driver answered the usual routine questions about his visit north of the border.

Due to the seriousness of Wendy's case, Castro

and his supervisors made arrangements to have the photograph sent to the Bellingham police detectives. When they received it, enhancements and enlargements showed a man with blond hair sitting behind the wheel. He appeared to have been calm and unruffled, but his general appearance matched the descriptions that Jarratt and Nolte had received from witnesses.

What had Johnson been doing in Canada? The detectives wondered. Had he gone there on Saturday morning, April 25, right after leaving the Lighthouse Mission? And where was Wendy? The fact that she was nowhere in the photograph gave them even more reason for concern. Had Johnson killed her at her house and then disposed of her body in Canada? If so, why would he have taken a chance on crossing the border with a corpse inside the car? That seemed like such a stupid thing to do, and they doubted that he would have done that. Yet here he was in the photograph, driving Wendy's car alone and crossing the border from Canada, leaving the detectives without a clue as to his purpose for having gone there in the first place. Had he disposed of her body elsewhere, somewhere in Washington, before crossing the border and had gone into Canada for another reason? Perhaps, they contemplated, he was planning to head south but had decided first to go north, taking a route in which he could avoid the much patrolled Interstate 5 corridor, choosing instead to travel through the central part of the state on secondary highways that were off the beaten path, highways where police and state troopers would be less likely to spot him driving Wendy's car. But he could have done that without making a risky crossing into Canada. It was also possible, they reasoned, especially if he had killed Wendy, that he had initially planned to flee to Canada, perhaps to hide out in that country's vast outdoors, but, for reasons known only to him, he had suddenly decided against it.

At any rate, Jarratt and Nolte decided that Johnson's actions only served to create more questions, not provide them with any immediate answers, and deepened the mystery surrounding Wendy's disappearance. That, they considered, simple as it was, might have been his plan all along. Create confusion and make the cops' jobs more difficult for them while buying time for himself to get out of the area. But in order to accomplish that, he would have to have known that he would be photographed by U.S. Customs upon reentering the country. Which would have been impossible since those chosen to be photographed are selected at random. It made more sense to presume that he had dumped Wendy's body somewhere in Canada. But where? With little else that they could do at this point, they updated their APB with the new information about the sighting of Wendy's car, and added their most recent description of Johnson: late twenties or early thirties, six feet tall, 160 pounds, with neck-length wavy blond hair and a mustache.

They would eventually see that Johnson's actions were consistent with the actions of one Darren

O'Neall, but information often traveled slowly between police agencies, and it would be at least a
week before the Bellingham detectives knew that
O'Neall and Johnson were one and the same.

Chapter 14

On Friday, May 1, the owner of Tiny's Tavern in Eugene, Oregon, called the police. He was sick and tired of seeing the old red and black Ford Torino parked in his tavern's parking lot, backed into a space next to the building. It had been there nearly a week, since Monday, April 27, and it was obvious that it had not been moved since it had been parked there. He had questioned all of his regular customers, but no one claimed ownership of the car. Neither did any of his employees. Unable to determine who it belonged to, he called the Eugene Police Department to have it towed away.

When a team of officers arrived, the first thing they did was to call the car's license-plate identification, in this instance Washington license plate HNB 826, in to their dispatcher, who ran it through the NCIC system. It was all a matter of routine, something that they always did before moving an abandoned vehicle. However, minutes later, when the information came back, the officers' early morning abandoned-vehicle case suddenly became everything but routine. Unlike what had occurred in Washington state regarding the stolen Chrysler that Darren O'Neall had been driving, the law enforcement data system worked as it was designed to do in this instance. The car, the officers learned, had been reported as stolen out of Bellingham, Washington, a city some 400 miles to the north, and was wanted in connection with the disappearance and suspected homicide of Wendy Aughe. As a result, a pair of Eugene detectives and number of crime lab technicians were dispatched to the tavern.

Inside the car's passenger area, the detectives found a number of paper items, mostly packaging from fast food and beverage items, one of which was a Burger King Whopper box. They also found a number of Camel filter cigarette butts in the ashtray, as well as other items. When they opened the trunk they found all of the usual items: a spare tire, jack, lug wrench, and so forth. But they also found a pair of black women's pants, made out of nylon and polyester, the type that would typically be worn by a woman who worked as a waitress in a cocktail lounge or restaurant or, as they would soon learn in this case, by a woman who toiled long hours in a beauty salon setting, a beauty school, to be precise.

Due to the type of case being investigated in connection with the car, as well as what the pants in the car's trunk implied, Detective J. T. Parr of the Eugene Police Department promptly notified his colleagues in Bellingham. He was assured that Lieutenant Dave Duthie, as well as detectives

Carlotta Jarratt and Fred Nolte, would travel to Eugene that same day.

Meanwhile, Parr and other detectives from his department began rounding up potential witnesses. After interviewing the tavern's owner they focused their attention for a while on three people, two of whom lived in an apartment above the tavern. The third person was a tavern employee. Because the apartment's windows looked out over the parking lot, Parr began by questioning the tenants. He reasoned, correctly, that they might have seen the car when it was driven into the parking lot or shortly afterward.

Tammy Burton* told Parr that on Monday morning she had seen a woman back the Torino into the spot where it was found abandoned. The car, she said, had attracted her attention because it was "extremely noisy," as if it had a faulty muffler, prompting her to look out of her apartment window. She didn't get a real good look at the woman, but was able to describe her as being 35 to 40 years old. Burton said that from the distance from which she had seen her, the woman appeared to have a "hard-looking face." She also said that her hair was cut short and swept back in the front. Dale Burton* told Parr that he had looked out, too, and had seen a woman standing next to the car. She looked around a bit, then walked away.

Anne Vaughn*, a tavern employee and a friend of the Burtons, told Parr that she drove a brown Honda that was very noisy and frequently backfired. She described how she had driven into the parking lot on that same Monday morning when she came in to work the day shift. Seeing the Torino and curious as to who it belonged to, she said that she walked over to the driver's side door and peered inside. Seeing nothing of significance, she turned and walked away.

Was the noisy car that Tammy Burton had heard really Anne's? And was Anne the woman that Dale Burton had seen? Parr pondered the possibilities, but somehow doubted both. After all, Anne was known to the Burton's, and he reasoned that they should have been able to recognize her easily. Besides, her physical appearance didn't match the descriptions of the woman offered by the Burtons. So who was this mystery woman? he wondered.

When Detective Jarratt arrived several hours later and reinterviewed Tammy Burton, her reliability as a witness came into doubt. Her story varied somewhat from what she had told Parr: she told Jarratt that she had never actually seen the woman driving the car. In Jarratt's mind, she figured that Tammy had initially only drawn that conclusion after seeing the woman standing in close proximity to the car. It soon became evident that neither of the Burtons had actually observed anyone inside the car, but had only seen a person near it. Still, the nagging question remained: who was that woman?

Wendy Aughe's car was subsequently towed to a secure police facility where crime lab experts examined it and its contents for fingerprints, hair and clothing fiber, signs of blood, and so forth. When they were finished, they had a considerable amount of evidence to analyze, but they declined to share any of the information publicly.

During that first week in May, word of Wendy Aughe's mysterious disappearance and the subsequent discovery of her abandoned car had filtered down from Bellingham and into Pierce County, mostly through news media sources. The similarities between the disappearances of Robin Smith and Wendy Aughe were obvious: there were two missing young women, both who had disappeared under mysterious circumstances after meeting a man in a bar or tavern; there were obvious signs of violence connected to both disappearances; two stolen cars, each driven by the suspected perpetrator, were involved in both cases; the cars in both cases had been found abandoned; and the physical descriptions of the suspect in both cases were chillingly similar to each other. Pierce County authorities had, of course, seen the APB issued by the Bellingham detectives. But their initial inclination had been to discount the possibility that Darren O'Neall was involved in Wendy's disappearance despite the fact that he clearly had been headed north out of Pierce County soon after Robin's disappearance, as evidenced by the discovery of the abandoned Chrysler at the rest stop north of Everett, a mere sixty miles south of Bellingham.

Edna Smith was one of the people who had been carefully following the news reports of Wendy Aughe's disappearance, just as she had in the disappearance of Kimberley Kersey in Clark County to the south. She saw the similarities in all three cases, but was quickly convinced that the cases of Robin and Wendy were even more alike. She stormed into the Pierce County Sheriff's Department on Monday, May 4, demanding to know why the police weren't investigating the cases as being related.

By that time the investigation into Robin's disappearance had been officially scaled back to one detective, Terry Wilson, who continued to follow up on reported sightings of O'Neall while Detective Walt Stout worked a number of other cases on their continuously growing crime roster. Although Stout was now officially off the case, he agreed to meet with her when she spoke with Wilson.

Stout, Wilson, and Lieutenant Jeff Edmunds basically told Edna that they had exhausted all leads in Robin's disappearance, and that O'Neall's trail had become cold. They discounted any connections between O'Neall and Mike Johnson, and tried to console Edna by telling her that the Bellingham Police Department had a history of Johnson being up there at the same time that O'Neall was in Pierce County. They were, of course, referring to the one night that Johnson had stayed at the Lighthouse Mission in Bellingham in February, and had presumed that he had remained in that area after checking out the next day. Edna, however, refused to accept that explanation in light of the case involving Wendy Aughe. The similarities between the two cases were just too persuasive to be brushed off so lightly.

"I've had my moments of a lot of anger," Edna told the lawmen. "I despise O'Neall for what he's done to my family. He has literally torn our family apart emotionally. He has taken something that does not belong to him. He had no right to do what he did. And now you're telling me that O'Neall and Johnson are not the same person?"

The next day, Tuesday, May 5, Edna and Jim Chaney drove to Bellingham, armed with mug shots they had obtained of O'Neall. They were determined to find out more about the possible connection between O'Neall and Johnson themselves. Their first stop was the La Paloma Restaurant, where they spoke with the owner, Loretta Lindquist, and explained the theory that they were working on. Edna pulled out the mug shots and laid them down on the counter for Lindquist to look at.

"Do you recognize this man?" Edna asked. "Is this the man who worked here?"

"They look like the man that was here," said Lindquist after studying the photos for several seconds. "I can't be sure, but they look like Johnson."

When Edna and Chaney showed up at the Bellingham Police Department and outlined their suspicions, they were met by resistance and literally ordered not to interfere in any of the ongoing investigations.

"It just doesn't piece together that well as far as being the same person," Lieutenant Dave Duthie said. "When the crime occurred in Pierce County, we have Johnson zeroed in up here."

But Edna persisted, pointing out that Loretta Lindquist had made a possible identification of O'Neall as being Johnson. She further stressed that both Robin and Wendy had met the perpetrator on a Friday, and then disappeared late Friday night or Saturday. The cars involved in both cases, she said, were dumped on a Monday morning. The two occurrences were exactly four weeks apart. Were the police going to wait until the fourth-week anniversary of Wendy Aughe's disappearance to see if yet another young woman disappeared?

"We've been going through pure hell, not knowing where Robin is and not knowing where Darren O'Neall is," Edna said, near tears. "It's been pure hell. I know that Robin was not the first, and I know that she's not the last. So who's he got now? Who is he doing this to now?"

Edna and Chaney left Bellingham grudgingly, all but ordered out of town by the police. They were now more frustrated than ever. Despite being run out of town, they took great satisfaction in knowing that they were on the right track. If only they could make the police see the case as they did, then maybe they had a chance in finding O'Neall and seeing justice served. That was all they could hope for at this juncture. They had all but given up hope of ever seeing Robin again, alive.

Although Edna and Chaney didn't know it yet, the Bellingham detectives had taken them both seriously, very much so. They just didn't want Edna and her family running around doing the detective work. It could cause problems, actually hinder their investigation. And they were more than a little embarrassed at not having seen the similarities in the two cases sooner themselves, something they didn't want to admit to Edna or to the media.

The Bellingham detectives, Jarratt and Nolte, began working closely with the Pierce County Sheriff's Department shortly after Edna's visit to learn as much as they could about Robin's disappearance and Darren O'Neall. Jarratt and Nolte also left promptly for Colorado Springs to interview O'Neall's parents and to study the case files involving O'Neall's alleged crimes there. It was at that time that Lieutenant Duthie issued the following announcement to the news media: "Both suspects [Johnson and O'Neall] have similar characteristics. There are also very strong similarities between statements made by and action taken by the two suspects."

When Jarratt and Nolte returned from Colorado, they traveled to Pierce County, where they met with Stout and Wilson. Together, they put together an updated wanted poster of Darren O'Neall, one that showed several different pictures of O'Neall side by side, and which illustrated how he was able to dramatically change his appearance by cutting his hair, growing or removing a beard and/or mustache, and wearing glasses.

Finally, the detectives had what they needed to positively confirm that the cases involving Robin and Wendy were linked. Fingerprints found on the

Whopper box in Wendy's car were positively identified as O'Neall's, as were fingerprints found inside Wendy's house and on the place mat "job application" he had submitted to the La Paloma Restaurant. The new evidence was frightening in that they could see a definite pattern developing, and for the first time Bellingham Police Chief Terry Mangan expressed his belief that both Robin and Wendy had been killed, likely by a serial killer. If O'Neall was in fact a serial killer, they feared that he could be preparing to kill again unless they could stop him first.

Armed with the new wanted posters, Jarratt and Nolte hit the streets and began distributing them to Bellingham homeless missions and to businesses such as bookstores and shops where wilderness and survivalist gear was sold. Because of the Louis L'Amour connection, Jarratt left her card and posters at every bookstore that sold L'Amour's books and asked of the clerks: "In case this person comes in and buys Louis L'Amour novels, would you please give us a call immediately?"

The now statewide effort also took investigators from a number of jurisdictions into beauty shops, because detectives had learned that O'Neall often had his hair permed, and into bars and taverns because he had met both Robin and Wendy in such establishments. In light of the new developments the FBI also became more actively involved in the investigation, expanding the manhunt for O'Neall nationwide.

"It's alarming to us that two women have disappeared in approximately one month," said an FBI spokesperson in Seattle. "That's why we're doing an extensive background check on O'Neall to Colorado, to Pennsylvania, to Oregon. There's a lot of missing people out there."

Utilizing the Violent Criminal Apprehension Program (ViCAP) and the computer system they reserve for tracking serial killers, the FBI began attempting to match up more unsolved murders from around the country that they felt they might be able to attribute to O'Neall. But in spite of all of their efforts, investigators from all of the jurisdictions involved readily admitted that they had no idea where O'Neall was or when they might capture him. They admitted that he might be difficult to find due to his ability to radically change his appearance with little effort. For all they knew, he could still be in the area, either in Bellingham or in Pierce County, done up in another disguise and enjoying the fact that the police would not be able to recognize him while he trolled for his next victim.

Chapter 15

On Wednesday, May 6, the day after Edna Smith and Jim Chaney had gone to Bellingham to convince the authorities that Mike Johnson and Darren O'Neall were one and the same person, O'Neall was spotted by two U.S. Forest Service workers, Daniel Peterson and Lawrence Proffitt, near the hamlet of Ashford, Washington, located near the south entrance to Mount Rainier National Park. Much to the chagrin of the Pierce County and the Bellingham investigators, the sighting proved to the law officers actively pursuing O'Neall that he was still in the area despite all of the publicity surrounding the cases of Robin Smith and Wendy Aughe.

The sighting occurred at about 3:20 P.M. when Peterson and Proffitt were working along Forest Service Road Number 59, three miles north of Washington Highway 7, the main south-southeast road that leads out of Tacoma and into Mount Rainier National Park's southern entrance. Although separated by many miles, the location was in an area parallel to Greenwater but on opposite ends of the park.

Greenwater, located on the park's north side, and Ashford, located on the park's south side, were nearly a straight line north to south from each other on the map. Peterson was driving his backhoe along the road when, as he rounded a corner, he saw a white male standing beside the road. As Peterson would later describe to Detective Terry Wilson, the man was approximately 25–30 years old, six feet tall, thin, with dishwater blond hair and a thin mustache. He also had a couple of days' growth of stubble on his face.

The man, Peterson observed, was bare-chested and was holding a dark blue shirt in his hand. At first glance it appeared to Peterson that he was using the shirt to wipe sweat off his arms, neck, and chest. Later, however, after having discussed the man's actions with his partner and with Wilson, it appeared more likely that he had just washed himself off in a drainage ditch that ran alongside the road and was using the shirt to dry himself. Besides, it wasn't hot enough up there in the higher altitude at that time of year for a man to be perspiring so heavily, even if he had been walking much of the day. The man was wearing dark brown corduroy pants, and Peterson observed that there was a dark green backpack lying on the ground beside him, with a light blue pad or mat, part of his bedroll, that was rolled up and tied to the top of the backpack. Peterson noticed what looked like a scar on his abdomen and a more recent-looking scar near one of his eyes. He was also wearing a silver necklace. At first the man seemed to be just another hiker of the thousands in the park each year. As Peterson drove by the man he waved at him and smiled, just as he had done with hikers on so many other occasions. The man, however, did not wave back. Instead he appeared startled, and a strange expression came over his face. On hindsight Peterson decided that the man had been ready to bolt into the woods when he realized that Peterson had gotten a good look at him.

Proffitt, following several yards behind Peterson in an old Forest Service pickup, also saw the man and was certain that he noticed a scar on the man's stomach as he drove past him. Peterson by then had stopped his backhoe about two hundred yards down the road and was waiting for Proffitt. When he caught up, Proffitt told his partner that the man looked familiar to him. Peterson readily agreed. In an attempt to figure out where they had seen him before, they discussed the man's features in detail. Afterward they both agreed that he looked very much like Darren O'Neall, the man depicted on the wanted posters that had been circulating throughout the area. Within two to three minutes Peterson and Proffitt returned to the area where they had seen the man, but he was gone. They looked up and down the road and peered into the forest on both sides, but there was no sign of him.

A short time later the two Forest Service workers, nosing around in the woods approximately a hundred fifty yards from where they had seen the man, discovered a stack of pornographic magazines, fourteen in all, stacked on a pile of rocks inside a thirty-two-inch culvert that ran beneath the road. It was a good place for someone who didn't want to be noticed to hide his belongings. The rocks, they figured, had been placed inside the conduit to keep the magazines elevated above the trickling water level so that they wouldn't get wet. The magazines consisted mostly of recent issues and included some of the more popular men's magazines such as *Hustler, Playboy,* and *Penthouse,* as well as many other lesser-known publications. There were also two sales receipts from an Albertson's grocery store in Des Moines, dated May 2, 1987.

When Detective Wilson arrived, followed a short time later by Detective Stout, Peterson and Proffitt turned all of the magazines and sales receipts over to the lawmen. Although Stout was still officially off the case at that time, he had some slack in his caseload and wanted to see firsthand what, if anything, was developing in the search for O'Neall. Wilson booked the magazines and receipts into evidence, and included a request that the Identification Section examine them for latent fingerprints. He also showed the two Forest Service workers the most recent poster on O'Neall, and both men positively identified him as the subject they had seen. They both emphasized that O'Neall had a "weird look" in his eyes, and said that his hair was not as curly and was actually a little thinner than it was depicted in the poster.

While they were relating their story to Wilson and

Stout, another Forest Service worker, Ed Powell, showed up and indicated that he, too, had some information to offer them. Powell had been running a front-end loader on the same Forest Service road, about forty yards from where Peterson and Proffitt had seen O'Neall, when a 1977 or 1978 yellow Datsun pickup passed him at a high rate of speed. Just before the pickup reached a nearby spur road that branched sharply off the main road to the right, its driver slammed on its brakes, turned onto the spur road, and sped up it. Powell explained that he had remained working in the area for about another thirty minutes, but the pickup never came back down the spur road. Unfortunately, he never saw the pickup's driver or how many people were inside it.

Had that been O'Neall inside the pickup? The detectives considered the possibility. But if it had been, where had he obtained the pickup? Had he stolen it? Why was he driving so fast? Had someone spotted him? And if so, why would he have driven up the spur road, a road from which there was no way down except by the same route the driver had taken when he went up? Would O'Neall have placed himself in a dead-end situation like that? They didn't think so. But then desperate men often do desperate things. And O'Neall was by now a desperate man.

Wilson and Stout ordered that Forest Service Road 59 be secured, and a number of deputies were posted to check the identification of all people who went in or came out. The two detectives then viewed the areas where O'Neall had been seen and where the men's magazines had been found. As they walked through the area, Wilson thought he detected the smell of wood smoke. He pointed it out to Stout, and together they followed the trail of smoke until they found its source. It was just as they had thought. The smoke had come from a fresh camp-fire, still smoldering after having been left unat-tended, likely by someone who had left the area in a hurry. The discovery, when combined with the sight-ings, was compelling evidence that O'Neall had been hiding out in the area. It wasn't surprising to Wilson and Stout. His mother had told them that her son was a drifter, and over the past several weeks he had indeed been drifting from one place to another.

Additional roadblocks were established at specific strategic locations, and for the next two days the for-est areas in and around Ashford were combed by de-tectives and deputies. A search plane carrying Wilson and Stout flew over the area for several hours in an attempt to spot suspicious movement or camp-sites from the air, and a number of deputies working undercover rented a room at a local motel and began checking all of the taverns along Washington High-way 7 just in case O'Neall decided he wanted a beer or some companionship. Another team of deputies parked in an unmarked car near the scene of the sighting and remained there around the clock, while other deputies notified all of the businesses and as many of the area residents as possible, warning them to be on the lookout for O'Neall. Everyone in the area was asked to report anything suspicious, no matter how trivial or unimportant it might seem to them.

A similar plan of action was in place the next day, with additional deputies driving the Forest Service roads in search of O'Neall. The effort involved a total of twenty-two vehicles that logged more than two thousand miles, and a total of ninety-one people who expended nearly a thousand man hours. Although searchers on foot found a number of interesting items, including another hammer—which, like the first, was found in a stream—there was no sign of O'Neall. They did find a number of beer cans and bottles, toilet paper, wash cloths, candy and food wrappers, a woman's empty purse, and a green dog leash, among other things, all of which indicated that someone had been spending a good deal of time in that area of the forest. Whether or not it had been O'Neall, or a number of people who had stopped there over a long period of time, remained to be seen. One thing was certain: if Darren O'Neall had been there, he was not there now. Despite the concentrated effort and additional searches from the air, Darren O'Neall was not seen in the area near Ashford again. He had slipped by the well-coordinated dragnet with relative ease.

Thinking that he might have headed back toward the Greenwater area, Wilson and Stout organized another coordinated effort in that locale. They first checked with the personnel office of the Crystal Mountain ski resort to determine if O'Neall had worked there or had applied for a job there, but quickly learned that he had not. A check of the personnel records failed to turn up anyone going by the name of O'Neall or similar spellings of that name; nor did they find anyone going by one of O'Neall's known aliases. The ski resort's employees were shown O'Neall's photo, but no one reported having seen him there.

The investigators again made a concentrated search of the more remote cabin sites and the trail heads leading to them, but found nothing suspicious. They also checked several of the hunting camp sites in the area, which often include cabins and other types of shelter, some of it temporary and erected only during the hunting season. They checked cabins and hunting sites at Silver Springs, Dalles, Deer Creek, and several other locations, and kept their eyes open for signs of recent car travel. The areas were all perfect for anyone wanting to dispose of a body or other evidence. However, after five days of searching, they found nothing to indicate that anyone had recently used any of the sites.

Meanwhile, a woman contacted Detective Wilson and told him about a trail of blood she had found the weekend that Robin Smith was abducted. It hadn't meant much to her, she explained, until she learned of Robin's disappearance and the subsequent search for O'Neall. Based on the information that she provided to Wilson, the blood trail was on Forest Service Road 74, just past the four-mile marker along the west fork of the White River. The woman accompanied Wilson to the area where she had seen the trail of blood, but he found nothing that looked *like* blood to him. If there had been any, the elements had effectively obliterated any visual signs of it.

On May 14 a blond, curly-haired man walked into a jewelry store in downtown Eugene, Oregon, and strode confidently up to the long glass display counter. His clothes were somewhat unkempt, and his general appearance was slovenly. The jeweler eyed him dubiously from behind the counter.

"How much can you give me for this?" asked the blond man as he pulled out a gold necklace.

The jeweler reached to pick it up, then hesitated when he saw the name "J-U-N-E" tattooed across the knuckles of the man's left hand. Recalling the police alerts on O'Neall from two weeks earlier, when Wendy Aughe's car had been found in the parking lot of Tiny's Tavern, the jeweler became nervous. Nonetheless, he examined the necklace briefly, then handed it back to the man.

"Sorry, I can't use this," he said without explaining.

The man, aware that the jeweler had seen the tattoo on his hand, glared at him for a few seconds, then turned and walked quickly out of the store. When he was certain that the man was gone, the jeweler picked up the telephone and reported the incident to the Eugene Police Department. When Detective J. T. Parr arrived and showed him a photo display of six similar men, the jeweler promptly picked O'Neall's photograph from among them as the person who had tried to sell him the gold necklace.

The following day, two downtown Eugene workers called the police and reported that they had been approached by a disheveled blond man who attempted to sell them a gold necklace as they left their workplace. Both of them turned him down, but because of the "J-U-N-E" tattoo that had by now been described in many news reports throughout the area, they suspected that the man was Darren O'Neall and reported him to the police. Like the jeweler had done, they too picked O'Neall's picture out of a photo throw-down.

When the information about the Eugene sightings reached the investigators in Tacoma and Bellingham, they began to admit that it was going to be difficult to find Darren O'Neall. They pointed out publicly how he changed his hairstyle and appearance frequently, and emphasized that the effect was dramatic. Fearing that O'Neall was a serial killer, the investigators suddenly stressed a sense of urgency: they now believed that he had killed twice, and in all likelihood would kill again. Because both Robin and Wendy had met O'Neall on a Friday night or early Saturday morning exactly four weeks apart, the investigators acknowledged that he seemed to be on a four-week rhythm of abduction and murder. If that theory proved to be true, they said, he was due to kill again within a week. But it was possible, they said, that his rhythm could change. Depending upon the circumstances facing O'Neall, such as the availability of a victim, his state of mind, or any number of other reasons, his killing rhythm could become more frequent or it could become spaced further apart. No one, of course, could say precisely when or where he would strike next. They only knew he would kill again unless he was stopped.

Chapter 16

By the third week in May, Edna Smith and her family had heard from a number of people that Darren O'Neall had been involved with another man, whose identity they were unable to uncover, in making pornographic videotapes. Since they had no absolute proof yet that Robin was dead, this new revelation gave them even more cause for concern. They felt that perhaps O'Neall was keeping Robin alive, holding her captive somewhere and using her against her will to make such tapes, or, if she was dead, had forced her to participate in the making of porno videotapes prior to killing her. The long and the short of it was that they had no answers, only fearful supposition, and they were willing to reach out anywhere they could in order to find clues that might show them what had become of Robin. In that vein they again turned to the psychic who had helped them earlier.

The psychic sat in a chair at a table and faced the group of concerned family members, and issued a stern warning that the results of their meeting might not be pleasant. Using a photograph of Robin, articles of her clothing and other personal items, and a map of the area where she had been last seen, she rapidly went into a trance-like state that bordered on the eerie. The trance, however, wasn't as melodramatic as those that have been depicted in made-for-television movies. Instead, she merely closed her eyes, gently tilted her head backward, then began to rotate her head from side to front to side to back, making a complete circle. This went on for some time in silence, without the aid of theatrics such as moaning and sighing, as she touched the items that Edna and her family had brought to her.

Finally she became still, and told them that she saw an image of a female tied to a chair, perhaps inside a cabin near the mountain. She thought that the girl was Robin, but she wasn't certain. It might have been another female, perhaps a girl that O'Neall had victimized before Robin, or perhaps it was the image of Wendy Aughe, the victim after Robin. She couldn't be certain, she told Edna. What she experienced had clearly frightened her, however, and she complained of being physically drained of her strength afterward. Edna and the others left the session wondering if the psychic had held back certain details in order to spare their feelings.

In the meantime Jim Chaney, Edna, and her family decided to recheck many of the mountain cabins near Greenwater, primarily because of what the psychic had told them. If the psychic had seen a girl or a woman tied to a chair in a cabin, they reasoned that another search was appropriate in order to leave no stone unturned. The sheriff's detectives told them that such an effort would likely prove useless, since the cabins had been checked twice already. But they were adamant that they would check them again, just in case they had missed one earlier or in the off-hand possibility that O'Neall had only now shown up at one of them. However, as Stout and Wilson had predicted, they found nothing.

Refusing to give up, Edna and Chaney carefully studied maps of northwest Washington, then went north in their search for Robin. They drove to the Mount Baker wilderness area near the U.S.–Canadian border, several miles northeast of Bellingham. They had decided to focus their search in that area due to the fact that Wendy Aughe had disappeared from Bellingham and because there was no longer any doubt that O'Neall, going under the name of Mike Johnson, had spent considerable time in that locale after Robin disappeared. Given his supposed penchant for the outdoors and the fact that it was now known that he had crossed into Canada through Washington state and had returned, they reasoned that he might have headed into the area around Mount Baker, perhaps with Wendy. They also reasoned that if he had gone there with her, he might have done so out of familiarity with the area, familiarity that he could have gained if he had dumped Robin's body out there.

It was truly backwoods country, they quickly realized as they wound around unpaved mountain roads, often barely passable due to considerable snow that had not yet melted away. They occasionally passed shanties, most of which were barely visible because they were set a considerable distance away from the road and into the woods. Some were inhabited by Native Americans, others by "earthy" white people. They occasionally stopped and showed O'Neall's photo to anyone who would look at it, but everybody they contacted said they hadn't seen him. The people, by and large, were unfriendly, and Edna and Chaney didn't like the vibes they were receiving. Nonetheless, they continued deeper into the expanse of the frontier-like wilderness that they had chosen to examine.

They stopped a number of times to inspect possible campsites, just as they had done in the Greenwater area, and often walked a hundred or so yards off the road and back into the woods. But they found few signs of human activity. If O'Neall had been in the area, the recent snowfalls had likely covered any tracks that he had made. All they were finding now were animal tracks, and they soon decided to call off their search effort in that area.

On the way back, Chaney abruptly stopped the car and parked in a narrow turnaround area. He had seen something out of the corner of his eye as he rounded the curve in the road, and he wanted to examine it closely. Not wanting to unduly alarm Edna, he merely explained that he saw an area that he wanted to check, an area where, from his vantage point, someone could easily pull over in a vehicle and toss a body over a steep slope. He told Edna to remain in the car, and hiked through the snow several yards to get a closer look. He was soon out of Edna's view, and that was when he saw a horrible sight.

There on the snow-covered slope lay two good-sized dogs, each neatly skinned and beheaded. The dogs, he observed with wild, wide eyes, had been skinned and tossed there only minutes earlier. Each was still steaming from their own body heat as it escaped into the cold atmosphere. Astonishingly, there was no blood on the snow anywhere near them. The only blood that Chaney saw was on the dogs themselves. Fear, as much as the bloody sight, made Chaney sick to his stomach. He had to get back to Edna, and they had to get out of there. Fast.

When they finally got back to civilization, they stopped and reported what they had seen to the authorities. They were promptly informed that they had unwittingly stumbled into an area dominated by a satanic cult, a group of people who valued their privacy highly. The slaughtered dogs were placed out where Chaney and Edna would likely see them as a warning to leave the area, a practice often used by the cultists to frighten strangers out of their territory. They promptly returned home, both pleased to leave the area but dismayed that their effort hadn't turned up any signs of Robin, Wendy, or O'Neall.

As the fourth-week anniversary of Wendy Aughe's disappearance came and went, law officers throughout the Pacific Northwest and the Rocky Mountain states were still no closer to nabbing Darren O'Neall. No one knew whether he had kept to his four-week cycle of murder and mayhem, and many investigators began to wonder openly about possible connections to other serial murder cases, including that of the Green River Killer, to which O'Neall might be linked.

Because of his purported knowledge of the outdoors, investigators from the Green River Task Force indicated their desire to talk to him when, or if, he was apprehended. All of the Green River Killer's victims had been found in outdoor locations, apparently dumped by someone who was familiar with the outdoors. According to the task force's spokesman, Dick Larson, O'Neall was being actively investigated but was merely one potential suspect out of thousands of names that had surfaced in that investigation. Nonetheless, the task force exchanged information with the Pierce County Sheriff's Office and the Bellingham Police Department so that all of the crimes could be studied in detail by all of the interested parties.

Although the Green River Task Force stopped short of completely eliminating O'Neall as a suspect in their case, they did say later that it was unlikely. He would have been almost too young to have committed the earliest murders attributed to the Green River Killer, and there was documented evidence that he had not been in the area when some of the other murders were committed.

* * *

As the month of May grew shorter, Edna Smith began pushing the Pierce County prosecutor to file some kind of charges against O'Neall based on the evidence they had so far accumulated. Although a $1,600 reward fund had gone unclaimed, which Edna and her family, in their belief that Robin was still alive, had hoped to use to buy information from someone about Robin's disappearance, Edna was slowly accepting the grim prospect that her youngest daughter was dead. As such she was beginning to take the approach that O'Neall must be apprehended no matter what it took, and she was applying pressure, lots of it, on the authorities to take action.

Much to her disillusionment, however, the Pierce County prosecutor's office told her that their office and the detectives had decided that it would not be prudent to issue a warrant for O'Neall's arrest just yet despite the fact that they felt they had enough evidence to do so. Their explanation was simply that they did not want to start the prosecution clock yet, which an arrest warrant would do. Instead, they told her, they would prefer to wait until O'Neall was either located and/or arrested.

To Edna Smith, however, that wasn't good enough. O'Neall might never be located, given his ability to change his appearance at will. And an arrest warrant, she reasoned, might more readily bring in other jurisdictions to assist in the case. But more importantly, Edna believed in her heart that O'Neall had killed before, and she knew that he would most certainly kill again unless he was stopped. A warrant for his arrest, she believed, would be the first step in preventing more young women's deaths at O'Neall's hands.

Chapter 17

Monday, May 25, 1987, was the day that Memorial Day was officially observed that year, and campers Kevin Hauser* and Meg Roberts,* both of Kent, Washington, were determined that they were going to enjoy the long weekend in the outdoors. On the previous Friday afternoon they had picked out what they considered to be an ideal location to set up camp, a site just off Huckleberry Creek Road, also known as Forest Service Road #73, a few miles east of Greenwater. It was secluded, which was what they wanted, and there were no other campers around for miles. The closest public or commercial campsite was located near Greenwater, but they didn't want to camp right next door to someone else. They could do that at home, in their own backyard. They planned to do a great deal of hiking that weekend, and part of their reasoning for choosing such an isolated area was that they simply wanted to make certain that they were off the beaten path.

Much of their weekend went as planned. Kevin and Meg tramped through the dense forest, following a previously uncharted course along the winding current of the White River and occasionally stopping to examine the abundant varieties of plant life or to observe a deer or other animal surviving in their natural habitat. It wasn't until Monday morning, their last day of hiking, that they made the macabre discovery, one so loathsome that it would forever change their lives and the view they held about the great outdoors.

When they awoke that morning Kevin rekindled the still smoldering campfire near their tent with several sticks of wood. After renewing the fire, Meg placed a large, blackened cast iron skillet on the burning embers and cooked them a hearty breakfast of sausage links and eggs. Admittedly not the healthiest of foods, it was a nourishing breakfast and was easy to prepare in their primitive setting. And eating in the outdoors always seemed to enhance the flavor and enjoyment of the food, no matter what the victuals. When they finished eating and had drunk the last of the freshly perked coffee, they packed their temporary canvas shelter and other camping gear and placed it in their car before heading out on their final hike.

Donning backpacks, Kevin and Meg looked out from their campsite and tried to decide which way to go. They had already been down the road to their left, past the large mound of dirt that made the road beyond that point impassable to passenger cars, and they had already followed the White River in both directions. Similarly they had also already followed

Boundary Creek, which occasionally crossed the small dirt road, for quite some distance. They hadn't, however, hiked into the dense patch of forest directly in front of them, the stand of woods situated next to a small clearing. The patch of forest seemed to glower at them across from their campsite, as if beckoning them to enter and explore the dark and vast reaches that they could not see from the road. There was a nearly unnoticeable animal trail that led into the forest, which they decided to follow. They reasoned that if wild animals could traverse the dense forest, so could they.

They had gone only about fifty feet east of the road, which barely placed them inside the patch of forest, when they both noticed the piece of white bony material off to their right. Their curiosity piqued, they veered toward it, reaching it within seconds. To their horror, they immediately recognized the white material as part of a human skull. Suddenly upset over their grim discovery and aware that additional human remains were probably nearby, Kevin and Meg quickly retraced their steps, packed up the rest of their gear, and left. When they reached Greenwater, they stopped and reported what they had found to the Pierce County Sheriff's Office.

Deputy Bob Hoffman was on duty that morning and became the first deputy to respond. He reached Greenwater in less than a half hour, at twelve-thirty, where he met Kevin and Meg and took a brief statement from each of them. The two campers then accompanied Hoffman to the location between White River and Highway 410 where they had found the skull. Hoffman examined it and confirmed that the skull was indeed human. Aware of the Robin Smith case and the fact that previous searches had been conducted in that same general area by the sheriff's department and Smith's family members, Hoffman promptly notified detectives Stout and Wilson about the discovery of the skull.

Stout and Wilson arrived at the Huckleberry Creek Road location at 2:40. Deputy Hoffman led the two detectives into the wooded area and pointed out the skull to them. Nearby, as they walked around and examined the adjacent area, Stout and Wilson discovered several additional bones that appeared to be human. It appeared to the detectives that the bones had been scattered about by animals. The most likely culprits were coyotes, which were abundant in the area. Aware that they were well within the perimeter of a potential crime scene, the detectives retraced their steps back to the road, where they were not likely to inadvertently disturb any evidence. Stout and Wilson promptly decided that a search of the area was necessary, but because of the late hour and the remote location it seemed unlikely that a proper search could be organized that day. However, unwilling to leave the bones that they had found overnight, fearing that animals might scatter them further, the two detectives decided that they had better collect everything that was of obvious importance that afternoon.

The search commenced a short time later after Identification Officer Van D. Victor arrived at the scene, accompanied by additional deputies from the Pierce County Sheriff's Office. Together, they reentered the wooded area and began searching in a careful, methodical manner. Before nightfall they located, in addition to the human skull, portions of a scalp and strands of blond hair similar in color to Robin Smith's. They also soon found a bone that looked like a femur, which is the longest, largest and strongest bone in the human body. Soon afterward they also found a mandible or lower portion of the jawbone, a nearly intact spinal column, a portion of the pelvic bone, and several other small bones that would take an expert to identify. They also discovered several beer cans, a rope knotted at one end, a blanket, and a white, orange, and blue crew sock, much like the socks that the naked girl in the trunk of O'Neall's car had been wearing as described by the helper at Frank Wilhelm's shop on Saturday, March 28.

As they prepared to recover each of the items, Victor first photographed each item where it was found. He also marked each object with stakes driven into the ground, and flagged each with corresponding article numbers and entered brief descriptions on official property sheets that would become part of the report. Only after each object had been marked, photographed, and logged onto a property sheet was it picked up and bagged as evidence. They picked up each item one by one, being careful not to cause any more destruction to each than had already occurred. It wasn't until they reached the portion of the spinal column that was still attached to the segment of skull that Stout noticed a small metallic chain dangling from it when he picked it up. It was only a thin chain, he noted, with nothing else attached to it. It was no longer hooked together. If something had dangled from it previously, such as a stone or jewel pendant, it was not there now.

Before calling it a day, Stout drew a preliminary sketch of the area where the items were found, using two Puget Sound Power and Light utility poles as points of reference. Later a more accurate sketch would be completed, one that would not only use the utility poles as reference points but which would include compass headings and precise distance measurements to enable the investigators to record accurately the locations where each piece of evidence had been discovered.

A Pierce County Sheriff's Office dispatcher reached Sergeant Tom Miner at home and advised him of the discovery of the human remains. Miner was instructed to report to the site near Greenwater and be prepared to spend the night. When Miner arrived, Stout briefed him on the items that had been found, and showed him an area of approximately 265 feet wide and about 250 feet deep that he wanted cordoned off and searched the next day. Stout told him that he wanted 50 searchers in the area by early the next morning.

Miner and Hoffman remained at the site throughout the night to provide security. During that time they developed a plan in which they would divide the area to be searched into 20-foot-wide sections using string lines attached to small stakes to maximize order and control of the nearly two-acre area. Each line would be numbered with odd numbers just in case a second cross grid became necessary. If so, those resulting control lines would be numbered using even numbers. One eight-man team would be assigned to each grid sector. The road would be used as the base line.

Washington State Patrol Crime Laboratory criminalist H. W. "Skip" Johnson arrived at the remote site early the next morning, just ahead of the Explorer Scouts, other search personnel, and a number of reporters trying to get a scoop on the story. He first made a walk-through of the area where all of the items had been discovered the day before. He took photographs from the road looking into the area, and additional photos were taken of the items that had already been discovered.

It was while making the walk-through of the area that the next discovery was made. Something in the periphery off to his right had caught his eye. When he turned his head to take a clearer look, Johnson saw an old rotted-out tree stump. Partially protruding beneath it was what had apparently caught his eye in the first place. When he approached the stump he saw that someone had attempted to bury or conceal articles of clothing.

After duly noting the discovery and photographing

the stump and surrounding areas, Johnson carefully removed the clothing. As he pulled it out he noticed that whoever had placed it there had done so carefully and neatly. The items had been meticulously folded, much as someone would fold their own laundry after it had been cleaned and dried. The items—a medium-size pink and white blouse, size thirty-six B tan bra, size twenty-eight blue jeans, a size eight web belt consisting of white, purple, and pink stripes, and size six tennis shoes—were packed into brown paper bags. Johnson and Stout commented to each other that the clothes likely belonged to the victim whose skull, vertebrae, and other bones they had found. The clothing, they noted, did not show any obvious signs of blood and did not appear to be torn. The clothing was also consistent with Robin Smith's physical characteristics, and clearly would have fit her. If the clothing was indeed Robin's, the fact that there were no blood stains on any of it added credence to the theory that Robin had been carried out and placed into O'Neall's Chrysler while nude. The absence of blood stains on the clothing also added credibility to the report of a naked girl purportedly seen beaten in the trunk of O'Neall's car across from Frank Wilhelm's shop. The manner in which the clothing had been folded and hidden prompted the investigators to theorize that they had been disposed of at the site separately from the victim's body.

Nearby and almost overlooked lay a woman's purse. In hopeful anticipation that its contents could help them identify their obvious victim, Johnson and Stout rushed over to it. After photographing it, they opened it and removed its contents one item at a time. Within seconds they found a Washington state identification card and a check-cashing card belonging to Robin Smith, both bearing her photograph. They also found an uncashed check in the purse made out to Robin in the amount of twenty dollars, a cloth makeup purse, and a hairbrush with strands of hair. However, it was apparent that the purse had been cleaned out. The hundred and twenty dollars that Robin's sister Laurie had paid her for baby-sitting the day she disappeared was missing, as was whatever additional money that Robin had been carrying. Also missing was Robin's prized gold dime, and for the first time since Stout had learned of its existence he wondered whether the gold dime that had turned up in the change of Robin's friend had really been Robin's.

By now the forest was buzzing with the news that Robin Smith's remains had likely been found, and the reporters from Tacoma and Seattle were busy trying to file their stories to their respective newspapers. Stout made arrangements with Wilson to contact Robin's mother to notify her of the possibility that the remains were Robin's, pending, of course, official identification. Stout emphasized that the official identification might be difficult since no dental, medical, or blood-type records existed for Robin, and as such they should be careful in approaching Edna with the information. Although it was not likely, it was still possible that the remains might not be Robin's.

As the grid search commenced that morning, additional items of evidence were discovered: a dark green dog leash, five feet nine inches in length; a zippered blue nylon bag; additional bones and teeth; a torn section of what appeared to be a wash cloth; a claw-type hammer with red paint on its handle; two Schmidt beer cans; and several other items, including soil samples. Many of the items, including the skull, vertebrae, bones, bone fragments, and teeth, were promptly transported to the Pierce County Medical Examiner's office, where they would be carefully studied by Emmanuel Q. Lacsina, M.D., M.E., a certified forensic pathologist.

In the meantime Edna and Laurie were sitting at home. Suddenly the telephone rang, and as usual, Edna jumped, startled by the ring and the news that might be delivered when she answered it. A woman on the other end identified herself as a newspaper reporter.

"How do you feel about the police finding your daughter's remains?" asked the reporter. The questions was abrupt and was posed as soon as the reporter had confirmed that she was speaking to Edna Smith.

"What?" Edna was shocked and frightened. "I don't know what you're talking about. I haven't heard anything from the police."

"Oh, you don't know," said the reporter.

"Know what?" asked Edna, nearly in tears.

"About your daughter's remains." The reporter, in her insensitivity, dragged the words out slowly, one by one.

"I don't know what you're talking about, and I'm not talking to the press until I find out what's going on," Edna blurted, angered by the reporter's callousness.

"I'm sorry, Mrs. Smith," the reporter said, suddenly realizing that she had jumped the gun. "I think I've made a big mistake."

"You most certainly have. I don't want to hear something like that from someone who doesn't know anything officially. You're talking about a person's life." Edna slammed the receiver down.

Only minutes later, as she was trying to recover from the shock over the telephone call, the telephone rang again. This time it was Detective Stout.

"Edna, I've got some bad news for you," he said. "I'm coming over. Please assemble your family so that we can talk."

For two months Edna had clung to a thin strand of hope, refusing to believe that Robin was really gone. But now her hopes were suddenly dashed. After receiving the call from the reporter and then the call from Stout asking her to assemble the family, she suddenly knew that she had to prepare herself to hear the worst. Robin, she finally realized, was never coming home again. She was dead.

Chapter 18

Forensic pathologist Emmanuel Q. Lacsina conducted the first examination of the human remains on Tuesday morning, May 26, 1987, in the cold austerity of the Pierce County Medical Examiner's Office in the Tacoma–Pierce County Health Building. Lacsina had previously inventoried all of the items, which had been brought to him in appropriately labeled brown paper sacks.

The first item consisted of strands of light brown, straight hair interspersed with twigs and leaves. The next item was the lower jawbone, or mandible, which contained thirteen teeth. Three were missing. Item #3 was the blanket with green and yellow floral print on a white background. It also consisted of a poly-filled inner lining with a mesh-like backing. The blanket was covered with dirt, twigs, insects, and what appeared to be dried blood. As Lacsina examined the blanket he found what appeared to be a phalanx. It was either a finger or toe bone, he wasn't sure which. He saved and labeled the phalanx, but returned the blanket to the property room.

Next he examined the skull that was attached to the upper spinal column. The skull was devoid of any recognizable maxillary bone and teeth, and the attached spinal column was largely intact with all of the cervical and thoracic vertebrae properly in place. There were no recognizable injuries or defects to the spinal column. However, Lacsina noted a circular fracture to the frontal bone of the skull, one inch in diameter. He also noted a slightly depressed comminuted, or splintered, fracture of the left temporal bone. Someone certainly could have struck the victim with a hammer, he reflected.

Item #5 consisted of a thin metal necklace tangled in scalp hair. There were several dead maggots attached to it, along with dirt, twigs, and leaves matted together by some unrecognizable material, possibly blood or putrefaction. Next was the knotted nylon rope, which measured 23 feet, 7 inches. It held a knotted loop at one end, 9 inches in diameter, and was covered with dark brown material that Lacsina figured was dried blood.

The remaining items consisted of the crew sock and several bones including the left scapula, long leg bones, pelvic bone, ten right ribs and nine left ribs, which were intact except for signs of animal gnawing, right ulna and right radius, several metacarpals, facial bones, and a tooth. Several of the bones had small amounts of dried soft tissue adhering to them, and there was evidence of bite marks from animals. Lacsina recalled that deputies had told him of four coyotes running through the area when they had set up their base camp at the site.

After surveying the various skeletal remains, Lacsina requested and obtained the assistance of William D. Haglund, chief medical investigator of neighboring King County Medical Examiner's Office. Two days later, on Thursday, May 28, Lacsina and Haglund worked together to reconstruct what everyone believed was Robin Smith's skeletal remains.

As they laid the remains in place, both pathologists noted a strong residual odor coming from the bones, and each had an oily feel to the touch that, they believed, indicated the presence of grease. With the exception of the fractures to the skull, the damage to the bones was consistent with carnivore scavenging. Based on the quality of the tissue and other findings, Lacsina and Haglund estimated that the victim had been dead for two to four months. The estimate, they concluded, was consistent with the time frame in which Robin had disappeared.

Based on the morphology, or structure, of the calvarium, which is the dome of the skull, and the innominate bones, which is either of the two bones that form the sides of the pelvis, the pathologists concluded that the sex of the victim was definitely female. Based on the epiphyses closure and tooth development, they also concluded that the victim's age was consistent with that of a woman 18 to 22 years old. They also calculated the victim's stature based on the length of various arm and leg bones to be between five feet to five feet four inches. Again, the height was consistent with the height of Robin Smith. But lacking dental X rays or other means of making a positive identification, neither pathologist was prepared to say that victim was without question Robin. They simply needed something more.

As a result Lacsina, Detective Walt Stout, and criminalist Skip Johnson returned to the Greenwater area the following day, Friday, May 29, to search for additional bones. Using a sifting screen, during the day-long search they found the following items: a thin, small piece of bone that appeared to have come from the facial area; a portion of the maxillary bone that consisted of an empty socket and two molars; an irregular, porous piece of bone that likely was from the end of a long bone; a segment of bone that was consistent with a phalanx; the "first" right rib; another small fragment of bone that likely came from the skull; a tooth; another segment of a phalanx; the "first" left rib; a large piece of bone that probably came from the base of the skull; a piece of bone that came from the orbital area; another tooth; and additional hair strands. Still, it was not enough. Despite all of the remains found at Greenwater, not to mention the identification and clothing that clearly belonged to Robin Smith, neither of the pathologists would commit themselves to officially identifying the remains as Robin's. They continued to tell Edna that more bones were needed, specifically more of the jawbone and teeth, to make a positive identification.

* * *

Edna, naturally, was outraged over the fact that the identification would not be made official. Again she wanted to help with the search for additional evidence, but again the police wouldn't allow it. The investigators told them again that they weren't trained in such matters and that they would just be a hindrance. So Edna waited until it was certain that the police were no longer planning to return to Greenwater. Finally, on June 9, they told her that they were finished. The department could no longer afford to continue searching at Greenwater. The budget had been cut, and they were short on manpower. Edna promptly called Jim Chaney.

"Jim, I have to get back up there to try and find some more of Robin," Edna said. Both agreed that they would return to Greenwater the next day, Wednesday, June 10. In fact, they would return there every day for the next 11 days, where they would spend eight hours a day searching for additional pieces of Robin's remains.

When they arrived at the Greenwater location on that Wednesday morning, Jim led Edna into the part of the forest where much of the remains had been found by the police. Jim had been up there the day before, but Edna didn't know it yet. He pointed out the spot where much of Robin had been found.

"Yeah, I know," Edna said. "I can tell exactly where her body was and how it had lain."

"What do you mean?" Jim asked, feeling a little eerie.

"Well, I can just tell," Edna responded, pointing at

a location on the ground. "I can see the outline of her body, the way her body had lain. Her legs were here, her head was here."

Jim, the hair rising on his arms and neck, glanced at where Edna was pointing. He had no difficulty seeing a moldy outline in the shape of a body. He could see it just as plain and clearly as Edna could. It stood out like a neon sign to him.

"Ma," said Jim, his voice shaky. "I've got to tell you something."

"What, Jim?"

"I was up here yesterday, and that outline was not there. This is crazy."

Although neither Jim nor Edna could explain why the molded outline had suddenly appeared, they took it as a sign of psychic phenomenon and began digging in the outline right where they believed Robin's head had lain. After trying larger tools and finding that they might cause more harm to the evidence that might be present, they began using small sticks the size of a little finger to scrape the surface of the forest floor. In some places the scraping went as deep as eight to ten inches.

As Edna searched for her daughter's remains, something about the quietude of the peaceful forest brought on a flood of memories, many that had been long suppressed. Edna, there on her hands and knees on the damp, soft earthen forest floor, tearfully recalled the difficulty that she had endured while giving birth to Robin. She suddenly remembered how she had hemorrhaged so severely and had almost died, and how Robin, when she was finally born with a premature birth weight, had arrived in the world with a strange-looking raised "raspberry" birthmark on the top of her head. Edna had often wondered about the birthmark and now, in retrospect, she reflected whether the mark had been some sort of a sign, some kind of a dark omen that something bad would happen to Robin someday. When she considered all of the mysterious, ethereal happenings that had occurred since Robin disappeared, she believed that it was entirely possible.

As Edna continued to dig, she couldn't get the memories of Robin out of her mind. She remembered how Robin had liked being an aunt, and how she had loved her nieces and nephews so much. She recalled how petite and feisty she had been, such a spontaneous person. Robin, in September 1984, while working at a painting job with her father in Texas, suddenly had left without warning and driven all the way home just so that she could be a bridesmaid at her sister Brenda's wedding. Edna also remembered how much Robin had loved animals, all kinds of animals—she had worked in a pet shop for a while, and had taken care of horses at a stable. She especially had loved cats, however.

Edna's thoughts were abruptly jolted back to the present when she and Jim began finding things as a result of their digging: teeth, small bones, fingernails, and so forth. At the end of each day they took what they had found and turned it over to Lacsina. Lacsina, as he accepted the items, only shook his head in disbelief. He couldn't believe that they were finding those things because he "and other professionals had gone over the area." Nonetheless, on June 11 he identified the first pieces that Edna and Jim turned over to him as a fragment of a maxilla, two maxillary teeth, fragments of bone from the cranium, and a fragment of bone from the mandible. On June 12, Edna and Jim submitted two additional teeth and miscellaneous bone fragments to Lacsina.

Finally, Edna and Jim went through the large pile of dirt that the police told them they had sifted through. After considerable digging and searching, they found another large bone, joints, knuckle bones, more fingernails, hair, and additional teeth. By the time they were finished on June 21, Edna and Jim had provided Lacsina with enough of the major missing pieces of cranium so that Robin's skull could now be reconstructed. Before leaving the Greenwater area, however, they constructed a small wooden cross and placed it on the area where the molded outline had appeared. The cross remains there to this day.

Detective Stout contacted Edna again, this time to ask about the availability of dental records for Robin. He would need them, he told her, in order for a forensic odontologist to conduct a dental comparison with the teeth that had been found with those of Robin's dental X rays. Much to his dismay, however, Edna informed him that no dental records existed, at least none to her knowledge. She reiterated how

Robin and her family had lived in Connecticut until 1975, when they had moved to Washington. Edna told Stout that as far as she knew, Robin had not seen a dentist since the family had moved to Washington. If Robin had, she said, she had no knowledge of it. Similarly, Stout was unable to come up with the name of a dentist that Robin might have seen while living in Connecticut.

On Tuesday, June 23, after the careful reconstruction of Robin's skull had been completed, including the placement of all of the teeth found at the Greenwater forest location, the teeth found in the trunk of the stolen Chrysler O'Neall had been driving were placed in the empty sockets. They fit perfectly. If there was still any doubt in Lacsina's mind as to the identity of the human remains, he kept it to himself. He formally identified the remains as those of Robin Smith, and his diagnosis of the injuries was finally stated in a permanent record. Lacsina made the following official opinion, which he turned over to the police and the prosecuting attorney's office:

"This twenty-one-year-old white female, Robin Smith, died of multiple blunt-force injuries to the head. The severity and nature of the injuries would indicate the use of a heavy, blunt object such as a hammer or other similar object. The absence of antemortem dental X rays and unavailability of soft tissue for fingerprints precluded positive identification. The anthropological examination, forensic dental examination, as well as other corroborative physical evidence recovered at the scene provided a very strong presumptive identification that the skeletal remains belong to those of Robin Smith. In consideration of the climatic condition as well as the presence of wild animals feeding on the remains, the degree of decomposition would indicate that death would have occurred shortly following the deceased's reported disappearance. The manner of death is classified as a HOMICIDE."

Due to the evidence found inside the trunk of the Chrysler, particularly Robin's jacket and some of her teeth, as well as the evidence found in the forest, Lacsina's conclusions, but mostly due to Edna's relentless urging, Deputy Prosecutor Tom Felnagle finally filed formal murder charges against Darren O'Neall and obtained a warrant for O'Neall's arrest. The arrest warrant, in the event of his capture, ordered that O'Neall be held in lieu of $500,000 bail. He was also charged with second-degree possession of stolen property in connection with the Chrysler that he had been driving.

As a result of the murder charges being filed and the arrest warrant being issued, it wasn't long before more wanted posters than ever began circulating among law enforcement agencies. As luck would have it, one of the posters landed on the desk of an FBI agent in Seattle. He immediately recognized O'Neall, but not in connection with the Robin Smith case. He recognized O'Neall's photograph from an earlier poster of police artist Jean Boylan's sketch of the man who had kidnapped, attacked, and sexually assaulted teenager Fawn Creswell in Portland.

The FBI agent promptly notified Portland Police Bureau Detective Bill Carter, who was in charge of Fawn's case. He obtained a mug shot of O'Neall from Pierce County authorities, sent it to Carter, who in turn showed it to Fawn in a photo throw-down. Even though six months had passed since the bearded man who had smelled badly had attacked her, Fawn had no difficulty choosing O'Neall's photograph from the six of similar men that were shown to her. As a result, O'Neall was promptly charged in Oregon with multiple counts under varying theories of law of first-degree kidnapping, first-degree rape, sexual penetration with a foreign object, third-degree rape, first- and third-degree sodomy, and sexual abuse. Although they continued to investigate the fact that O'Neall was driving a semi-trailer when the attack occurred, they continued to draw a blank. The investigators presumed that he had stolen it, and because no stolen truck reports had turned up, they guessed that perhaps he had returned it before it could be reported missing.

Meanwhile, with the finality of Robin's death now indisputable, Larron became even more despondent despite the fact that he knew that he had done everything that he could to help the police find her killer. Nonetheless, he blamed himself for Robin's death, and told nearly everyone he talked to that

Robin would still be alive had he not left her at O'Neall's apartment when he went fishing. Edna did not blame him, however, and in fact did everything that she could to comfort him and tried to convince him that Robin's death wasn't his fault, to no avail. Larron finally got to the point where he couldn't work, even for short periods, and he had no choice but to seek psychiatric help. Despite the fact that he was promptly placed on medication, his condition continued to deteriorate.

Since there were no clues to O'Neall's whereabouts and therefore little else that she could do in the search for her daughter's killer, Edna Smith went public once again. Knowing that O'Neall was well versed in Scripture passages, since he had quoted them to impress workers at the mission in Bellingham, and recalling how he had written on his "pioneer" list of goals that he wanted to learn more about the Bible, Edna thought that she would try to reach his Christian side, if it still existed. This time her public plea was in the form of a letter she had written to O'Neall, which was broadcast on television and appeared in the print media. It read:

I sense very strongly in my spirit that you are not the Darren D. O'Neall that you had intended yourself to be. You had a very different plan for yourself and for your life. But somewhere something went wrong and out of control. Things began eating away at you and there was a lot you needed to talk about.

And in making the decision to either get help or to handle it on your own, you chose the wrong direction. God knows that if you had made the decision to get help, things would be different for you today and perhaps you could be living the life you really wanted to live, raising animals and living off the land.

What went wrong, Darren? You know what you've done and what you are guilty of. You can run from the law, but you can't run from God. I cannot forgive you at this time. Robin had the right to live her life to the fullest, just as you do. Knowing the things you have done, Darren, and going down deep into your heart, don't you feel that facing the law will be easy compared to what you have to face when you meet the Lord? Don't wait until it's too late, Darren. Take the Lord's hand and let Him guide you and help you to do what is right. Please turn yourself in to the law, get the help you need, and turn this situation around.

Edna never knew whether O'Neall ever heard her plea to come forward and turn himself in. It was her hope, of course, that her plea might appeal to his biblical background and at least bring him out into the open.

In the meantime, O'Neall's killing cycle was overdue. Or so everyone thought.

Chapter 19

While Edna Smith and Jim Chaney were busy digging and searching for Robin's remains in the forest near Greenwater, and detectives in Washington and Oregon continued running down leads to Darren O'Neall's whereabouts, pretty 22-year-old Lia Elizabeth Szubert set out alone on a trip from Twin Falls, Idaho, to Boise, where she lived. Lia's fiancé, Jeff Parker,* was arriving at Boise's airport from San Diego in the afternoon. Lia had taken time off from her job as a waitress at the Heartbreak Cafe first to make the trip to Twin Falls to visit her family, then to return to Boise to pick up Jeff. She hadn't seen Jeff for some time and was naturally excited about his visit. She left Twin Falls at about 1:30 P.M. for the two-hour, 129-mile drive back to Boise. But she never made it there, and Jeff was left waiting at the airport wondering what had become of her. It was June 9, 1987, a Tuesday, a beautiful late spring day. It was also the same day that Pierce County officials had decided to abandon their efforts in their search for Robin Smith's remains and the day that Edna and Jim had decided to take over the endeavor.

Lia had driven for about an hour and twenty minutes and had gone approximately eighty-five miles when her car engine began to misfire. She was just outside of Mountain Home and, having made the trip several times, she knew that there was a truck stop just ahead, aptly named the Gear Jammer. Her car, clearly malfunctioning, chugged along slowly as she exited the freeway. Low on gas, she decided to stop for a fill-up and a rest room break, which would also give the car's engine time to cool off a bit. She hoped it would run better later, when she restarted it and resumed her trip. However, as she steered the car into a gas pump island it continued to lose power, and Lia suddenly realized that she might not be able to make it all the way to Boise. But she knew that she had to try. It was only another 45 miles or so.

Some twenty minutes later, with a full tank of gas, Lia started up the car and drove away from the Gear Jammer. At first the car seemed to be running fine. But its recovery would be short-lived. As she pulled onto the on-ramp to the westbound lanes of I-84, her car stalled out. She steered it to the on-ramp's shoulder and tried several times to get it started again, to no avail. She realized that there was no reviving it this time, not without help.

Lia walked back to the Gear Jammer and went promptly to a telephone booth outside the truck stop's cafe, from where she called a friend and explained what had occurred. She didn't have enough money to have it repaired at the truck stop, and with her limited knowledge about cars she didn't want to commit herself to having it repaired without having someone she knew and trusted present to make certain that she didn't get taken for a ride by a mechanic. After making the telephone call, Lia apparently decided to wait inside the restaurant until help arrived or until someone called and advised her what to do next. When she hung up, she likely hadn't noticed the shaggy-looking, bearded man as he watched her leave the phone booth. Not at first, anyway.

That was the last time that anyone heard from Lia. Precisely what happened after she made that telephone call is not known. What is known is that she disappeared from the truck stop's restaurant before the person she called could send someone to help her. Telephone calls to Lia at the truck stop went unanswered, and it was at first presumed that she must have gotten her car started and had continued on to Boise, or that someone must have offered her a ride. But she never showed up at the airport, nor did she make any additional phone calls.

After waiting at the airport for a considerable time, Jeff finally called Lia's family and explained that she hadn't shown up as planned. Her family in turn notified the Twin Falls Police Department and set the wheels of a missing-person investigation into motion. Detective James Howells was assigned to the case and promptly took a report from the Szuberts.

According to the information that the missing woman's family provided to Howells, Lia was born on February 25, 1965, in Flint, Michigan. She and her family moved west to Idaho in 1979, where they settled in Twin Falls. Active in cross-country running, other sports, student government, and debate, Lia graduated from Twin Falls High School in 1983. Afterward she attended the College of Mount Saint Vincent at Riverdale, New York, and also worked for a time at a Wall Street brokerage firm. When she returned to Idaho, she took a job as a waitress at the Heartbreak Cafe and was preparing to return to school at the time of her disappearance.

Expediting procedures due to the mysterious and suspicious circumstances surrounding Lia's failure to show up at the airport to pick up her fiancé, Howells sent out a regional all-points bulletin to alert the agencies between Twin Falls and Boise of Lia's disappearance. By then the police had learned of the telephone call that Lia had made from the Gear Jammer. As a result it wasn't long before an Idaho Police trooper found Lia's yellow car parked along the shoulder of the on-ramp with its emergency lights still flashing.

After tagging and sealing the car and having it towed to a secure location in case it held clues to what had happened to Lia, investigators from the Idaho State Police, the Mountain Home Police Department, and the Twin Falls Police Department converged on the Gear Jammer. Over a period of a couple of hours, they located several people who reported having seen Lia within the time frame that she had made the telephone call to her friend. They also described a grubby-looking man with long, unkempt hair, a scraggly beard, and the letters J-U-N-E tattooed across the fingers of his left hand. The man, said the witnesses, had been hanging around the truck stop for some time prior to Lia's arrival. The man was also seen in Lia's presence for only a short period, but was not seen again after she disappeared.

Due to the fact that news of Lia's disappearance and the description of the man that she was seen with ever so briefly at the truck stop had been rebroadcast to include law enforcement agencies all over the Pacific Northwest, it was only a matter of days before the APB landed on the desks of the Pierce County investigators. Both Stout and Wilson, after reading the description of the man with the tattooed knuckles, suddenly knew that O'Neall had struck again, this time in Idaho.

Knowing that one of a serial killer's most effective weapons against capture is his mobility, which makes it more difficult for investigators from different jurisdictions to communicate effectively with each other when people start disappearing and bodies begin turning up, Stout and Wilson promptly contacted the authorities in Idaho and brought them up to date on what they had accumulated so far on O'Neall. They couldn't be certain, of course, that O'Neall was responsible for Lia's disappearance, but they felt that there was sufficient likelihood that they should provide their colleagues in Idaho with all of the details on Robin Smith and Wendy Aughe, as well as the Colorado connection and the known and the possible crimes that O'Neall had committed there.

Also, knowing that serial killers typically monitor a police department's movements by reading newspapers and watching television news reports, which sometimes prompts such a killer to change his modus operandi to avoid being detected, it was decided that only a minimal amount of news surrounding Lia's disappearance would be released to the media. It was during this same time frame that Stout and Wilson also learned of two rapes that had been reported in Oregon along I-84 within the past three months. They couldn't help but wonder whether their man had been involved in those assaults as well.

While authorities in Idaho were busy looking for clues that would lead them to Lia Szubert's whereabouts, reliable reports of likely sightings of Darren O'Neall continued to pour into the Pierce County Sheriff's Department. Although some of the callers had difficulty providing specific dates of the sightings, most had occurred in the days and in some cases weeks prior to Lia's disappearance in King and Pierce counties. Some of the sightings had also occurred in Oregon. If O'Neall had done Lia in and had committed the two rapes along I-84 in eastern Oregon, and was in and out of Pierce and King counties, he had been a busy boy indeed, prompting Stout and Wilson to wonder how many other crimes he might have committed that they knew nothing about yet.

One of the reports from Oregon was from a man who had heard about the cases involving O'Neall and had called to tell the investigators that he knew O'Neall from a plasma center in Eugene. The same individual said that he had also seen O'Neall at a Eugene mission, at a plasma center in San Francisco, and had seen him in the outdoors camping near Cougar Hot Springs in Oregon. The man could not recall specific dates for the detectives, but said that he had last seen O'Neall in November 1986 in Eugene, at which time they had exchanged Louis L'Amour books. It was clear to Stout and Wilson that O'Neall had traveled considerably on the West Coast, at least in Oregon and California, prior to moving to Washington. The last encounter that the man had reported, they noted, had likely been right after O'Neall had left Idaho driving the Chrysler that he had stolen from Barry Fenwick.

A woman called in to report that her girlfriend had seen O'Neall. The woman's girlfriend had refused to call the police herself and had forbidden her friend to divulge her identity. She was planning just to forget the incident, but with all of the publicity that the Robin Smith case was getting and the fact that O'Neall was still on the run prompted her to have her girlfriend call in the report for her. The caller's girlfriend claimed to be an acquaintance of O'Neall's and had seen him at a telephone booth outside a Safeway store in south King County in late May or early June. They had made eye contact, resulting in the witness being fearful to contact the police. The caller's friend had made a positive identification, she said. Since she knew him personally, there was no doubt in her mind about his identity. The caller told the investigators that her friend had said that O'Neall had straightened his hair and had cut it just below the ear. He was also wearing clear glasses.

Another caller, an employee at a convenience store in south King County, reported seeing a man who looked very much like the picture of O'Neall that was being displayed everywhere on the Pierce County Sheriff's Department flier. The caller said that she had seen the man inside the store several times, on and off over several weeks, and that he had been harassing her 16-year-old niece. She said that he had called himself Denny O'Brien. Relating to the harassment of her niece, the caller explained that the man had left several bizarre notes for the teenage girl and on one occasion had left a rose. He also somehow had obtained the niece's home telephone number and had called her asking questions about her life. Some of the things he had said indicated that he had been stalking her. The harassment had begun about the time that Robin Smith had disappeared, and had continued ever since except for a short interim of a couple of weeks. Stout and Wilson didn't know whether O'Neall's use of the name Denny O'Brien was simply to taunt them or whether he was merely just unimaginative.

Yet another report placed a man matching

O'Neall's description at a Seattle Mariners baseball game. The man was with another man of similar age and build, and both men began harassing an elderly black male employee of the Kingdome who had asked them to extinguish their cigarettes. After complying, the two men threw peanuts at the employee when his back was turned, then tried to keep straight faces when the employee turned around to see where the peanuts were coming from. The caller said that he had pointed at the two men to show the employee who was throwing the peanuts. Afterward, the employee notified the police and three uniformed officers responded. The man accompanying the man who looked like O'Neall had "put on a big show" by acting very drunk and obnoxious. The caller, however, said that he had only drunk two beers at the game. While the police were dealing with the obnoxious man, the man who looked like O'Neall quietly slipped away and left the stadium.

A man who refused to give his name called to report that a "Michael O'Neal" and a "Michael Johnson" had applied for food stamps at the Puyallup Welfare Office. The man was adamant that "O'Neal" and "Johnson" were one and the same. He had dubbed the man "the Teardrop Kid" because of a small tatoo below one of his eyes. The call had been traced to a home in Spanaway, but when the residents were contacted by the police they refused to provide any further information and demanded that their names not be given out.

A police dispatcher from Bellevue called to report

that an anonymous tipster had contacted their department about a man who looked like Darren O'Neall that had been seen attempting to pick up young girls from the Pioneer Square area of downtown Seattle. He was seen leaving the area driving a white 1979 Ford LTD.

During this same spate of reports, a man who had taken a trip on a Trailways bus called the Pierce County detectives to inform them that, weeks earlier in May, a man fitting O'Neall's description had boarded the same eastbound bus in Bend, Oregon. He had sat next to the caller and had complained that his legs were hurting him because he had been hiking in the woods. The man was wearing hiking boots and was carrying a sleeping bag with him. He claimed to have been going to Kansas but left the bus in Denver.

A short time later a Burien, Washington, resident called to say that she had seen O'Neall in Colorado Springs during the second week in May. When Stout and Wilson checked the earlier report, this sighting had occurred during the same time frame in which O'Neall had been seen getting off the Trailways bus in Denver. He had relatives there, so it fit that he might have gone there seeking their help but had left shortly thereafter to return to the Pacific Northwest. He was effectively avoiding capture, Stout and Wilson conceded, by staying on the move.

On Thursday, June 11, two days after Lia Szubert had disappeared, a Seattle resident on business in the Spokane area, in the eastern part of the state, reported to Spokane authorities that he had been held up and robbed by two hitchhikers, a man and a woman, that he had picked up. He described the man as a white male in his late twenties or early thirties, five feet ten inches tall and a hundred sixty pounds with light brown or dishwater blond hair. He was clean-shaven, but had a small teardrop or possibly a star tattoo beneath his left eye, and J-U-N-E tattooed across the knuckles of his left hand. He described the man's companion as a white red-haired female, about thirty years old, five feet nine inches and a hundred fifty pounds.

A man matching O'Neall's description was seen again and again in the same vicinity over the next few days, both east and west of Spokane, according to Joe Smith of the FBI's Seattle office. Smith and other federal investigators were confident that the sightings were of O'Neall—nearly all of those who had reported seeing him also reported seeing the telltale tattoos. Because O'Neall had friends and relatives in the area, stakeouts were strategically placed near homes and businesses where the investigators felt he might show up. However, much to their dismay, he slipped away from Spokane as easily as he had slipped in. As was his custom, O'Neall had vanished again without a trace.

It was nearly dusk at nine o'clock on Saturday, June 13, when a middle-aged male motorist heading west on I-84 toward Portland decided that he had to urinate. He was about 10 miles outside La Grande,

Oregon, located in the eastern part of the state. He pulled over in a safe and secluded area near Ladd Canyon, exited his car, and relieved himself near the side of the road facing the canyon.

It was while peering down the embankment and into the canyon that something frighteningly familiar caught his eye lying near a creek bed. It appeared lily white, giving it an almost ghostly appearance in the last rays of sunlight, but as he continued to stare at it he suddenly recognized it as a human body. From his vantage point it appeared to be a female, and several times as he dumbfoundedly stared at it he was struck by a foul odor as the light breeze occasionally shifted direction. Someone, he quickly reasoned, must have killed her and tossed her down the embankment. Suddenly terrified at the thought of finding a murder victim, the man ran back to his car and drove into La Grande, where he notified the Oregon State Police of his unnerving discovery.

Chapter 20

Early the next morning Oregon State Police (OSP) investigators, along with criminalists from their own department and accompanied by investigators and deputies from the Union County Sheriff's Department, converged on the crime scene at Ladd Canyon and relieved the state troopers who had been posted there as sentries overnight. Overhead, area photographs were taken of the scene from an OSP helicopter. It was immediately evident to Lieutenant Gerald Hays, who headed the investigation, that they were dealing with a homicide of the worst sort.

Hays and the other investigators observed that the body was clearly that of a young female, completely nude and rapidly decomposing. The odor of putrefaction was very strong, making it difficult for them to do their work. They guessed that the body had been lying there for a few days, since maggot activity was already present. The body was also beginning to bloat. Although no one would comment publicly about the corpse's condition or cause of death, sources close to the investigation indicated that "horrible things" had been done to her prior to her death. The detectives refused to reveal the specifics, however, in order to preserve the integrity of the investigation. Certain things about active homicide investigations have to remain known only to the police and the killer, for obvious reasons. Aware of the missing-person report on Lia Szubert and recognizing that the victim generally fit Lia's description, Hays promptly notified his colleagues in Idaho.

Shortly after Detective James Howells of the Twin Falls Police Department and Detective Ken Smith of the Ada County Sheriff's Department in Idaho arrived in Oregon, the victim was positively identified as 22-year-old Lia Szubert. With no way to know precisely where she had been killed, the detectives guessed that she had been murdered shortly after being abducted from the Gear Jammer and her body driven approximately 150 miles, where it had been dumped like refuse into Ladd Canyon. It was pure luck that her body had been found so soon. If not for the motorist who had stopped to urinate, her body might have lain there for weeks, months, or even years without having been discovered, leaving it available for animals to feed on and scatter just as with Robin Smith.

Few additional details were released following the definitive autopsy on Lia's body, performed the next day in Pendleton by pathologist Robert Connell. The authorities would only say that homicide was ruled as the cause of death and that Lia had been dead approximately three to five days when her body was found. But sources in a position to know revealed that she had been strangled.

In the days following the discovery of Lia's body, despite the fact that investigators openly stated that there was nothing to suggest that the killer was from the area or was still at large in the vicinity, officials in eastern Oregon and Idaho began to downplay the possibility that she had been slain by a serial killer. Nonetheless, they were privately conferring with Stout and Wilson in Pierce County, Jarratt and Nolte in Bellingham, and additional investigators in Colorado. It was clear in law enforcement circles that Darren O'Neall was being looked at, hard, as a suspect. Their investigation had turned up several people who had seen a man closely matching O'Neall's description, right down to the tattoos on his face and knuckles, who recently had been in the area. They had even turned up witnesses who reported that he was believed to have been driving a late 1960s or possibly an early 1970s model Camaro with Oregon license plates. Maroon in color, witnesses said that it was noisy and in poor condition.

As in the cases of Robin Smith and Wendy Aughe, fliers with Lia's picture were printed up and distributed to restaurants, truck stops, and rest areas along I-84 in Oregon and Idaho. They hoped that the fliers would bring people with information forward. While the flier did produce people who wanted to help, unfortunately the information those people offered did not bring the police any closer to nabbing O'Neall.

* * *

When Edna Smith and Jim Chaney heard about Lia Szubert's murder, they immediately drove to Oregon and Idaho to learn what they could from the various law enforcement jurisdictions. Although the investigators were willing to talk to them, they weren't willing to reveal many details surrounding the murder. It did become clear to Edna and Jim, however, that O'Neall was the prime suspect in Lia's case. According to Chaney, an OSP trooper he spoke with had some pretty strong feelings about O'Neall, which Chaney interpreted to have been created by whatever the killer had done to Lia before killing her.

"He'd better hope that he never crosses my path," Chaney said the trooper told him. "If he does, I won't waste the taxpayers' money by bringing him in. I'll blow his ass away and dump his body in a ditch."

When Edna and Jim viewed photographs of Lia that had been provided to the police by Lia's family, they were stunned at how beautiful she was, and were haunted at how similar Lia's smile was to Robin's. O'Neall, they reasoned, was like other serial killers in that he seemed to pick his victims based on similar physical characteristics. They knew, too, as did the police, that O'Neall's ability to express himself and to make contact with women in a number of given situations lay at the heart of his crimes. O'Neall had effectively learned how to put on an acceptable face, even a friendly, often desirable face, a mask, in order to lure his victims in. By then, however, it was often too late to escape his clutches. It had been too late for Robin, Wendy and now Lia, and only God and O'Neall knows how many others.

At four o'clock on July 25, 1987, a Saturday, Willis Haynes* was sitting in the Cowboy Bar on Main Street, located in the dusty and somewhat secluded town of Joseph, Oregon. Geographically Joseph is situated in the northeast corner of the state, well off the beaten path, near the Eagle Cap Wilderness Area. It was just the sort of place that Darren O'Neall might fancy.

Haynes noticed the stranger when he walked into the bar. He was puffing on a cigarette. Sipping a beer, Haynes stared at the man from a few feet away. He recognized the stranger from the wanted posters of Darren O'Neall that had been distributed throughout the area after Lia Szubert's murder. Haynes didn't approach the stranger, but instead watched and listened.

The stranger ordered a drink and began talking to a few of the other men standing at the bar, smoking one cigarette after another. He overheard the man say that he owned a "spread" in Echo, Oregon, about 18 miles west of Pendleton. Haynes observed that he was making a halfhearted attempt to act rugged, like an outdoorsman. To Haynes, he looked just like one of the five photos of Darren O'Neall that he had seen side by side on the wanted poster. Haynes never spoke to him the entire time he was in the bar, but saw him a short time later walking in town. He didn't see a vehicle associated with the man that he believed was O'Neall.

When Haynes reported the sighting to the authorities, he described O'Neall as having short, curly hair with a mustache that didn't extend beyond the corners of his mouth. It was cut very close, and he was wearing gray wire-rimmed glasses. Haynes said that he was wearing a black jacket with white trim, Levi's, a cowboy hat and cowboy boots. Haynes described him as wide and well built.

As was his custom, however, O'Neall disappeared from the cowboy town as quietly as he had appeared. No one saw how he left or when. He was simply nowhere to be found in Joseph by the time the police took Haynes's statement. He may have hitched a ride, or he may have driven out on his own, likely in a vehicle that he had stolen somewhere. The investigators considered that he might have gone north out of town on Highway 3, toward Washington or northern Idaho, or east toward the Hells Canyon National Recreation Area. They didn't know that he had actually doubled back and headed west until a report of another sighting came in some two and a half weeks later.

Betty Fife,* 25, told Oregon investigators that she had picked up a hitchhiker who fit the description of Darren O'Neall on August 14, 1987, a Friday, along Interstate 5 near Eugene. She said that she dropped him off a couple of hours later near the intersection of Highway 217 and Highway 10 in Beaverton, Oregon. Betty described him as 29–30 years old, five feet nine inches tall, thin, with sandy or light brown hair and light blue eyes. She also said that he had a mustache, and had tattoos on the knuckles of his left hand. He had another tattoo between the thumb and first finger of his left hand. During the trip Betty said that the man had told her that he had come from Crescent City, California, and was going to take I-84 east to Wyoming.

Despite the fact that existing APBs were updated with the latest information and sent out all over the western states, O'Neall remained elusive. Unfortunately, no one could figure out where he was heading. The only thing that was certain at this point was that he was on the move.

Chapter 21

Even though the FBI had entered the case due to the fact that Lia Szubert had been kidnapped and transported across state lines, the federal agents as well as the investigators from the multi-state agencies were still no closer to locating and apprehending Darren O'Neall. At first, right after the FBI added O'Neall to their Ten Most Wanted list in August, federal agents thought that they had gotten a lead on him in Ketchum, Idaho. He was linked to the abduction and assault of a woman that had gone awry. Fortunately, the woman had managed to escape and was able to report the incident to the authorities. From the description that she had provided, it certainly seemed that O'Neall had been the perpetrator. But again he slipped through their dragnet with ease.

Because the various law enforcement agencies throughout the western states had received teletypes about Lia Szubert's death and were now actively communicating with one another, the FBI was able to use many of the information exchanges to aid them in developing a standard profile of the killer they were looking for utilizing standards introduced when the Violent Criminal Apprehension Program (ViCAP) was placed in operation by their own Behavioral Sciences Unit. Among the characteristics that figured into the profile was the fact that O'Neall always seemed to select his victims from public places. He had first seen Robin Smith at a tavern, Wendy Aughe at the bar where he worked, and Lia Szubert at a truck stop. The ages of the victims, all in their twenties, was another factor they considered. Each had similar hair lengths. It was known that two of the victims, Robin and Lia, had had their clothing removed prior to being dumped at outdoor locations; the same was in all likelihood true with Wendy, but her remains hadn't been found to prove it. In the case of Robin and Lia, the remains of both were found in areas in which O'Neall had become very familiar. He had learned his way around Washington shortly after moving there, and he knew his way around Idaho and eastern Oregon from having lived with Barry Fenwick. The outdoors, particularly wilderness areas, always seemed to figure importantly in the scenario, even all the way back to Colorado. As with most serial killers that have been studied, O'Neall's crimes always appeared to be fantasy-driven.

For the most part O'Neall, like most serial killers, appeared very normal to those around him. It was an unsettling thought, but true, making it impossible for anyone to identify a serial killer by appearance alone.

In studying O'Neall's method of operation, it was evident to investigators that O'Neall always selected victims less powerful than himself. However, women in and of themselves, they noted, did not satisfy that characteristic. If he perceived a woman as potentially strong-willed or physically strong, he left them alone. He preyed only on the women that he considered vulnerable, easy targets. His crimes, like those of all serial killers, were sexual in nature, and were a game of power and domination in which he made the decisions. Ultimately, he alone held the power over the life or death of his victims. In O'Neall's case it was usually death, as he seemed consumed with committing murder.

Stout and Wilson realized early on in the investigation that they were not experts on serial murder. They also soon recognized that there were not any real experts, despite the fact that many law enforcement and mental health professionals, and even a few authors, claim to be experts. The closest thing to expertise, they found, was their own learning by doing, seeing, and studying firsthand what serial killers do. And even that wasn't going to be enough to bring their man in. Trying to predict his next move, his next killing, had not worked. He didn't stay in one place long enough for them to catch up to him. They knew by now that the only way they were going to catch Darren O'Neall was when he slipped up and made a mistake.

In the meantime Edna Smith butted heads with the judicial system again, and was becoming more and more disillusioned with it each time that she was forced to deal with it. Although Edna and her family had already held a memorial service for Robin with family and friends, she now wanted Robin's remains released to her so that she could give her a proper Christian burial and lay her to rest. But when she asked the Pierce County Medical Examiner's Office to turn over Robin's remains, they refused. A spokesman for the medical examiner's office told Edna that they had to "hang onto the bones" as evidence until O'Neall was arrested and brought to trial.

"I don't know why you have to hold her there," cried Edna. "My God, you've got all the evidence you need!"

Unable to obtain and bury Robin's remains, Edna and her family vowed to fight the system for their return. In the meantime, having experienced the loss of a loved one through an act of violence, Edna and her family saw the need for assistance, moral and financial, to the families of other crime victims. As a result they established the Victims' Memorial Burial Fund and convinced the Pierce County Chaplaincy, a nonprofit organization that provides support for victims of violence and their surviving families, to administer it. It not only kept Edna and her family busy, it helped them to unite and grow even stronger in the aftermath of their loss.

"It's hard for the families," said Brenda Baker, Robin's sister. "They're not prepared for things like this. It's bad enough to realize you've just lost a loved one, and now you have to figure out how you're going to pay for a funeral."

"Until we get Robin's remains back, it's hard," said Edna. "There is no peace of mind. It's sad because we know the reality of what lies ahead of us."

For the time being, Robin's bones were kept in paper bags inside a locker at the morgue.

The FBI soon acknowledged that O'Neall had been seen in Utah after the incident in Ketchum, Idaho. Although their efforts to pinpoint his whereabouts failed, they did learn that three young women had been shot to death in the Salt Lake City area in the past year. Each had been killed with a small-caliber gun, and an examination of the spent slugs showed that they had been fired from the same gun. And even though several people had reported seeing a man who fit O'Neall's description in the vicinity, right down to the J-U-N-E tattoo on his knuckles, there was nothing that conclusively linked him to the women. Unless the investigators came up with something more substantial such as a witness who actually saw him in the presence of one or more of the women, they were going to have a tough time pinning the slayings on him, and they knew it.

Chapter 22

Even before the tragedy of Robin's murder struck, Edna Smith had always held life, especially the lives of her own children, as something sacred, something never to be taken for granted. She knew from the furthest reaches of her heart and soul that being a mother was far more than a mere word or title. It was a bond *for life* between a woman and her child, a life that she would be attached to forever. Despite the dreadful and intense pain of giving birth to each of her children, Edna always knew that the pain would go away the second that she held each newborn child in her arms and knew that she was looking at a miracle. To her, each was "a blessed gift from God." Each child, from her first to her last, was special and provided her a new joy in life. She had spent the best years of her life nursing them, feeding them, nurturing them, loving them, and always had done the best that she could to teach them right from wrong based on the values of her own Catholic upbringing. Each time one of them would fall she would pick them up, attend their wounds, "kiss them all better," and every day of their lives the bonds of love only grew stronger between them. She watched them with loving, adoring eyes as they grew, each helping the other over the hurdles of life and through the mistakes that would inevitably be made, getting through life's up and downs with an ever strengthening bond, if such a thing was possible, between them.

Then one day a frightening thought overcame Edna. Knowing that the day would eventually come that she would have to let her children go out into the world on their own, she began to wonder what her life would be like without them. She began to question whether she had done a good job of teaching them to survive on their own in the world, a world that she knew could at times be cruel and hard. But she had to let them go, and could only hope for the best. One by one they left the shelter of Edna's love, and with each departure the pain of letting go did not subside. It only grew worse, and she finally knew what her life was going to be like without them. Empty. She survived by knowing in her heart that she would never truly let go of any of her children. Even though they would no longer be physically living with her, they were her life, her joy, her happiness. They were hers to love forever, no matter what happened. No one could ever take that away from her. Or so she had always thought.

When Robin was murdered, Edna's world began to fall apart. She was not ready to face the death of one of her children. Children, she thought, were supposed to bury their parents. It wasn't supposed to be the other way around. Edna had given Robin life, and in the space of only seconds in time someone else had taken that life away from not only Robin, but from Edna and all those who loved Robin. No one had the right to do that. With Robin's death, a part of Edna died along with her, and she began to withdraw from life. When the reality of the permanence of death had finally sunk in, Edna began to deteriorate further, both emotionally and physically. She was in so much pain that she had put aside her own life and the lives of her other children. Life, as she knew it, had suddenly stopped, and Edna knew that she would never be the same person that she once was.

Edna felt and tried to grasp the pain that her other children experienced over Robin's murder. All of the pain that they felt, she felt too. At first she had tried to ease their pain and bring it unto herself until finally it became too much for her to bear. She soon became afraid to embrace her other children, and her fear of the possibility of losing another child caused her to put up a barrier between herself and her children. She thought an unspoken distance would lessen her pain over Robin's death. But she was wrong, and every part of her heart and soul ached not only over the loss of Robin but for the closeness of the children that she held at a distance. She finally realized that she was out of control, and she turned to the only thing that she felt she had left: her faith.

One day while crying out to God to help get her through her grief, Edna suddenly felt an overpowering urge to obtain a statue of the Virgin Mary. If the criminal justice system wouldn't turn over Robin's remains so that she could provide her with a proper burial, and could only pay her respects and vent her grief by making weekly trips to Greenwater to place flowers on the site where Robin's body had lain, she would build a shrine of sorts to Robin in her own backyard.

Edna spent weeks looking for the statue that she wanted. She finally found an unpainted statue at a local store, bought it, and took it home. She carefully painted it, being meticulous with the detail, and placed it in her backyard. She planted a variety of flowers and yellow rose bushes, which had small yellow buds and were not mature enough to bloom yet, all around it. The statue of the Holy Mother became Edna's private memorial for Robin. She went out to it often to pray, and though it gave her some peace of mind and the feeling that she was closer to Robin, the pain of Robin's murder remained.

One day, while she was praying in front of the statue, the pain of loss returned. It was stronger, more intense than it ever had been. Edna lost what little control that she had been hanging on to.

"Why, God? Why her?" Edna screamed, tears streaming down her face. "I don't understand. I need some answers. I can't take this pain anymore! God, where are you when you're needed? I loved her so much, I can't let her go. I need your help. I can't do it alone."

Edna sobbed uncontrollably and was nearly hysterical. The line between reality and delusion was fast disappearing. Soon Edna heard a small voice speak to her, and she briefly wondered how she had been able to hear it over the sound of her own wailing. The soft voice said: "Go back inside your home."

As she turned to walk back inside, Edna thought that she must be losing her mind. She began screaming out again and again, "God help me! I can't take this pain!" By the time she had made it back inside her house, she was crying so hard that it had become painful for her to breathe. Then she heard the soft voice again, inside her head: "Stop. Look over at your plant on the table."

Edna stopped crying, and her tears abruptly ceased as she stared at the plant set atop her dining room table. It appeared to her to be crying, dripping tears from its blossoms, and she didn't know if what she was seeing was real or delusional. Was she hallucinating? She didn't know. It seemed real enough. Suddenly she felt as if the plant had somehow picked up or absorbed all of her pain and suffering. There was no longer a single tear in her eyes. Her eyes were, in fact, now dry. Then she heard the voice again: "Go back outside to your statue." Edna obeyed.

When she reached the icon of the Holy Mother and kneeled before it, a warm, peaceful feeling came over her. She somehow felt different, that she was not alone. She believed that there was a holy presence there with her. When she looked toward the yellow rose bushes, they were no longer buds. They were not yellow, either. Instead large white roses were blooming from where the yellow buds had been only minutes before. She gasped in awe as she stood up.

This cannot be, she thought. She had planted yellow roses there, and they had not been ready to bloom. Then it came to her. She was in the presence of the Holy Mother, the mother of God, the mother of Lord Jesus. She fell to her knees, and felt the pain being lifted from her soul as she said, as much to the icon as to herself:

"Of course. The Mother of God. Who better could know another mother's pain? You and you alone know. You were the first mother ever to feel the pain of loss. You suffered the greatest pain of all. You had no control, nor could you lift a hand to help him. You could not change God's plan for your son, and you lived with the pain all those years knowing his destiny and that you would watch him die. You stood at the foot of the cross in such pain as life left him so that we might have life. There is no greater pain than that. You knew also that it was not the end. It was the beginning. You knew that you would see him again. As a mother you gave us all the gift of love, your son Jesus. I will take comfort from you, Holy Mother, that I will see my daughter again, and that I will never be separated from her or any of my children."

Even though she is somewhat hesitant to recount

it for others, the experience that day in her backyard and inside her house was very real to Edna, and it burned a place in her heart that will last forever. It also gave her the strength that she needed to carry on and the courage that she would need to face the days, weeks, and years that lay ahead.

Chapter 23

By early September the FBI was still searching for Darren O'Neall in Utah, but was also reporting to its colleagues in Oregon, Washington, and Idaho that O'Neall had been linked to the deaths of women in Anchorage, Alaska, and Las Vegas, Nevada, as well as in various locations in Colorado and Texas. The body count attributed to the actions of Darren O'Neall was now into double digits, but in most of the cases being examined he was merely a "person of interest" due to the lack of eyewitnesses and physical evidence.

"We want him badly," said T. C. Brock, the FBI's agent-in-charge in Idaho. "He has become a very high-priority issue to us."

"The crimes appear to be increasing in frequency and becoming more violent," said Dan Pence, the FBI's agent-in-charge in Denver. "We are trying to catch him before more violence occurs."

What they didn't know was that Darren O'Neall had headed south after passing through Utah, and had begun living under a number of aliases, as was his custom. All the while that they were searching for him in Utah he had, in fact, arrived in the state of Louisiana, where he had begun running scams in and around New Orleans. His illegal activities ranged from selling drugs to working as a drug enforcer, in which he collected drug debts from junkies for some of the local dealers in return for drugs and/or money, to creating and selling forged passports to other criminal types. He was by now using the name John A. Mayuex [*sic*], and another variation of that name, Zhohn Arronel Mayeaux.

It was approximately 7:30 A.M. on Monday, August 31, when Officer E. L. Brown, badge number 2496, received a call about an auto theft from a resident in the 2400 block of Ninth Street in Harvey, Louisiana, a New Orleans suburb. The Jefferson Parish Sheriff's Office deputy responded promptly and arrived within minutes at the home of Connie LeFevre,* 59. LeFevre was clearly upset over the theft of her nearly new 1987 Mercury Marquis.

"Can you tell me what happened here this morning?" Brown asked. "How did you come to know that your car had been stolen?"

"A friend of mine, June Smith,* came over this morning and got me out of bed," Connie replied. "June asked me where my car was. When I looked I noticed that it was not parked outside where it should have been. I then looked under my bed and saw that my purse was also missing."

"Was there anyone else in the house with you?" Brown asked.

"Only my boarder, John," Connie said.

"What is John's full name?" Brown asked as he looked up briefly from his note pad.

"John A. Mayuex." Connie spelled the last name for Brown. "He's about thirty years old, maybe older, five feet eleven inches tall, about a hundred sixty-five pounds with blond hair and blue eyes."

"What else can you tell me? What were the contents of your purse? What did the purse look like?" Brown asked.

"The purse was black and gray," Connie replied. "It was worth about forty-five dollars. I had about two thousand dollars in cash and uncashed checks inside it, along with several credit cards. There was a Visa, an Exxon card, a couple of others."

"What did your car look like?"

"It was a four-door, silver over gray." Connie told Officer Brown that it had Louisiana license plates, number 518A853, with tags that didn't expire until 1991. She also went to a drawer where she kept her important papers and provided Brown with the car's vehicle identification number. She placed the value of the car at twenty thousand dollars.

"When was the last time that you saw John?" Brown asked.

"About four o'clock this morning," Connie said. "He was lying on the couch. I went into the living room after June came over to tell me that my car was gone, and that's when I saw that John was no longer there. My car keys were also missing from the kitchen table, where I left them when I went to bed. That man took my car and purse."

"What relationship is John to you?" Brown asked.

"None. Like I said, he was just a boarder. He paid rent when he worked."

"Do you wish to press charges against him?" Brown explained that if she did, a warrant would be issued for his arrest and that an APB would be sent out for the car. The information would also be added to the National Crime Information Center's computers.

"Yes indeed."

Connie added that John had taken most of his clothing with him, but had left a few items behind. He had also left behind the key to her house.

Unknown to law enforcement agencies from Louisiana to Washington, Darren O'Neall was by now using the alias Zhohn Arronel Mayeaux and had headed north to Nashville, Tennessee. He hit the tavern and bar scene, as was his custom, and for the first few nights he slept in cheap motels using the cash that he had stolen from Connie LeFevre when he wasn't sleeping in her silver Marquis.

It wasn't long, however, before he met Nadine Quinn,* 23. Nadine, at five feet four inches tall and 125 pounds, was an attractive woman with brown hair and brown eyes. She was alone, visiting Nashville from Lakeland, Florida, but was returning home soon. O'Neall, seizing the opportunity, told her that he was heading for Florida, too, and offered to drive her there. She could have said she was going anywhere, and O'Neall would have said he was going there, too. She naively accepted his offer, unaware that he was merely setting her up to use her for sex and anything else that he could get from her, and they left Tennessee together for the drive to Florida shortly after meeting each other.

Shortly after their arrival in Lakeland during the early part of September, O'Neall took advantage of the situation and moved what few things he had, mostly clothes, into Nadine's apartment. While staying with Nadine he began running scams out of taverns and bars, and within days he had positioned himself as a drug dealer's enforcer and had effectively worked his way into Lakeland's drug underworld. Not only was he selling drugs and skimming the profits as well as the "products" for his own use, he was breaking fingers and busting jaws to collect bad drug debts for his newfound drug-dealing associates. And he was enjoying every minute of it.

On Tuesday, September 22, at a few minutes before 9:00 A.M., O'Neall and Nadine turned westbound on Carver Street from North Kettles Avenue in Connie LeFevre's Mercury Marquis. They were in an area of town commonly referred to as the "Bottoms," a neighborhood known for its gangs, drug activity and used as a dumping site for stolen vehicles. But they weren't there to dump Connie's Marquis. They were there looking for Curt Hinkle,* 31, a slender man with a medium build whom they had taken there to score some drugs for O'Neall. They finally found him walking northbound from the intersection of Crawford and Lincoln. He was easy to spot because he was wearing a bright blue Hawaiian print shirt. O'Neall and Nadine weren't the only people who had spotted him, however. Officer Gary A. Swank of the Lakeland Police Department saw Hinkle as he drove by in his patrol car. He also noticed how the silver Marquis had slowed down as it approached Hinkle from the opposite direction, and how the car's occupants and the man in the Hawaiian shirt looked at each other. They seemed to know one another.

Swank, suspicious of their activities, drove on by, planning all the while to turn around down the block so that he could position his car behind the silver Marquis to stop it for identification purposes. But before he could get his cruiser turned around, the Marquis had picked up the man on the street, had turned around, and was driving toward Swank. O'Neall, aware that Swank was suspicious of them, pulled alongside Swank's patrol car and asked him for directions to another street, hoping to allay the officer's suspicions with the ruse. Swank, however, was not about to be bullshitted. Not in that neighborhood.

"Pull your car around the corner there and stop," Swank demanded.

"Okay," O'Neall said.

Before Swank could get his car turned around, O'Neall sped off. Swank, in pursuit, called in for a backup and reported the Marquis' Louisiana license plates. As he hit the siren and turned on his overhead lights, O'Neall turned the Marquis into the parking lot of a funeral home. He exited onto Kettles Street from the other side of the parking lot and began turning corners as he accelerated. First north onto Lincoln Avenue, then west onto Crawford Street. O'Neall continued driving in this manner for some time, turning corner after corner, hoping to shake Swank off his tail. But Swank stayed on him.

Finally, O'Neall lost momentary control of the car at the intersection of West Eleventh Street and Carver Avenue, causing him to drive into a high concrete curb and onto the sidewalk. The impact caused the front right tire to blow out, effectively disabling the car. With Swank close behind, O'Neall and the other occupants fled the car on foot.

O'Neall ran westbound in the 900 block of West Eleventh Street, with Swank now pursuing him on foot. At first he was making considerable headway, and for a few moments it seemed that he might outrun Swank and escape over a nearby fence. However, before he could reach the fence, an alert citizen who could see that O'Neall was being chased by a policeman stepped into his path and effectively knocked him down. He held O'Neall there on the sidewalk on West Eleventh Street until Swank caught up to him and placed him in handcuffs. Before placing O'Neall in the patrol car, Swank frisked him and found two credit cards in O'Neall's right front pants pocket. Both bore Connie LeFevre's name. O'Neall was not carrying any identification of his own, nothing that revealed that he was really Darren O'Neall. All that Swank could get out of him was that his name was Zhohn A. Mayeaux. Moments later a communications dispatcher reported to Swank that the Marquis had been reported stolen out of Louisiana. After Swank advised "Zhohn A. Mayeaux" of his Miranda rights, O'Neall responded that he could not speak English.

A short time later, after K-9 units were brought into the area, Nadine Quinn and Curt Hinkle were apprehended at separate locations in the Bottoms, not far from where Darren O'Neall had been arrested.

During booking procedures, "Mayeaux" told officers that he was born in Schweinforrt, Germany, that he had no Social Security number, and that he was currently employed as a laborer for a local storm door company. He stated that the Marquis belonged to his adopted mother, Connie LeFevre, and that she had allowed him to use the car as well as the credit cards. When they informed him that LeFevre was pressing charges against him for grand theft of the automobile, as well as for the theft of the credit cards and money, he stated that he did not want to talk any further. In addition to the charges in Louisiana, "Mayeaux" was charged in Florida with grand theft, resisting an officer without force, possession of stolen credit cards, fleeing to elude police, and driving without a license.

In an attempt to learn more about their mystery

man, Officer Swank and Detective R. D. Hardee took Nadine Quinn into an interrogation room. She had already waived her Miranda rights and seemed eager to cooperate with the police.

"Officer Swank stopped you this morning on the north side of Lakeland, or tried to stop you and you were in a vehicle, correct?" Hardee asked.

"Yes," Nadine quietly replied.

"Who was in this vehicle with you?"

"Just Zhohn and Curt and me." She spelled Zhohn Mayeaux for them.

"How long have you known Zhohn?" Hardee asked.

"Less than a month. Probably two or three weeks."

"Where did you meet him?"

"While I was on vacation in Nashville."

"Did he have the car at that time?"

"Yes. We came back to Florida in that car."

"And he's been staying with you since your return?"

"Yes."

"What did he tell you about the car?"

Nadine explained that Mayeaux had told her that the car was his, that he had purchased it from a former associate or coworker, she couldn't remember which, for nineteen thousand dollars. She also explained that she did not know the car was stolen until the police had informed her that it was. She said that she wouldn't have normally fled as she had, but when the tire blew out Mayeaux had said, "When I stop, everyone jump out and run."

"Do you know anything about these credit cards?" Hardee asked as he displayed them for Nadine to see.

"No."

"Have you seen Zhohn use the credit cards? Yes or no?"

"I didn't see him use them, no."

"Do you know if he's used them to purchase gas?"

"I guess so, yes. He's bought gas at Exxon, here in Lakeland. I just assumed they were his. But I never actually watched him use them."

"What do you know about Curt Hinkle?"

"Nothing. I just met him last night."

"Does he know that the car is stolen?"

"No, I don't think so."

Following additional questioning, and turning up nothing significant in a routine background check, both Nadine Quinn and Curt Hinkle were cited for eluding police officers and released on their own recognizance. They had to appear in court later, but got off lightly with a fine and probation.

With no identification on Mayeaux's person, Lakeland police had little choice but to take him at his word that he was in fact John Mayeaux. They ran his name and physical characteristics through the usual computers, but no outstanding warrants came back under that name or any variations of it. Since they had little way of proving otherwise at this point, the

Florida authorities figured that the guy really must be John Mayeaux. Despite the charges pending against him in Florida and Louisiana, no one thought to run his fingerprints through the federal computerized data banks. If they had, they would have known right away whom they had lodged in their jail.

Chapter 24

September and October passed uneventfully for Edna Smith and her family. Edna had made additional attempts to get Robin's remains released from the medical examiner's office so that she could get her daughter buried before the holidays set in, but again they had refused her requests. Even though she had threatened to obtain a court order for the release of the remains, she was repeatedly told that if and when O'Neall was apprehended, his lawyer could request that forensic experts examine the remains, which would mean that she would have to have them dug up. It was bad enough holding the earlier memorial service for Robin with the empty lavender coffin she had purchased, but the thought of having to exhume the remains later, she decided, would be far worse. Edna decided to wait to provide Robin with a proper burial, and for the time being continued to pray for her daughter's soul at the memorial in her backyard.

The holidays were especially difficult for Edna and her family that first year without Robin. She remembered, much too easily, how Robin had loved the holidays, especially Thanksgiving. One of the first things that Robin would do on Thanksgiving was to walk over to the oven and get into the turkey and the stuffing to sample it before Edna could get it onto the platter for serving. Now Edna didn't know how she could even get through the holidays in light of all that had happened.

Christmas that year was particularly empty for the Smiths. Without Robin it just didn't feel like Christmas. Looking back on it, Edna would remember it as the worst Christmas any of them had ever experienced. Most of the family didn't care whether or not they even celebrated Christmas that year. But as the holiday drew near, they finally decided to bring everybody together at Edna's house simply for the sake of having the family together.

A few days before Christmas, however, Edna began to lose control again. She went out and bought Christmas gifts for the entire family, including gifts to each member of the family from Robin. She placed the labels on the presents in Robin's name to each of them. When questioned about what she was doing, Edna tearfully explained that she just couldn't let go of Robin, not yet. She was so accustomed to buying gifts year after year for everyone that she just couldn't bring herself not to include Robin, too. It was a futile attempt to keep Robin alive in the minds and hearts of her family, and it didn't work.

"Mom, try to forget about her," Brenda had said.

"She'll always be inside us. She'll always be a part of us. We have the memories of her."

Edna, however, just couldn't accept the fact that Robin was not there that Christmas, and would never be there again. To her it was like a part of the family circle was no longer complete. It had been broken, leaving a gap that could not be closed no matter how hard they tried.

Tears came that Christmas. Everybody cried at one time or another during their holiday gathering. They went their own way, found their own corner or place where they could cry alone.

Chapter 25

Darren Dee O'Neall, still insisting that his name was Zhohn Arronel Mayeaux, was eventually extradited to Louisiana from Florida on Wednesday, December 30, 1987, after several delays. Shortly after his arrest in Lakeland, Florida, he had pleaded guilty to fleeing an officer and for driving without a license, for which he was sentenced to thirty days in jail. He was also sentenced to another forty-five days in jail after pleading no contest to credit card theft and resisting arrest. He had fought the extradition, but it was finally approved by a Florida judge who decided that he must face the charges in Louisiana. With his true identity still unknown to the police, he was booked into the Jefferson Parish Corrections Center in Gretna, a New Orleans suburb, to await trial. Compounding the confusion over his true identity, he was booked in Gretna under the name John Mayeux.

Upon his arrival in Gretna, O'Neall was routinely fingerprinted. Afterward, his fingerprint cards were sent to the Louisiana State Police Bureau of Criminal Identification in Baton Rouge. Nearly a month later and only a few days before "Mayeux" was to go before a judge for a bail hearing, the fingerprint cards landed on the desk of Kathleen Dremillion, 32, an astute rookie officer with a keen eye for detail.

When she reviewed the cards she nearly processed them in the normal manner, and in which case she would have merely filed them away. But something about the name Mayeux bothered Dremillion. It sounded fictitious to her. Acting on a gut feeling, Dremillion began examining hundreds of sets of fingerprints in the state's files, including many of criminals wanted nationally by the FBI, aided by a magnifying glass and a computer. Finally, on Wednesday, February 3, 1988, Dremillion scored big time. She positively identified "Mayeux's" fingerprints as those of Darren O'Neall's. She was pleased that she had made the "knockoff," as such discoveries are called by the police, but she was shocked to learn that she had found a criminal on the FBI's Ten Most Wanted list.

"We call it a 'knockoff' to get one, and she got him," said one of Dremillion's coworkers. "Once she verified him, everybody had a big celebration. It gave her the thrill of her life."

Everyone concerned was naturally delighted over the fact that O'Neall had been identified, not only because he was one of the FBI's Ten Most Wanted but because it meant that he would be kept behind bars. Keeping him incarcerated effectively broke his repetitive cycle of killing, which had up to his arrest in Florida been driven by fantasy and impulse.

Breaking the pattern of a serial killer was something that behavioral scientists still had been unable to accomplish except by keeping them behind bars and out of circulation.

After noting that O'Neall was wanted for murder in Pierce County, Washington, the Louisiana authorities notified Detective Walt Stout of the identification. Stout in turn notified Edna of the news. Although crying uncontrollably, she was ecstatic upon hearing the details of O'Neall's identification, and she took comfort in knowing that he was now behind bars where he could not hurt another woman.

"I'm so happy, I'm overjoyed," Edna told Stout. "But you know, there's something drastically wrong with our system if a guy like Darren O'Neall, a top ten criminal, with all the tattoos he's got, can sit in jail for so long without anyone knowing who he really is."

Stout, along with Bellingham detectives Carlotta Jarratt and Fred Nolte, flew immediately to Louisiana to interview O'Neall. Much to their dismay, however, O'Neall would not speak to any of them beyond relating that he hadn't made up his mind whether or not he would fight extradition to Washington.

Nonetheless, by Friday, February 5, in an effort to be the first in line to obtain custody of O'Neall, Washington Governor Booth Gardner signed the necessary extradition papers to have O'Neall returned to Pierce County. The paperwork was shipped off to Louisiana the same day.

Detective Walt Stout, meanwhile, retired from the Pierce County Sheriff's Department shortly after making the trip to Louisiana to interview O'Neall. He had put in his twenty-five years of service, reached the minimum age, and decided that he'd had enough. He turned in his shield and his service revolver, and in effect turned the remainder of the investigation over to his partner, Terry Wilson.

When Nadine Quinn and her mother heard the news about Zhohn Mayeaux's true identity, they were naturally shocked. Neither had had any idea that Zhohn was really Darren O'Neall and that he was wanted for murder in the Pacific Northwest.

"That kind of made my stomach do flip-flops because he stayed in my house for two nights," said Nadine's mother. "He seemed to be a very intelligent young man. The way he talked, he wanted to get a job and settle down here ... he was very gentlemanly. It was yes ma'am, no ma'am. He was someone you enjoyed talking to."

In the weeks that followed, Darren O'Neall began playing games with the system. Despite his fingerprint identification, he insisted that he was not Darren O'Neall. Everyone knew better, of course, but O'Neall forced the issue into the courts in order to delay his extradition. To make matters even worse, the state of Louisiana didn't want to give him up to the state of Washington until after he had been tried for stealing Connie LeFevre's car and money.

Edna, of course, became infuriated upon hearing of the delays. She began hounding the authorities in Pierce County, and after being told that there was little they could do for her, she began writing letters to Louisiana Governor Buddy Roemer. She made it clear that she wasn't going to stand for any more bullshit from a system that seemed to her to be more interested in protecting Darren O'Neall's rights than in seeing that justice was properly served.

"I want him brought back here," Edna told everyone, including the news media. "I want the justice system here to start dealing with this man. He's a murderer."

Nonetheless, weeks passed and quickly turned into months. Everyone seemed to keep putting off doing anything about O'Neall's extradition, right down to the governor's office in Louisiana. To Edna, no one seemed to care about the victims or their families. Everything that was being done seemed to be only in the interest of protecting Darren O'Neall's rights. Edna went public again, this time to collect signatures for a petition that she would send to Governor Roemer's office.

Edna, assisted by Jim Chaney and her sons and daughters, collected more than three thousand signatures during the petition drive to bring O'Neall back to Washington. She sent them to Roemer, and he sympathetically replied that he would do everything within his power to expedite the extradition process.

Even though Roemer kept his promise, it took until early June to see the results.

When a Louisiana judge finally did sign the extradition order, O'Neall's attorney, to make matters worse, appealed the order to the Louisiana State Court of Appeals in New Orleans, claiming that Washington's Governor Booth Gardner had included improper paperwork in his extradition warrant. One of the papers was a photocopy of the original. It was a frivolous appeal, and was filed only to delay O'Neall's extradition.

Edna was outraged. More than four months had passed since O'Neall had been positively identified, yet he still sat in a Louisiana jail awaiting trial for auto theft while the family of one of his victims waited for justice.

"There isn't a day that goes by that I don't think about my daughter," Edna tearfully told a group of reporters. "I can't go to a gravesite and bring flowers and pray and talk to her. I have to go to Greenwater, where she was found, and plant flowers. Something has to be done. Louisiana has to stop dragging their feet, stop playing games with this man. A stolen car is nothing compared to a human life. What if he escapes? I know that my daughter wasn't the first, and I know that she wasn't the last. How many more victims is it going to take to open the eyes of the people to get this man brought back here and get him into court and get him into prison where he belongs? And maybe even get him the death penalty? Louisiana is treating him like a car thief, and not a murderer."

The appeals process surrounding the extradition order didn't take long, in part because of all the noise that Edna and her family was making. It was quickly determined that everything was legal, and the order was signed and executed.

O'Neall arrived at the Tacoma–Seattle International Airport aboard Delta Airlines flight 1012 at 2:50 P.M. on Thursday, June 24. After allowing the plane's other passengers to disembark, O'Neall was led by two Pierce County detectives out of the plane and down a flight of outdoor stairs to avoid going inside the terminal. Halfway down the stairs O'Neall paused, looked up, and smiled smugly at a crowd of reporters and television news crews who were held back inside the terminal but were videotaping and taking photographs from behind the glass-enclosed concourse waiting area.

He appeared unkempt. His hair was long and in disarray, and he had grown another beard that was no longer neatly trimmed. He was dressed in a black, sleeveless T-shirt and a pair of camouflage pants. His hands were handcuffed in front of him. When he paused on the stairs and smiled, it appeared that he had done so for Edna's benefit to taunt her, knowing that she would most likely be watching the evening news. The detectives ushered him across the tarmac and placed him inside a waiting police car that would take him to the Pierce County Jail in Tacoma.

O'Neall appeared in Pierce County Superior Court for the first time the following day for his arraignment on the charges that he had kidnapped and murdered Robin Smith. Edna, her family, Larron, and Jim were all there, too, and for the first time they would see O'Neall, the man who had destroyed their lives, the man they hated, face to face.

Edna tried to control herself during the twenty-minute proceeding, but it was difficult. She took a seat in the front row of the gallery, right behind O'Neall. As she watched O'Neall, who sat there quietly with his lawyer, Edna kept asking herself, "Why?" The question repeated itself again and again inside her mind, and all she could do was visualize him hurting Robin. The visual image just kept coming into her mind until she lost control emotionally. She stood up, crying uncontrollably, and began screaming at O'Neall and the judge.

"No more mistakes!" she sobbed. "This system has been bad enough through this whole thing, and I've had to plead tooth and nail to get this man back from Louisiana. Now he's finally here. I'm going to see this man pay for what he's done to my daughter and others. He'll *pay!*"

Larron and Jim led Edna out of the courtroom and into the hallway. While sitting on a wooden bench trying to relax and regain her composure, she sensed that someone was looking at her. When she looked up she noticed a woman approximately her own age staring at her from another bench across the hall. The woman eventually stood up and approached Edna.

"I just have to tell you that I love you," the

woman, near tears, told Edna. "And God bless you. I have to hug you."

As the woman placed her arms around Edna, she added: "Please keep doing what you're doing. It's remarkable what you've done. God bless you for what you're doing for victims' rights. I've been fighting to get things done and am getting nowhere. My son was murdered four years ago."

"Please just hang in there and don't give up," Edna told the woman as she embraced her again. "You have to fight. You have to fight the system."

Edna was still upset, but she felt a little stronger after her encounter with the stranger in the hallway. Edna, although trembling, returned to the courtroom, where she watched O'Neall plead not guilty to murdering Robin. The judge ordered that O'Neall be held on five hundred thousand dollars bail. His trial was set to begin on Monday, August 15. O'Neall never turned around, and he tried to avoid making eye contact with Edna as he was led out of the courtroom.

Chapter 26

When August 15 rolled around, there was yet another delay—and more anger—in bringing Darren O'Neall to trial. O'Neall's attorney had requested that an independent pathologist, somebody from outside Pierce County, conduct an examination of the remains. The pathologist was located in Oklahoma, which meant that Robin's remains would have to be shipped there. The judge granted the request. The additional delay and the judge's ruling was almost too much for Edna to take. Although a representative from the prosecutor's office tried to comfort her, words were not enough and she broke down in another emotional outburst directed at the judge.

"I wish the victims would get some attention instead of the criminals all the time," she screamed. "Everything's done for the criminal, right down the line. But for the victim there's nothing. There's no mercy. I'm tired of it. I want my daughter's remains!"

A week later, on Monday, August 23, Edna was back in Pierce County Superior Court again. After it was learned that the defense would not ask their expert to travel from Oklahoma to testify at O'Neall's trial, chief criminal deputy prosecutor Tom Felnagle filed a motion on Edna's behalf for the release of Robin's remains. When O'Neall's attorney, Ray Thoenig, didn't object to the motion, Judge E. Albert Morrison approved the release of Robin's remains.

"We're just thrilled to finally have her," Edna said, glowing, when Morrison approved the release. "The family can have peace of mind now in knowing where we can go to be with her."

The following Saturday, fifteen months after Robin disappeared, her remains were finally laid to rest in the lavender coffin that Edna had purchased. Edna, clutching a small tree branch adorned with an ornamental robin that was symbolic of her daughter, wept as the casket was lowered into the ground following an emotional funeral service and prayers at the Washington Memorial Park and Mortuary.

"We hope that our family can now be put back together," Edna said, fighting back tears. "We're hoping that justice will be served."

"Rockin' Robin," as her name was engraved on the headstone, was finally at peace in Edna's eyes. Larron Crowston, Robin's fiancé, however, was not.

"I'll never be at peace until Darren O'Neall is put where he belongs," Larron said after the service.

O'Neall's new trial date had been set for Monday, November 7. However, a week earlier, on Monday, October 31, O'Neall's attorney, Ray Thoenig, requested a continuance to allow him more time to prepare O'Neall's case. Judge Morrison approved the request for the delay, and set a new trial date for Wednesday, January 4, 1989. This time Edna was not upset over the delay but was, in fact, relieved.

"I'm a little bit relieved because we can go through the holidays without something heavy hanging over us. We won't be at rest until this comes to an end, but at least it'll give us a little peace through the holidays."

Edna, however, could not have been more wrong.

With the holidays fast approaching again, Larron Crowston became more and more depressed over Robin's murder. Despite being under a psychiatrist's care and taking prescribed medication, Larron continued to blame himself for Robin's murder. He had talked about suicide a number of times, but Edna had always managed to convince him that suicide would only make matters worse for everyone. She continued to show him love and insisted that no one blamed him for Robin's death and that he shouldn't blame himself, either.

Nonetheless, on Friday, November 11, Larron went out drinking with some of his friends. He had been drinking more and more, some people said, to mask the pain and depression over Robin's death. He had taken his prescribed medication that evening before going out, which should not have been mixed with alcohol, and drank heavily that night. When his friends dropped him off at home sometime after midnight, he lay down face up on the couch and apparently passed out.

At some point during the night Larron began vomiting, regurgitating everything in his stomach from earlier that night. But he was unconscious from the alcohol and the medication, and could not turn his head or move his body. As a result he began choking on his own vomit, and when he was found later that morning he was dead.

Some people tried to say that Larron had committed suicide, but Edna didn't believe that at all.

"He at one time talked about taking his own life," Edna said to quell public speculation that he had committed suicide after the news broke about Larron's death. "But we talked him out of it. He promised us faithfully that he would not do it. It was an accident, not suicide. He lost what he had loved the most. Larron was literally dying of a broken heart, day by day by day. He's with Robin now, but not by his own hand."

Larron was buried next to Robin.

Chapter 27

Wednesday, January 4, 1989, despite the shadow of Larron's untimely death, was going to be a big day for everyone in Pierce County Superior Court. Even though Larron had been one of the state's major witnesses against O'Neall, deputy prosecutors Tom Felnagle and Jack Nevin were ready. They were going to introduce all of Larron's statements to the police, and they had a forensic anthropologist, a forensic dentist, and a blood-spatter expert lined up to testify. In all they had more than thirty witnesses set to testify in what they considered a "textbook" case. There was even talk that the prosecutor would ask for the death penalty.

Several jurors were picked during the morning session, and everyone concerned was hopeful that the jury could be seated by the end of the day or by the next day at the latest. Then, shortly after jury selection resumed following the lunch break, O'Neall indicated that he needed to talk to his attorneys. Although the selection process was interrupted as he conferred privately with his attorneys for several minutes, no one thought too much about it as they huddled in conference. Minutes later, however, a hushed silence fell over the courtroom when O'Neall's attorneys asked to approach the bench. O'Neall, they said, wanted to plead guilty to first-degree murder.

Following the initial shock of the surprise announcement, Judge E. Albert Morrison accepted O'Neall's plea and set sentencing for February 6. Prosecutor Nevin informed Morrison that no deals had been made with O'Neall.

"There has been absolutely no reduction of the charges," Nevin said, "and we are recommending the maximum punishment that the legislature has allowed in the state sentencing range."

When Edna realized what had transpired in a matter of just a few moments and was informed of the sentencing range and that the maximum sentence that O'Neall could get was twenty-seven years and nine months, with time off for good behavior, she became outraged.

"There's no time that he can get that will justify Robin's death in our eyes," Edna said. "We have to make sure he can't get back on the street. That's the only satisfaction we can get."

Edna was clearly angry at the prosecutors, and blamed them for not conferring with her before accepting a guilty plea arrangement. But Felnagle and Nevin were defensive, and told her that they were just as surprised as she was by O'Neall's decision to plead guilty.

"We were all geared up to go," Felnagle told her.

"We had sheriff's deputies out at the scene today, tromping through the snow, putting the finishing touches on diagrams. We were expecting three hard weeks of battle. Not this."

Nonetheless, Felnagle told Edna, it was in the best interest of justice to accept the guilty plea. Not only were they now assured that he would be sentenced to prison with the risk of possible acquittal or a conviction on lesser charges removed, but forgoing a trial would save the county a lot of money.

However, Detective Terry Wilson, present in the courtroom, sided with Edna and was angry over the decision to accept O'Neall's guilty plea. He said that he felt cheated, like Edna, and was certain that Walt Stout and the other investigators who had worked on the case would feel cheated, too. He said that the case would have been interesting because it was based almost entirely on circumstantial evidence, much of which was obtained by Edna and her family and corroborated by investigators and forensic experts. The investigation, according to Wilson, was one of the county's most intensive and costliest cases.

"I highly suspect that was why he pleaded guilty," Wilson said. "Although no one saw him do a thing, that's not always necessary. We had all that we would have needed. This would have been a good case to lay on a jury. I could see no way how he was going to get out of this one. That's why I feel cheated."

Afterward, Edna lost what little faith she had left in the criminal justice system. She had desperately wanted O'Neall to stand trial for Robin's murder, and was actively pushing the prosecutors to seek the death penalty. She viewed O'Neall's action that day as an attempt to prevent the sordid details of his crimes from being told in open court.

Epilogue

At his sentencing on Monday, February 6, 1989, Darren O'Neall faced Pierce County Superior Court Judge E. Albert Morrison and apologized for murdering Robin Smith. During his declaration of sorrow, he occasionally looked off to the side and would not face Edna, who had gotten up from the gallery to stand right beside him. He calmly explained that Robin had engaged in sex with him willingly following his party. Edna again lost control of her emotions.

"Robin wouldn't have gone to bed with you 'cause you're a sleaze and you're a liar," Edna cried. "Be honest, Darren, please!" Edna looked at Judge Morrison and tearfully added: "Please don't ever let him do this to another girl."

Edna showed snapshots of Robin to the judge, and described how Robin had wanted to have a normal life, to get married and have children of her own someday. She wanted the judge to see the real person that Darren O'Neall had destroyed.

"I wish I could take Robin's place, but I can't,"

O'Neall said, never once looking toward Edna. "I was wrong. I'm sorry for it."

O'Neall fooled no one. He was cold and calculating at his sentencing, and it was clear to everyone present that he was laying part of the foundation that he knew he had to have firmly in place to manipulate the system later on. He knew that he had to have certain people hear him say that he was sorry, but it wasn't personal, he didn't mean it. True sociopaths rarely express remorse or admit their crimes unless it is self-serving, as was the case with O'Neall. It was all merely a part of his game plan, something that he knew the parole board would read later without having any faces or emotions present. When the time came for him to be considered for parole, the parole board was only going to be reading the words on paper.

"Personally, I'd be inclined to impose the death sentence on you," Judge Morrison told O'Neall. "But my personal feelings have no place in this."

Morrison then sentenced O'Neall to twenty-seven years and nine months in prison, to be served at the Washington State Penitentiary in Walla Walla. Morrison noted that O'Neall could be eligible for parole after serving only eighteen years and six months, according to a provision for time off for good behavior that O'Neall had heard about. O'Neall stood expressionless as sentence was passed.

By law in Washington State, victims of violent crime or their survivors are allowed to face the perpetrator and to address the court. Although Edna felt that O'Neall's sentence "stinks," she said that she wouldn't have missed the opportunity to face her daughter's killer under any circumstances.

"As soon as I learned that I had the right to do this," Edna said after the sentence was meted out, "I knew that I would. I had to face this man and describe the girl who was a living, breathing person, looking forward to marriage and children. She wasn't just 'the victim,' or 'the deceased' to any of us. I wanted to show some snapshots, give a sense of who she was beyond the bones they found in the woods after the animals had gotten through with her. How else can you form a picture of someone whose face has been taken out with a hammer?"

In May of the following year, O'Neall was brought to Portland to stand trial for the kidnapping and rape of fourteen-year-old Fawn Creswell. He had steadfastly maintained his innocence, and through his attorney, Scott Raivio, attempted to shift the blame onto the girl for what had happened to her. Even though investigators had never turned up the big rig allegedly used by O'Neall that night in January 1987, Multnomah County Deputy District Attorney Charles Sparks demonstrated through statements that O'Neall had made to others regarding his knowledge about driving semi-trailers. After pleading guilty to murdering Robin Smith, O'Neall had talked about riding cross-country with truck drivers and how he had frequented truck stops. By the time Sparks summed up the case, the jurors could see for themselves through O'Neall's own bragging about his past association with truckers that he knew how to drive a semi. They also saw, again through his bragging, that he knew how to steal them. That, coupled with the eyewitness identification of O'Neall by Fawn as her attacker, was enough for the jury. Under varying theories of law, they convicted him of two counts of first-degree kidnapping, three counts of first-degree rape, sexual penetration with a foreign object, three counts of third-degree rape, and single counts of first-degree sodomy, third-degree sodomy, and sexual abuse.

At his sentencing hearing on Thursday, August 3, 1990, before Multnomah County Circuit Court Judge Kimberly Frankel, O'Neall's attorney claimed that there was a connection between O'Neall's criminal history and his abuse of cocaine and amphetamines.

"Whenever he is away from drugs," said his attorney, "Mr. O'Neall has polite middle class values."

Frankel didn't buy it and sentenced O'Neall to a hundred and thirty-five years in prison, to run consecutively with his sentence in Washington for the murder of Robin Smith. If and when he made parole in Washington, she ordered that he be immediately transferred to the Oregon state correctional system. However, Frankel noted that it would be up to the Oregon State Parole Board to decide when he would be eligible for parole on the Oregon convictions. According to Deputy D.A. Charles Sparks, O'Neall will almost certainly spend a minimum of thirty years at the Oregon State Penitentiary before being considered for parole. Edna Smith and her family have vowed to attend all of his parole hearings, both in Washington and Oregon, to urge the respective parole boards to vote against granting O'Neall parole.

To date, the whereabouts of Kimberley Kersey remain unknown. A known psychic has told this author that someone close to Kimberley knows what happened to her, but insists that that person did not harm her. Clark County investigators have all but dismissed Darren O'Neall as a suspect in her disappearance and probable homicide, and the investigation, while still open and active, seems to be at a standstill.

Similarly, the whereabouts of Wendy Aughe remain unknown, though investigators are certain that she fell prey to O'Neall's murderous impulses. Despite the overwhelming circumstantial evidence implicating O'Neall in Aughe's disappearance and probable murder, the Bellingham police and the Whatcom County prosecutor's office have declined to charge him without first finding the remains. He was, however, charged and eventually convicted in the theft of Aughe's car.

In Oregon, Lia Szubert's murder also remains on the books due to a lack of physical evidence linking O'Neall to the crime. It is almost ironic. Bellingham police have a considerable amount of evidence linking him to Wendy Aughe's death, but no body. Oregon state police and Idaho investigators, on the other hand, have a body but no evidence.

Many of the other homicides initially linked to O'Neall in other jurisdictions, including Colorado, remain open and active. To date, O'Neall has expressed no sincere remorse for any of his crimes, and reportedly has resigned himself to spending the rest of his life in prison.

To Edna Smith and her family, the only question that never seems to get answered is, "Why?" Deep down she knows that O'Neall killed Robin, and likely the others that he's suspected of killing, because he lacks a conscience. He wanted to be able to satisfy himself regardless of the cost to others. It was selfishness to the extreme. He clearly did not care for anyone except himself, and did not care how his actions affected others or how many lives his actions destroyed. She wishes that there was a better answer for Robin's death, but realizes, sadly, that there isn't.

To this day, when Edna is down in the dumps or starts thinking about Robin, whether at home or at work, she can look down at the floor or ground and nearly always find a dime. And she always bends down to pick it up, sincere in her belief that it's Robin's way of staying in touch, and a reminder to all of them that her gold dime was in fact significant.

Whenever Edna finds one of those dimes, she always says to herself: "Okay, Robin, thank you, I know you're thinking of me and I love you, too."